Ecoviolence

Ecoviolence

Links Among Environment, Population, and Security

edited by
THOMAS HOMER-DIXON
and
JESSICA BLITT

ROWMAN & LITTLEFIELD PUBLISHERS, INC.
Lanham • Boulder • New York • Oxford

ROWMAN & LITTLEFIELD PUBLISHERS, INC.

Published in the United States of America
by Rowman & Littlefield Publishers, Inc.
4720 Boston Way, Lanham, Maryland 20706

12 Hid's Copse Road
Cumnor Hill, Oxford OX2 9JJ, England

British Library Cataloguing in Publication Information Available

Library of Congress Cataloging-in-Publication Data

Ecoviolence : links among environment, population, and security /
    edited by Thomas Homer-Dixon and Jessica Blitt.
        p.   cm.
    Includes bibliographical references and index.
    ISBN 0-8476-8869-0 (cloth : alk. paper).—ISBN 0-8476-8870-4
(pbk. : alk. paper)
    1. Developing countries—Environmental conditions—Case studies.
    2. Environmental sciences—Social aspects—Developing countries—
Case studies.   3. Renewal natural resources—Social aspects—
Developing countries—Case studies.   4. Human ecology—Developing
countries—Case studies.   I. Homer-Dixon, Thomas F.   II. Blitt,
Jessica, 1974–
GE160.D44E28   1998
363.7'03'091724—dc21   98-24369
                                                                              CIP

ISBN 0-8476-8869-0 (cloth : alk. paper)
ISBN 0-8476-8870-4 (pbk. : alk. paper)

Printed in the United States of America

∞ ™ The paper used in this publication meets the minimum requirements of
American National Standard for Information Sciences—Permanence of Paper for
Printed Library Materials, ANSI Z39.48-1984.

Contents

1

Introduction: A Theoretical Overview

Thomas Homer-Dixon and Jessica Blitt

By the year 2025, world population will be nearly 8 billion.[1] This figure represents an increase of almost 2 billion in just over 20 years. As a worldwide figure, the number is disturbing enough, but the implications of rapid population growth for specific regions are sometimes truly alarming. Over 90 percent of the expected growth will take place in developing countries, in which the majority of the population is often dependent on local renewable resources like cropland, forests, and fresh water supplies. In many places, these resources are being degraded and depleted: soil is eroding from farmland, forests are being logged and burnt away, and rivers are being damaged by pollution. The resources that remain are often controlled by powerful interest groups and elites, leaving even less for the majority of the population. What, if any, are the links between this increasing scarcity of renewable resources—or what we call "environmental scarcity"—and the rise in violent conflict within countries in recent years?

In this book, we investigate these links by exploring in detail environmental scarcity's role in conflicts in Chiapas, Gaza, South Africa, Pakistan, and Rwanda. We hope that the information from these cases will help resolve the ongoing debate between those who maintain that environmental scarcities play only a minimal role in conflict and those who argue that this role is much more significant (and who, in the process, often sensationalize the issue and overstate the contribution of environmental pressures). We show that the answer lies somewhere between these two extremes.

Environmental scarcity is scarcity of renewable resources. Natural resources, in general, can be either non-renewable (for example, oil and iron ore) or renewable (for example, forests, soil, lake and river water, and the stratospheric ozone layer). A non-renewable resource consists of a "stock," which is the total quantity of the resource available for consumption. A renewable resource has both a stock and a "flow," which is the incremental addition to, or restoration of, the stock per unit of time. Renewable resources can be further subdivided, roughly, into those that provide "goods" and those that provide "services." Coastal fisheries are a renewable resource that provide the good of fish; similarly, underground layers of rock that hold water, commonly called aquifers, provide the good of water when tapped by wells. In contrast, the stratospheric ozone layer provides the service of protection from high levels of ultraviolet radiation. Some renewables provide both goods and services: surface bodies of fresh water—like lakes and rivers—provide water, but at the same time they often absorb pollution from cities, industries, and farms, which is a very important service for society. Similarly, soil provides the good of nutrients for plant growth and the service of a site for the roots of plants (often called "rooting depth").[2]

Non-renewables are usually independent from one another—in other words, depletion of one body of a non-renewable resource (such as a seam of iron ore) does not usually affect other bodies of non-renewables. In contrast, renewable resources are highly interdependent. A good example is the interdependence between a forest and its surrounding ecosystem of renewable resources. Severe regional forest loss from logging can significantly affect other renewables in the neighborhood: it can change the local cycles of rainfall, the stability of soils on hillsides, and the productivity of local fisheries (which are damaged when silt washes off the hills into rivers, lakes, and the sea). As a result, depletion of renewables often produces unexpected effects—effects sometimes much more severe, complex, and difficult to manage than originally anticipated.

Types of Environmental Change

This book focuses on the social consequences of renewable resource scarcity in developing countries. In many of these countries, large populations are highly dependent for their day-to-day well-being on local cropland, forests, water supplies, and fisheries. Under certain circumstances, we argue, scarcity of these resources causes violent conflict.

For our purposes, six major types of environmental change deserve particular attention: water and land degradation, deforestation, decline in fisheries, and, to a lesser extent, global warming and stratospheric ozone depletion. The latter two, despite the amount of attention they receive in popular media, are less important in our analysis. They are unlikely to have a large effect on people's well-being in the near future, and so are unlikely to be immediate causes of violence. But global warming and ozone depletion still deserve mention here, because when they do eventually have an impact, they will probably interact with already present environmental and demographic pressures, thus making those pressures much worse.[3]

Water

If we were simply to add up all of the freshwater resources available world-wide, we would be hard pressed to argue that any sort of scarcity exists or could ever exist. Around the world each year, about 41,022 cubic kilometers of renewable water resources are available;[4] of this amount, humans withdraw annually some 3,240 cubic kilometers (as of 1987). Unfortunately, the total availability and consumption of water are only a small part of the story. There are large disparities in water availability and consumption among regions and, in some places, water quality is extremely poor and getting worse.

Many areas—including much of Europe, large parts of the United States, the Ganges basin in India, and the northwestern provinces of China—are using virtually all of their river runoff. In other regions, particularly dry, developing countries, increases in population growth threaten to reduce per capita availability of water to levels that are inadequate to meet basic household, industrial, and agricultural needs.[5] At the same time, the poor quality of fresh water resources is a hazard to a large portion of the world's population. Water-borne diseases like yellow fever, malaria, and river blindness infect a large fraction of humanity.[6] Despite a seeming abundance of water, there are significant problems with the quantity and quality available to much of the world's populations.

Cropland

The potential amount of cultivable land is another statistic that is misleading at first glance. Only 1.5 billion of an estimated 3.2 to 3.4 billion hectares of potential cropland is being used worldwide. However, most of the unused land is of inferior quality and not easily accessible. In fact, the largest reserves of unused arable land are underneath the rain forests of the Congo and the Amazon basins. Not only are these forests important repositories of biodiversity (that is, they host a diversity of plant and animal species), but the land is ill suited for agricultural development and becomes quickly degraded when converted to farmland.

If we look at regional rather than aggregate figures, the story is even grimmer. A country is generally considered land scarce when 70 percent or more of its potential cropland is being used. Yet Asia, which encompasses four out of five of the world's most populated countries, is using about 82 percent of all of its potential cropland.[7] Moreover, large sections of land disappear every year due to a combination of factors ranging from the expansion of cities to erosion and loss of nutrients.

Forests

In the early 1990s, about 17 million hectares of tropical forests were logged each year, an increase of almost 6 million hectares over the deforestation rate in the early 1980s.[8] Between 1980 to 1990, an area of tropical forest almost three times the size of France was converted to other uses. Today, three countries—Brazil, Indonesia, and Malaysia—account for half of the world's tropical rain forest loss.[9]

Deforestation of large areas is not the only issue, however. Forest fragmentation threatens biodiversity by shrinking the size of habitats so that they can no longer support indigenous plants and animals, while forest degradation can lead to erosion and cause changes in the local environment that harm local wildlife.[10]

Fisheries

The Food and Agriculture Organization (FAO) estimates that 100 million metric tons of fish can be sustainably caught each year from the world's oceans, lakes, and rivers. In 1993, humans were catching about 86 million metric tons per year.[11] As human extraction approaches the limits of sustainability, there are signs of a worldwide fisheries crisis. The FAO now estimates that 69 percent of marine fish stocks are "fully exploited, overexploited, depleted, or in the process of rebuilding as a result of depletion."[12] In many places around the world, from the coasts of New England to the seas around the Philippines, overexploitation has caused a dramatic decline in the productivity of regional fisheries. These events have not only harmed ocean ecosystems but have produced widespread human hardship and unemployment.

Global Warming

Scientists agree that humans are releasing large amounts of carbon dioxide and other gases that help trap heat within the Earth's atmosphere. There is controversy surrounding the rate, effect, and importance of the resulting global warming. Nonetheless, scientists have achieved a consensus of sorts on the issue—a consensus expressed in the findings of the Intergovernmental Panel on Climate Change (IPCC). By 2100, these scientists estimate, the Earth's atmosphere will warm on average between 1 and 3.5 degrees Celsius.[13] Although this amount may not seem significant, the earth has warmed only about 5 degrees since the coldest period of the last ice age. Furthermore, even minimal warming could sharply increase the frequency of extreme weather events, such as droughts, floods, storms, and heat waves. Some infectious diseases might become more widespread, since the insects that carry them could range over larger territories.[14] Global warming could also interact with, and worsen the impact of, other environmental stresses. For example, when soil is eroded and rooting depth lost, crops become more vulnerable to the drought that global warming may cause.

Stratospheric Ozone

Ozone depletion is a classic example of a "threshold" or "nonlinear" response of an environmental system to human perturbation: slow incremental changes accumulated over time to produce a sudden and unexpected shift in the character or behavior of the system. In the 1980s, the scientific community was surprised by the discovery of a hole in the stratospheric ozone layer over the Antarctic. Data from satellites indicating that a hole had appeared were, in fact, available as far back as the 1970s. However, a sudden loss of ozone was regarded as so unlikely that these data were ignored by computers designed to disregard anomalous results.[15] Scientists had assumed that there would be a more or less linear—or incremental—relationship between chlorofluorocarbon (CFC) emissions and ozone depletion. Instead they discovered that, under the right conditions, CFCs could destroy multikilometer-thick layers of ozone in a matter of weeks.[16] The nonlinear character of environmental systems is one of the most powerful reasons why humans should show prudence when dealing with these systems: there is so much that we clearly do not understand and cannot predict that it is folly to assume that we can successfully manage all aspects of the global environment.

Meanwhile, we live with the consequences of an increasingly depleted ozone layer. The World Meteorological Organization (WMO) has estimated that global ozone losses will peak in the late 1990s at about 12 to 13 percent at northern midlatitudes in the winter and spring, at 6 to 7 percent at northern midlatitudes in the summer and fall, and at about 11 percent at southern midlatitudes on a year-round basis.[17] Researchers believe that, on average, a 1 percent depletion of stratospheric ozone causes a 1.6 percent increase in the amount of UV radiation reaching the surface of the earth.[18] This increase boosts the risk of skin cancer and may affect other environmental systems such as crops, forests, and the ocean food chain.

Causes and Interactions

All of the above-mentioned environmental changes can produce "scarcities" of vital renewable resources. Such changes are, however, only one cause of the more general phenomenon of "environmental scarcity." Environmental scarcity is also caused by increased demand for resources (either because of population growth or greater per capita resource consumption) and unequal distribution of resources. In other words, environmental scarcity is a function, jointly, of "supply-induced," "demand-induced," and "structural" scarcities.

Supply-induced scarcity (often called "environmental change") is caused by the kind of degradation or depletion of environmental resources discussed in the previous section of this chapter. Ecosystem sensitivity determines, in part, the amount of depletion or degradation caused by a given amount of human activity like logging, fishing, or extraction of water: the more fragile the resource system is to begin with, the quicker it will be depleted or degraded. For example, agricultural activity that produces soil erosion will have a bigger impact in regions were the topsoil is shallow than in those where the soil is deep. In some cases, fragile resource systems become irreversibly degraded; in these cases, even if the human activities causing the degradation are stopped, the system cannot recover. *Demand-induced scarcity* is caused by either population growth or an increase in per-capita consumption of the resource; either factor serves to increase the overall demand for the resource, which, if the supply of the resource remains constant, increases its scarcity. *Structural scarcity* arises from the unequal social distribution of a resource, as occurs when a resource is concentrated in the hands of a small percentage of the population while the rest experiences shortages.

A "pie" metaphor best illustrates these three sources of environmental scarcity: supply-induced scarcity, arising from a reduction in the quantity or quality of the resource, shrinks the size of the resource pie as a whole; demand-induced scarcity arising, for example, from growth in the number of people competing for the resource pie, causes the average size of each person's slice of the pie to shrink; and structural scarcity, arising from unequal distribution, puts large slices in the hands of a few, thus diminishing the amount available for the rest.

These three types of scarcity often occur simultaneously and interact.[19] Two patterns of interaction are especially common. *Resource capture* occurs when demand- and supply-induced scarcities interact to produce structural scarcity: powerful groups within society, anticipating future shortages due to increased population growth and a decrease in the quantity and quality of the resource, shift resource distribution in their favor, which subjects the remaining population to scarcity. *Ecological marginalization* occurs when demand-induced and structural scarcities interact to produce supply-induced scarcity: lack of access to resources caused by unequal distribution forces growing populations to migrate from regions where resources are scarce to regions that are ecologically fragile and extremely vulnerable to degradation.[20]

Resource capture occurred in the Senegal River Basin during the 1970s and 1980s. The lands of Mauritania, to the north of the Senegal River, consist mainly of arid desert and semiarid grassland. The country had a high population growth rate. In an effort to boost agricultural production during a time of drought and impending food shortfalls, the governments of countries in the region built a series of dams along the river. The change in water flow in the river significantly raised the value of the riverside land. It led Mauritanian Moors to abandon their cattle production, which they had been operating on highly degraded land to the north of the Senegal River, and migrate south to the river basin. The land was already occupied, however, because black Mauritanians had historically farmed and herded along the river. In order to lay claim to the resource, the Mauritanian government, controlled by the Moor elite, rewrote the legislation that governed land ownership. Black Mauritanians were effectively barred from farming in the area, subjecting them to further scarcity. This became a contributing factor to the high levels of violence that later arose between Mauritania and Senegal.[21]

Ecological marginalization is one of the factors that played a significant role in the recent communist-led insurgency in the Philippines. In the decades following World War II, peasants were generally denied access to the country's best cropland, which lies in the coastal zones of the islands in the Filipino archipelago. Since colonial times, this land has been controlled by a relatively small elite of powerful landlords. When this skewed distribution of good land was coupled with rapid population growth in the 1960s and 1970s, many peasants had no choice but to move into marginal upland areas in the interior of the island. They brought with them neither the knowledge nor the capital to preserve these fragile areas, and their slash and burn farming practices caused severe environmental damage—water erosion, landslides, and changes in the hydrological cycle. These changes invariably led to their further impoverishment, because the degraded land generated smaller and smaller agricultural yields. Grievances increased and the peasants were easily mobilized to support the insurgents of the New People's Army.[22]

Adaptation Failures

Environmental scarcity does not inevitably or deterministically lead to social disruption and violent conflict. If society can generate enough social and technical ingenuity—in the form of institutions like efficient markets and also in the form of technologies like genetically engineered grains—it might be able to adapt to resource scarcity. Yet, market failure, social friction, and the limited availability of capital tend to reduce the supply of ingenuity while simultaneously raising the requirement for it.[23]

Market Failure

Traditional economic models assume that an economy will supply the ingenuity it needs to deal with its resource scarcities if resource prices accurately reflect scarcity. In response to profit opportunities, entrepreneurs will find new sources of scarce resources and will develop new technologies to substitute relatively abundant resources for scarce ones. Consumers will conserve increasingly expensive resources. In other words, if the market works properly, the price mechanism will ensure that necessity is the mother of invention; an adequate flow of adaptive ingenuity will permit the economy to respond to scarcity without a significant decrease in the population's standard of living.

But prices often do not fully reflect the degree of scarcity experienced by an economy or society. Such "market failures" occur in two important ways. First, many renewable resources—like hydrological cycles or productive seas—cannot be physically controlled or divided into saleable units for trade in a market. It is therefore hard to assign property rights to the resource, and they remain "open-access," which means that anyone can use them. This situation tends to skew price signals and produce overexploitation. Second, even when clear property rights exist, market prices often do not take account of the "negative externalities" of resource exploitation; these externalities are costs borne by people who don't participate in the market transactions affecting the resource in question. For example, deforestation can cause siltation of rivers and damage to waterways and fisheries, yet these consequences are rarely incorporated in assessments of logging's costs.

Social Friction

Increased environmental scarcity often provokes vigorous action by powerful groups and elite members to protect their interests.[24] The economist Mancur Olson calls these groups "narrow distributional coalitions," because they are more interested in distributing the economic pie in their favor than increasing the overall size of the pie so that everybody benefits.[25] They tend to be small, with a disproportionate amount of political power relative to their size, and they are invariably motivated by narrowly defined self-interest that does not take account of society's needs as a whole. Therefore, they hinder efforts to reform existing institutions when these reforms do not coincide with their own interests. In so doing, they "interfere with an economy's capacity to adapt to change and to generate new innovations."[26] This "social friction" caused by environmental scarcities can thus impede the generation and implementation of solutions to the very same scarcities.[27]

Capital Availability

Both financial and human capital are essential for an adequate supply of ingenuity. Financial capital is needed to fund research into ways to adapt to scarcities and to build the infrastructure of roads, communication networks, and electrical grids that makes government response to scarcities possible. Yet many of the countries that face the worst environmental scarcities are very poor and do not have the financial capital they need for an adequate ingenuity supply in response to scarcity. Human capital—trained scientists, engineers, and corporate and government managers—also tends to be in short supply in these countries. The brain drain is a particularly serious problem throughout the developing world, as a significant percentage of highly skilled labor emigrates to rich countries, leaving critical shortages of talent and expertise in their countries of origin.[28]

Key Social Effects

If market failure, social friction, and capital availability prevent a society from supplying the amount of ingenuity that it needs to adapt to environmental scarcity, then five kinds of social effect are likely: constrained agricultural productivity, constrained economic productivity, migration, social segmentation, and disruption of legitimate institutions. Environmental scarcity is not the sole or sufficient cause of these social effects; rather it *interacts* with various contextual factors to cause these social effects. Contextual factors range from the nature of relations among ethnic groups to the state's degree of autonomy from outside pressure groups.

Much research shows that various kinds of environmental scarcity— including loss of topsoil, deforestation, water scarcities and, potentially, global warming—can have a strong negative effect on both agricultural and economic production. However, in most developing countries the weight of this hardship is not carried equally across society, because of structural inequalities in wealth and power. Much of the negative effect of environmental scarcity on agriculture and the economy is felt by the least advantaged groups in society, especially those who are most dependent on local renewables for their day-to-day livelihoods. In contrast, more powerful groups can often shift laws in their favor and take advantage of profit opportunities that scarcities present.

If environmental scarcity hurts agricultural and economic production, some people will become poorer, and they may try to improve their situation by migrating to cities or to regions where environmental resources are more plentiful. Experts often focus on the relative strengths of "push" and "pull" factors as causes of migration. Push factors are unpleasant conditions at home that make people want to leave, and pull factors are attractive conditions elsewhere that tempt people to move there. This language implies that we can distinguish clearly between push and pull factors. In fact, however, it is the *gap* between the migrant's current quality of life and the potential quality of life offered in the new region that is important. Push and pull factors do not exist in isolation from each other; they are linked by the migrant's implicit comparison between the relative benefits of "here" and "there."

The combination of these first three types of social effect—constrained agricultural productivity, constrained economic productivity, and migration—can make the "segmentation" of society much worse. Segmentation arises when groups respond to scarcity by hardening the already existing religious, class, ethnic, or linguistic divisions that separate them. Competition among these increasingly distinct groups worsens, which reduces both their interactions with each other and with the state. Fragile bonds of civil society become disrupted, thereby making it harder for groups to articulate their needs nonviolently through established networks.

ᐟAll these developments can seriously disrupt legitimate institutions at every level of society—including village and community based organizations, labor markets, class relations, and even the state itself. Environmental scarcity increases state vulnerability by threatening the delicate give-and-take relationship between state and society. Falling agricultural production, migrations to urban areas, and economic hardship increase demands on the state. At the same time, scarcity can interfere with state revenue streams by reducing economic productivity and therefore taxes; it can also increase the power and activity of small coalitions of elites, known as rent-seekers, that seek to profit from monopolizing scarce resources. These groups become ever more able to avoid paying taxes on their increased wealth and to influence state policy in their favor. Environmental scarcity therefore increases society's demands on the state while decreasing the state's ability to meet those demands.[29]

Conflict

The five key social effects of environmental scarcity described above—constrained agricultural output, constrained economic production, migration, social segmentation, and disrupted institutions—can, either singly or in combination, produce or exacerbate conflict among groups. They do so by simultaneously increasing the grievances of the affected populations and changing the structure of political opportunities so that it is more rational to act violently upon those grievances.

Reduced agricultural and economic production can cause objective socioeconomic deprivation, which can make grievances stronger in the affected populations. But objective deprivation does not always produce strong grievances. Instead, grievance tends to be correlated with "relative deprivation." According to conflict theorists, individuals and groups have feelings of relative deprivation when they perceive a gap between the situation they believe they deserve and the situation that they have actually achieved.[30]

Even if people feel relatively deprived and, as a result, have powerful grievances, widespread civil violence is not inevitable. At least two other factors must be present: the aggrieved individuals need to participate in groups with strong collective identities, and these groups must have good opportunities for violent collective action against authority. When individuals are members of groups that are already organized around clear social cleavages—such as ethnicity, religion, or class—it is more likely that their grievances will be articulated and acted upon at the group level. Thus, to the extent that environmental scarcity exacerbates social segmentation in developing societies, it makes civil violence more likely.

In addition, serious civil strife is likely only when the structure of political opportunities facing aggrieved groups keeps them from peacefully expressing their grievances but at the same time offers them openings for violent action against the perceived cause of their grievances. The balance of power among actors is key here. Perceptions regarding the relative strengths and weaknesses of the state, challenger groups, and their respective allies will affect these actors' calculations of the costs and benefits of the different courses of action they can pursue. For example, a state debilitated by corruption, falling revenues, rising demand for services, or factional conflicts among elites (all of which are potential consequences of environmental scarcity) will be more vulnerable than a strong state to violent challenges by aggrieved groups.[31]

A number of other contextual factors can affect *both* grievances and opportunities, including rapid urbanization, international economic shocks (such as sudden changes in oil prices), and the organization and leadership capacity of challenger groups. Leaders help bring about the "cognitive liberation" of their groups by helping their followers understand that their situation should and can be changed.[32] Leaders change their followers' conception of justice—that is, their conception of the "social good"—thus encouraging them to see the current situation as illegitimate and needing change. Consequently, the followers' sense of relative deprivation rises.[33] In much the same way, leaders can influence perceptions of the social balance of power and the opportunity structure facing challenger groups, which can make violent action by these groups seem more likely to succeed.

By making some people poorer and weaker and others richer and more powerful, by causing people to move to new locations where they are often not wanted, and by weakening key institutions such as the state, environmental scarcity boosts grievances and changes the structure of opportunities facing challenger groups. This conjunction of grievance and opportunity in turn raises the probability of major civil violence, such as insurgency, ethnic clashes, and coups d'etat. Research shows that this violence tends to be subnational, diffuse, and persistent—exactly the kind of violence that conventional military institutions have great difficulty controlling.[34]

Project on Environment, Population, and Security

The Project on Environment, Population, and Security (EPS), a collaborative effort of the University of Toronto and the American Association for the Advancement of Science, investigated the causal processes described above. Between July 1994 and December 1996, a team of researchers based in Toronto gathered, evaluated, and integrated existing data on causal linkages among population growth, renewable resource scarcities, migration, and violent conflict. This effort was guided by three key questions:

- Does environmental scarcity contribute to violence in developing countries?
- If it does, how does it contribute?
- What are the critical methodological issues affecting this type of research?

The EPS Project produced detailed case studies of civil violence in Chiapas, Gaza, South Africa, Pakistan, and Rwanda. These studies, which form the core of this book, show the importance of environmental factors in some instances of social instability, and the limited role of these factors in other contexts.

The decision to analyze cases that exhibit both environmental scarcity and violence—in other words, cases that exhibit a prima facie link between these factors—provoked some controversy. According to standard scientific method, researchers should select cases that are largely similar in their characteristics but that differ in their values of the independent variable; then the researchers should see if these cases also differ in their values of the dependent variable. In the environment-conflict research program, this means that researchers should compare cases where environmental scarcity (the independent variable) is severe with cases where scarcity is not severe to see if these cases vary consistently in their levels of civil violence (the dependent variable). Importantly, the cases should be selected to control for all variables other than environmental scarcity that might be significant causes of violence. If this procedure is not possible, an alternative is available: researchers can choose cases that hold the independent variable constant and that vary only the dependent variable; in other words, researchers can compare cases with similar levels of environmental scarcity but with different levels of violent conflict.[35]

However, in the early stages of research into the links between environmental scarcity and violent conflict, there are significant problems with both these methods. The ecological-political systems under study are extraordinarily complex, and complex systems are often characterized by large and unanticipated responses to small changes in variables not initially recognized as important. Under such circumstances, it is almost impossible to conduct truly *controlled* comparisons of cases—that is, to select cases that are the same on all except the variables of interest.

Moreover, it is grossly inefficient to make a large investment of resources early in environment-conflict research to study "null" cases in which environmental stress is present but violent conflict does not occur. Before closely examining such cases, analysts need a good understanding of the boundary conditions governing their hypotheses about environment-conflict links, an understanding that can best be gained from an exacting study of the causal processes in cases in which environmental scarcity appears to lead to conflict.[36]

EPS researchers therefore selected cases for study that appeared to exhibit a causal relationship between scarcity and violence. They then used a methodology known as "process tracing": they carefully traced the individual causal steps between environmental scarcity and its varied social effects, and they weighed the (often scanty) evidence available to determine whether the society's violence was somehow a consequence of its environmental scarcity and, if so, *how* it was a consequence. Process tracing allowed the EPS researchers to determine which environmental factors, if any, were causally important to the outbreak of violence and how they interacted with the complex variety of political, social, and economic conditions unique to the society under study. The methodology did not prejudice the research in favor of finding that environmental factors were important causes of violence. In fact, in the case of Rwanda, it led EPS researchers to the conclusion that environmental factors were not key in the country's recent experience of genocide.

As research on the links between environmental scarcity and violence progresses, and once the role of environmental factors is better understood across a range of cases, investigators can turn to cases that exhibit high levels of environmental scarcity without violence. Such a comparison will help analysts identify factors that promote successful adaptation to environmental scarcity.

Case Studies

The case studies in the following chapters were written from 1994 to 1996 as part of the Project on Environment, Population, and Security. They do not, therefore, address some of the more recent developments in the countries or societies in question. Nonetheless, their analyses of the causes of conflict in these cases remain highly relevant.

We begin with the case of Chiapas, the southernmost state in Mexico. This study identifies the different forms of environmental scarcities that affect the people of Chiapas. In recent years, these scarcities—especially of cropland and forest materials—have become acute. Increased demand for cropland and fuelwood arising from high population growth and an influx of migrants occurred within the context of a long-standing inequitable distribution of land resources. The contribution of cropland degradation to land scarcity was localized in the state's Central Highlands. Cropland and forest scarcities did not cause civil strife by themselves; in interaction with other factors, however, they multiplied the grievances of the campesino and indígena communities. At the same time, economic liberalization reduced the governing regime's capacity in Chiapas and provided greater opportunities for violent challenges by opposition groups.

We then turn to the case of Gaza, which shows how scarcity of fresh water can influence economic development and social change. The achievement of limited autonomy for Palestinians in Gaza and Jericho in 1993 engendered hope for peace in the Middle East, yet violence persisted. The links between environmental scarcity and conflict are complex, but in Gaza, water scarcity has clearly aggravated socioeconomic conditions. These conditions, in turn, have contributed to the grievances behind ongoing violence against Israel and emerging tensions among Palestinians in Gaza.

The South Africa case follows Gaza. It clearly demonstrates the hurdles that democratization and social change have to overcome when environmental scarcity is serious. Although South Africa experienced a relatively stable transition to democratic rule, violence within the black South African community escalated steadily in the 1980s and early 1990s. This violence increased at precisely the same time that many anticipated the transition to a more peaceful society—upon the release of Nelson Mandela, the end of the ban on political activity, and the official end to apartheid. Conflict became more intense and spread throughout the country. This chapter provides a new perspective on these events by analyzing the link between South Africa's environmental scarcity and its social turmoil. It examines state-society relations in South Africa and how the changing nature of these relations affected resource access, perception of grievances, and opportunities for violent action. Once again, environmental scarcity was not the sole cause of the country's recent turmoil. But policy makers and social analysts who ignore environmental problems risk missing a factor that powerfully contributes to violence.

The Pakistan case study shows that the country's varied and worsening environmental scarcities interact with the structure and operation of the Pakistani state to trigger processes that heighten ethnic, communal, and class-based rivalries. This combination of forces encourages resource capture, the marginalization of the poor, rising economic hardship, and a progressive weakening of the state. These processes, in turn, culminate in increased group-identity (for example, interethnic) and deprivation conflicts, particularly in the country's urban areas.

The Rwandan genocide is the fifth and final case. Following the assassination of President Juvenal Habyarimana in April 1994, violence gripped the country. Approximately a half-million people were killed and over two million people became refugees between April and August 1994. Until this violence, Rwanda had a population of 7.5 million, a population growth rate estimated at about 3 percent per year, and a population density among the highest in Africa. Ninety-five percent of the population resided in the countryside, and 90 percent relied on agriculture to sustain themselves. Land scarcity and degradation threatened the ability of food production to keep pace with population growth. Rwanda could be described as a country with severe demographic stress relying for subsistence on a limited resource base. Yet, although environmental scarcities were significant development issues, the case study concludes that they had at most a limited, aggravating role in the conflict.

The last chapter of this book derives a set of key findings from the above case studies. These findings recapitulate and extend the main theoretical arguments in this introductory chapter.

Conclusions

The research conducted by the EPS Project and others has definitively shown that severe environmental scarcities often contribute to major civil violence. Poor countries are more vulnerable to this violence, because large fractions of their populations depend for their day-to-day livelihoods on local renewable resources, such as cropland, forests, lakes and streams, and coastal fish stocks. Moreover, poor countries are often unable to adapt effectively to environmental scarcity because their states are weak, markets inefficient and corrupt, and human capital inadequate. If adaptation does not occur, marginal groups dependent on environmental resources will suffer economically; many will try to move to cities or to regions with more abundant renewable resources. Segmentation along existing social cleavages will increase, and key social institutions will further weaken. These changes contribute to rising grievances and shift the balance of power among key social groups. The result is often chronic and diffuse subnational violence that is exceedingly difficult to control using conventional means, that undermines development, and that sometimes jeopardizes the security of neighboring countries.

Notes

1. Alex Marshall, ed., *The State of the World Population 1997* (New York: United Nations Population Fund, 1997), 70.
2. Thomas Homer-Dixon, "Environmental Scarcities and Violent Conflict: Evidence from Cases," *International Security* 19, no. 1 (summer 1994): 8.
3. Ibid., 7–8.

4. World Resources Institute (WRI), *World Resources 1996–97* (New York: Oxford University Press, 1996), 306.

5. Thomas Homer-Dixon, *Environmental Scarcity and Global Security,* Headline Series, no. 300 (New York: Foreign Policy Association, fall 1993), 26.

6. Terry L. Anderson, "Water Options for the Blue Planet," in *The True State of the Planet,* ed. Ronald Bailey (New York: The Free Press, 1995), 275.

7. World Resources Institute (WRI), *World Resources 1990–91* (New York: Oxford University Press, 1990), 5.

8. World Resources Institute (WRI), *World Resources 1992–93* (New York: Oxford University Press, 1992), 118.

9. World Resources Institute (WRI), *World Resources 1994–95* (New York: Oxford University Press, 1994), 129.

10. Ibid., 130–33.

11. Food and Agriculture Organization (FAO), *The State of World Fisheries and Aquaculture* (Rome: FAO, 1995), 47.

12. WRI, *World Resources 1996–97,* 309.

13. See J. T. Houghton et al., eds., *Climate Change 1995—The Science of Climate Change,* contribution of Working Group I to the Second Assessment Report of the Intergovernmental Panel on Climate Change (IPCC) (Cambridge: Cambridge University Press, 1996); and Robert T. Watson, Marufu C. Zinyowera, and Richard H. Moss, eds., *Climate Change 1995—Impacts, Adaptations and Mitigation of Climate Change: Scientific-Technical Analyses,* contribution of Working Group II to the Second Assessment Report of the Intergovernmental Panel on Climate Change (IPCC) (Cambridge: Cambridge University Press, 1996).

14. WRI, *World Resources 1996–97,* 182, box 8.1.

15. See S. Schneider, *Global Warming: Are We Entering the Greenhouse Century?* (San Francisco: Sierra Club Books, 1989), 226.

16. See Owen Toon and Richard Turco, "Polar Stratospheric Clouds and Ozone Depletion," *Scientific American* 264, no. 6 (June 1991): 68–77; and Richard Stolarski, "The Antarctic Ozone Hole," *Scientific American* 258, no. 1 (January 1988): 30–38.

17. World Meteorological Organization, *Scientific Assessment of Ozone Depletion: 1994,* Global Ozone Research and Monitoring Project, Report No. 37 (Geneva: World Meteorological Organization, National Oceanic and Atmospheric Administration, National Aeronautics and Space Administration, and United Nations Environment Programme, 1995), xxxiii.

18. Gert Kelfkens, Frank de Gruijl, and Jan van der Leun, "Ozone Depletion and Increase in Annual Carcinogenic Ultraviolet Dose," *Photochemistry and Photobiology* 52, no. 4 (1990): 819–23.

19. Homer-Dixon, "Environmental Scarcities and Violent Conflict," 8–10.

20. Ibid., 10–11.

21. See Thomas Homer-Dixon and Valerie Percival, "The Case of Senegal-Mauritania," in *Environmental Scarcity and Violent Conflict: Briefing Book* (Washington, D.C.: American Association for the Advancement of Science and the University of Toronto, 1996), 35–38.

22. See Thomas Homer-Dixon and Valerie Percival, "The Case of The Philippines," in *Briefing Book,* 49.

23. For a more detailed description of ingenuity see Thomas Homer-Dixon, "The Ingenuity Gap: Can Poor Countries Adapt to Resource Scarcity?" *Population and Development Review* 21, no. 3 (September 1995): 587–612.

24. Ibid., 600.

25. Mancur Olson, *The Rise and Decline of Nations: Economic Growth, Stagflation, and Social Rigidities* (New Haven: Yale University Press, 1982).

26. Ibid., 62.

27. Homer-Dixon, "The Ingenuity Gap," 600–601.

28. Ibid., 602–603.

29. The authors would like to thank Valerie Percival for her insights on these matters.

30. Ted Gurr, *Why Men Rebel* (Princeton: Princeton University Press, 1970).

31. Homer-Dixon, "Environmental Scarcities and Violent Conflict," 26–27.

32. Doug McAdam, *Political Process and the Development of Black Insurgency 1930–1970* (Chicago: University of Chicago Press, 1982).

33. Thomas Homer-Dixon, "On the Threshold: Environmental Changes as Causes of Acute Conflict," *International Security* 16, no. 2 (fall 1991): 111.

34. Homer-Dixon, "Environmental Scarcities and Violent Conflict," 6.

35. Marc Levy, "Time for a Third Wave of Environment and Security Scholarship?" *Environmental Change and Security Project Report*, issue 1 (Washington, D.C.: Woodrow Wilson Center, spring 1995), 45.

36. See Thomas Homer-Dixon and Marc Levy, "Correspondence: Environment and Security," *International Security* 20, no. 3 (winter 1995–96): 194.

2

The Case of Chiapas, Mexico

Philip Howard and Thomas Homer-Dixon

Overview

In the hushed morning after San Cristóbal's New Year's celebration in 1994, hundreds of masked rebels moved through the empty streets, cutting phone lines, immobilizing the local security apparatus, and establishing an alternative political order. This revolutionary Zapatista government lasted only four days in San Cristóbal and other urban centers of the Central Highlands of Chiapas, Mexico. However, in the next two years, the Ejército Zapatista de Liberación Nacional (EZLN), or Zapatista National Liberation Army, would bring the plight of Chiapan peasants to the attention of Mexicans, foreign investors, and the international community, challenging anew the legitimacy of the ruling Partido Revolucionario Institucional (PRI).[1] Commentators have attributed a range of revolutionary objectives to the Zapatistas, often obscuring the insurgents' principal goal: relief from escalating environmental scarcities that have impoverished their communities.[2]

There are three common explanations for the conflict in Chiapas. First, orthodox political-economic explanations emphasize broad—and often external—forces driving the conflict.[3] These include the PRI's neglect of peasants as a client group, the difficulties of economic restructuring, the inadequacies of Mexican electoral reform, the fear of the North American Free Trade Agreement (NAFTA), the class basis of land concentration, resurgent Mayan identity, and generalized poverty. Although these explanations sketch the national and international context in which the crisis evolved, they obscure the role of ecological and demographic forces.

Second, environmental explanations suggest that the rebellion is somehow connected to deforestation, soil erosion, and biodiversity loss.[4] However, these explanations fail to specify the links between degradation and the Zapatista rebellion. The Zapatistas are not fighting for conservation issues as they are commonly understood by Northern environmentalists, even though the Lacandón Rain Forest is one of the last large tropical rain forests in North America and is the focus of many Mexican and international conservation efforts. As a group, these environmental explanations of the conflict are often ideologically biased, describing the main actors, for example, as evil landowners and innocent peasants.

The third group of explanations falls between these two perspectives. A growing and insightful body of literature emphasizes the maldistribution of natural resources—especially land—as the central grievance of the EZLN and its sympathizers.[5] This literature argues that the development model used by the Mexican government has generally failed. The government's focus should be on microeconomic and micropolitical issues, such as market access, peasant agriculture, local corruption, and the control of PRI political bosses. The virtue of these studies is that they analyze both the structural inequities of land distribution and the history of impediments to real reform.

We show below that the insurgency was a product of three simultaneous factors: rising grievances among peasants caused largely by worsening environmental scarcity, a weakening of the Mexican corporatist state by rapid economic liberalization, and efforts by churches and activist peasant groups to change peasants' understanding of their predicament.

An accurate understanding of the roots of the Chiapas conflict is important for U.S. and Canadian policy makers. The conflict helped trigger an economic crisis by reminding the world that Mexico is a developing country that has yet to solve many underlying economic and social problems. Moreover, the EZLN inspired campesinos, indigenous people, labor, and the urban poor of central and northern Mexico to express discontent with the PRI regime by engaging in violent protest and grassroots democratic campaigns. Mexican authorities have been forced to devote substantial resources to keep similar insurgencies from flaring up elsewhere.

Background

Geography

The southernmost state in Mexico, Chiapas shares a 962-kilometer international border with Guatemala and internal borders with the states of Tabasco, Veracruz, and Oaxaca. Chiapas has an area of 7.6 million hectares administered by 112 municipios, which are administrative areas centered on principal towns. Chiapas can be roughly divided into three regional bands running from northwest to southeast across the state: the Soconusco Coast along the Pacific Ocean, the Central Highlands, and the Eastern Lowlands (see map 2.1). The Soconusco Coast is dominated by great plantations of cash crops for export and some light industry served by modernizing port facilities. The Central Highlands rise 900 meters from the coast to the fertile lands of the Grijalva River and its tributaries. The Highlands encompass two major urban centers, Tuxtla Gutiérrez, the state capital, and San Cristóbal, a former seat of colonial

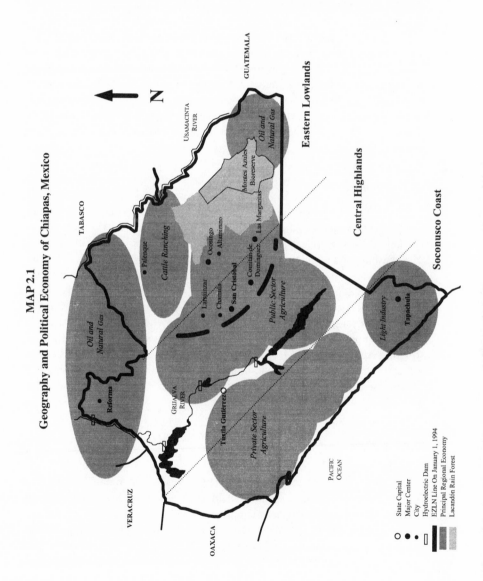

MAP 2.1

Geography and Political Economy of Chiapas, Mexico

power and now a popular tourist destination. Also in the Central Highlands is the municipio of Reforma, with abundant oil and natural gas reserves. The Eastern Lowlands include the Lacandón Rain Forest, which is bounded by the Usumacinta River and Guatemala to the east, the vast deforested area of the Marqués de Comillas in the south, and the increasingly populous area of the Cañadas at the foot of the Highlands. It is in this frontier region between the Highlands and the Eastern Lowlands that people have been most severely affected by environmental scarcities, and it is from here that the EZLN draws its support.

The southern states of Mexico are rich in oil, natural gas, forests, and farmland. In most southern states, and particularly in Chiapas, these resources are extracted by the national government for the use of Mexico's central and northern states. Chiapas produces 5 percent of the nation's oil, 12 percent of its natural gas, 46 percent of its coffee, and 48 percent of its hydroelectric power, yet only a tiny portion of the wealth generated from these resources is returned to the state for development programs—leaving it one of the poorest in Mexico.

Demography

Since 1970, the population of Chiapas has grown 3.6 percent annually, though the rate for the indígena population—speakers of the Mayan family of languages—has been 4.6 percent.[6] According to official Mexican statistics, the total indígena population in Chiapas is currently over 700,000. A full demographic assessment, however, must also include 60,000 indígena refugees who fled Guatemala between 1980 and 1985 and the annual fluctuation of another 60,000 to 120,000 Guatemalan migrant laborers.[7] Most of the Chiapan and Guatemalan indígenas live in the Eastern Lowlands, a socially and economically marginalized region with inadequate educational and health infrastructure (see appendixes 1 and 2). Adding migration from Mexican states to the north, the population growth in the Cañadas and other frontier communities has been between 8 and 12 percent annually for the last two decades (see map 2.2).[8]

Class Relations

In the story of the Zapatista uprising, six groups are important. As mentioned above, the indígenas are the native peoples of this region. One-third of indígenas are monolingual speakers of an indigenous language, and 70 percent live in towns of 1,000 people or less. Spanish is at best their second language, and indígena cultures and languages cut across state and municipio boundaries. The state and municipio governments try, but often fail, to contain and manage these groups. The largest groups are the Tzeltal, Tzotzil, and Chol.

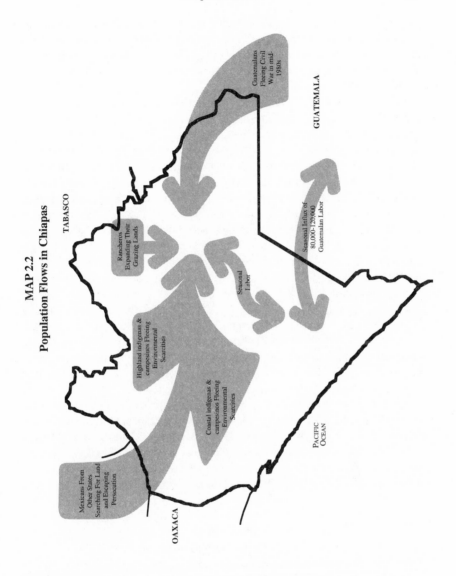

MAP 2.2
Population Flows in Chiapas

TABASCO

GUATEMALA

Guatemalans Fleeing Civil War in mid-1980s

Seasonal Influx of 80,000-120,000 Guatemalan Labor

Seasonal Labor

Rancheros Expanding Their Grazing Lands

Highland indígenas & campesinos Fleeing Environmental Scarcities

Coastal indígenas & campesinos Fleeing Environmental Scarcities

PACIFIC OCEAN

Mexicans From Other States Searching For Land and Escaping Persecution

OAXACA

The vast majority of the EZLN members are indígena coffee growers. The insurgents do not represent all of the people of the Eastern Lowlands; they represent the most marginal of those who have colonized the Lacandón in the past forty years.

The campesinos usually speak Spanish as their first language. As with the indígenas, they are generally subsistence farmers who produce their own food on their own small plots, on commonly owned plots, or on illegally occupied land. Their monetary income is derived from several sources, including raising cattle for large ranches in the region, producing small tradable items, working in tourist industries, engaging in seasonal labor in developing areas of the state, and growing cash crops that are sold to local marketing boards or directly exported.

The latifundistas are a relatively small class of landowners that has long controlled vast territories in the state. In the Eastern Lowlands, most of this land is devoted to capital-intensive cash crops for export: mainly coffee, cocoa, and citrus fruits. Distinct from but similar to the latifundistas are the rancheros, a relatively new group that has taken control of huge tracts of land with the encouragement of state subsidies. They are largely responsible for converting forestland into pastures for grazing, particularly around Palenque at the northern edge of the Lacandón. In Chiapas, both groups have withstood federal attempts at political reform and land redistribution and have retained control of state politics. Working for the PRI, affiliated parties, and the latifundistas are the caciques, political bosses who mobilize communities to support the PRI, exact tithes for traditional festivals, and benefit economically by containing opposition to the ruling regime.

Finally, a group of intellectuals and church and opposition leaders has helped organize indígenas and campesinos and encouraged them to express dissatisfaction with the unfulfilled political promises of the caciques and the oppression of the latifundistas. Many of this group fled political persecution in other parts of Mexico, and some sought refuge in the Chiapan Central Highlands after the 1968 student massacre in Mexico City.

According to the National Statistics and Geographical Information Institute (INEGI), in 1992, 44 percent of Mexico's 84 million people lived in poverty, with 16 percent in extreme poverty. Fifty-six percent of the extreme poor are engaged in agriculture in rural areas.[9] Class distinctions in Chiapas are acutely evident in statistics on the distribution of education, infrastructure, fuel supplies, wages, and economic activities (see appendixes 1 and 2).

Race Relations

Distinctions of race in Chiapas are even more sharply defined than those of class. Statistics show that subordinate racial groups systematically receive less public investment in infrastructure, education, and health than the state or national average. Indígena populations are rigidly confined to a limited number of occupations, mainly in agriculture; most indígena workers earn the minimum wage or less. Poverty statistics reveal striking economic marginalization: in municipios where the indígena population is less than 10 percent, 18 percent of the people are at or below the poverty line; for municipios where the indígena population is between 10 and 40 percent, 46 percent of the people are poor; and for those where more than 70 percent of the population are

TABLE 2.1
Four Main Forms of Landholding in Chiapas

Ejidos: Land vested in peasant communities by agrarian reform, portions of which are often worked by individual campesinos. Until a constitutional change in 1992, the land could not be sold, rented, or used as collateral.

Comunidades agrarias: Primarily land reclaimed by indígena communities from private owners who had seized their land in the late nineteenth and early twentieth centuries.

Private landholdings: Throughout Mexico, privately owned estates not exceeding five thousand hectares, except in Chiapas, where state legislators extended the limit up to eight thousand hectares. In Chiapas, illegal renting or "name lending" (assigning neighboring land titles to family member) increases the actual size of many estates beyond the legal limit.

Official bioreserves and national parks: Areas set aside for the conservation of local ecology, often superimposed upon already existing land titles.

indígena, over 80 percent are poor.[10] These figures suggest that racism has consistently affected the design and implementation of public policy in Chiapas. Policy elites have rarely consulted indígena communities during the planning of welfare programs.

The combined effect of class and racial barriers faced by indígenas and campesinos drives them to rely increasingly on wage opportunities within the rapidly expanding market economy. The market generates an incentive structure that redirects this labor into the production of cash crops or into local industry to supplement subsistence agriculture. As a result, smallholders become bound to the prices and economic fluctuations of distant markets. In addition, the labor demands of oil exploration and production in the north, of industrial and hydroelectric projects on the coast and in the Central Highlands, and of latifundios on the coast provide many with seasonal cash income.[11] Some workers use this income to buy consumer goods or fertilizers and herbicides for their farms. Elites—especially plantation owners and industrialists— have often profited from this increasing supply of cheap, competitive, and largely unorganized labor. Labor competition is accentuated by migrations from other states and Guatemala.

Environmental Scarcity

As discussed in the introductory chapter, there are three types of environmental scarcity: demand-induced scarcity is caused by population growth or increased per capita resource consumption; supply-induced scarcity is caused by degradation and depletion of environmental resources; and structural scarcity, the type most often stressed by political analysts, is caused by an unbalanced distribution of resources that severely affects less powerful groups in the society.[12]

Demand-Induced Scarcity: a Growing Population on a Limited Land Base

From 1970 to 1990, the population of Chiapas doubled, from 1,570,000 to 3,200,000, with an average annual growth rate of 3.6 percent. During this period, the growth rate for indígena populations was a percentage point higher, with the total almost tripling, from 288,000 to 716,000. Although these indígenas are spread throughout the state, many are concentrated in the Eastern Lowlands, especially the Lacandón. There, migrations of poor farmers from other parts of the state and of indígenas from Guatemala have combined with natural population growth to boost the total from 12,000 in 1960 to over 300,000 today.[13]

The 1983 eruption of the Chicón volcano in the northern Central Highlands displaced thousands of people into the Eastern Lowlands. Over the next few years, as many as 300,000 Guatemalans moved across the border during the civil conflicts in that country. Additionally, before several huge hydroelectric projects flooded high-quality farmland in the Grijalva basin, the government forcibly relocated tens of thousands of smallholders into the Eastern Lowlands.[14] These people now live in one of the most marginal parts of the state, often without potable water, electricity, or infrastructure.[15] In the 1960s and 1970s, the movement of seasonal labor to other parts of Chiapas relieved the increased population pressures on small farms, but with economic downturns in the mid-1980s, this option was no longer as easily available.

Although anecdotal evidence suggests that the Eastern Lowlands and the Central Highlands suffer the highest demand-induced scarcities of cropland, good data are available only for the state as a whole, as shown in figure 2.1. This graph demonstrates that land availability per capita increased for much of this century as new lands, especially forestlands, were opened to cultivation. Around 1975, the curve turned sharply downward. There are significant regional differences, however, among the Soconusco Coast, the Central Highlands, and the Eastern Lowlands. Great plantations of coffee and maize have existed in the coastal region since before the Revolution, and labor demands of the coastal latifundios have helped absorb population growth and migration. In contrast, the Central Highlands have seen ever-higher population densities on marginal farmland.[16]

Particularly in and around San Cristóbal, the growing population has consumed much of the forest and occupied most of the potentially arable land, greatly changing the local landscape. Even the expansion of municipio boundaries by some ten-thousand hectares every twenty years has not offset the demand for cropland reflected in the dramatic rise in the percentages of worked and pastoral land and the decrease in the percentage of forested area (see table 2.2).[17]

Supply-induced Scarcity: Deforestation and Soil Erosion

Supply-induced scarcity arises from degradation or depletion that shrinks the pool of resources. In Chiapas, the critical environmental resources are forests and cropland. Land degradation often begins with forest removal, continues with unsustainable agricultural practices, and ends with overgrazing by cattle, sheep, and goats.

Deforestation

When the Spanish found the Lacandón Rain Forest along the Usumacinta River and its tributaries, they called it the Desierto de los Lacandónes—a "desolate" forested area of about 1.5 million hectares. Five hundred years of use have reduced the virgin forest by two-thirds, to about 500,000 hectares.

FIGURE 2.1
Decline in Cultivated Land per Capita in Chiapas

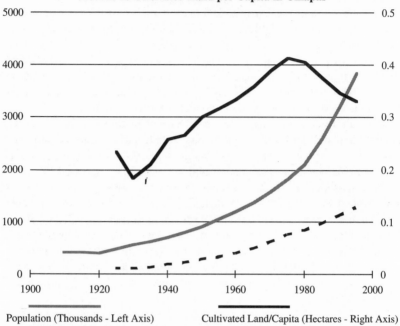

Population (Thousands - Left Axis)   Cultivated Land/Capita (Hectares - Right Axis)

Cultivated Land (Thousands of Hectares - Left Axis)

Sources: Thomas Benjamin, *A Rich Land A Poor People* (Albuquerque: University of New Mexico Press, 1989), 225, fig. 4, and 231, fig. 5; Instituto Nacional de Estadística, Geografía e Informática, *Anuario Estadístico del Estado de Chiapas, Edición 1991* and *Edición 1994* (Mexico, D. F.: Instituto Nacional de Estadística, Geografía e Informática, 1991 and 1994); Instituto Nacional de Estadística, Geografía e Informática, *VII Censo Ejidal* (Mexico, D. F.: Instituto Nacional de Estadística, Geografía e Informática, 1994); Coordinación General de Estadística, Geografía e Informática, *Chiapas Básico 1987* (Coordinación General de Estadística, Geografía e Informática, 1987); and George Collier, Personal Communication, 25 May 1995.

Much of this deforestation has taken place in the last twenty-five years. The largest unfragmented tract of forest—and the largest remaining tract of tropical rain forest in Mexico—is in the Montes Azules Bioreserve. The reserve is also the most diverse ecosystem in Mexico and contains the only Mexican habitats for many endangered mammals.[18]

Over the years, the Lacandón Rain Forest supplied wood for local harvesting and international export and topsoil for monocultural production and cattle grazing. Each of these natural services is now seriously taxed. While the average annual rate of deforestation for tropical forests since the 1950s in Mexico has been 2.44 percent, some parts of the Eastern Lowlands have been deforested at 4 percent per year, and Palenque in the northeast has lost a total of

TABLE 2.2
Population Size, Density, and Land Use in San Cristóbal and Periphery,
1950–1990

	1950		1970		1990	
Population						
San Cristóbal	23,054		32,833		89,335	
Periphery	86,541		132,606		278,191	
Total	109,595		165,439		367,526	
Density	People/km^2		People/km^2		People/km^2	
San Cristóbal	47.6		67.8		228.3	
Periphery	38.8		54.9		81.9	
Total	45.4		68.5		97.0	
Land use	Hectares	%	Hectares	%	Hectares	%
Worked Lands	66,264.9	28.5	71,479.9	29.8	103,956.9	41.5
Pastoral Hills and Plains	43,223.2	18.6	70,569.7	29.5	80,993.2	32.3
Forests	103,466.1	44.5	59,095.5	24.7	45,535.7	18.2
Other/Unproductive	17,135.8	7.4	40,099.7	16.7	19,973.0	8.0
Total	230,090.0	100.0	241,245.0	100.0	250,458.8	100.0

San Cristóbal's periphery includes the municipios of Amatenango, Chalchihuitan, Chamul, Chanal, Chenalho, Huixtan, Larrainzar, Mitontic, Oxchuc, Pantelho, Tenejapa, Teopisca, and Zinacantan.

Sources: Compiled from *Censo Agricola Ganader Y Ejidal, 1950, 1970* (Direccion General de Estadistica) and *VII Censo Ejidal* (Mexico, D.F.: Instituto Nacaional de Estadística, Geografía e Informatíca, 1994).

76,000 hectares at 12.4 percent per year (map 2.3).[19] Moreover, the Lacandón Rain Forest has been increasingly fragmented by squatters' settlements and rancheros, boosting the amount of pastureland within the forest by 200 percent between 1980 and 1988.[20] According to the most comprehensive study of forest loss, between 1974 and 1986 the Lacandón Rain Forest was reduced by 7.7 percent a year. In all, 42 percent of the newly exposed area was converted to pasturelands, 42 percent was overtaken by secondary forests, 6.7 percent was lost to severe soil erosion, and only 3.7 percent was ever used for agricul-

MAP 2.3
Deforestation in Chiapas, 1950–1970

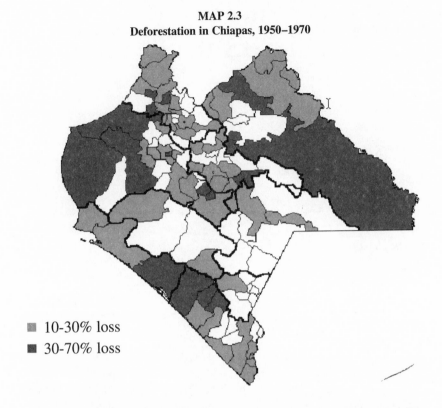

■ 10-30% loss
■ 30-70% loss

Source: George Collier, *Basta! Land and the Zapatista Rebellion in Chiapas* (Oakland, Calif.: Institute for Food and Development Policy, 1994), 42, fig. 2.2.

ture.[21] The fragmentation of forests by road construction, hydroelectric and oil projects, logging, and slash-and-burn or pastureland agriculture has also disrupted the overall integrity of the forest ecosystem. In general, as forests are lost, grassland spreads, as indicated in map 2.4.

In the Central Highlands, deforestation has led to firewood shortages. Highland Mayan communities use oak, madrona, and cedar to cook, to fire ceramic goods, and to distill moonshine.[22] Many communities have exhausted nearby supplies and must travel high into the hills for wood. These "cloud forests," which are home to flora and fauna only found at the crests of hills permanently engulfed by tropical mists, are now the prime target of firewood gatherers.

Soil Erosion

Soil erosion occurs when land is stripped of vegetative cover, tilled or overgrazed, and exposed to the energy of the wind, rain, and runoff. Highland

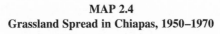

MAP 2.4
Grassland Spread in Chiapas, 1950–1970

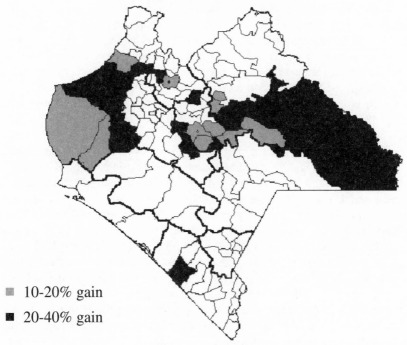

▨ 10-20% gain

■ 20-40% gain

Source: George Collier, *Basta! Land and the Zapatista Rebellion in Chiapas* (Oakland, Calif.: Institute for Food and Development Policy, 1994), 42, fig. 2.2.

soils are particularly vulnerable to erosion, because the steepness of the land makes it easier for wind and rain to dislodge soil particles. Fine-grain eroded soil often contains three times more organic matter and nutrients than the coarse-grain soil left behind. Erosion also reduces soil depth, the diversity of soil biota, and water infiltration and holding capacity.[23]

The rate of erosion is strongly influenced by the kind of processes that expose land to the elements. Logging, road construction, swidden agriculture, and prolonged overgrazing, especially by goats and sheep, all make erosion worse. For example, long-term study of the hillsides of La Fraylesca and Motozintla on the Chiapan border with Guatemala found high levels of soil loss—twenty-five tons per hectare per year—for maize fields that have been stripped of forests, burned, and grazed; losses of fifteen tons for fields that were burned but not grazed; and losses of less than three tons for fields that were neither burned nor grazed.[24]

Much peasant farmland in Mexico is vulnerable to degradation. Neil Harvey notes that the ejidos and communidades agrarias make up about half of Mexico's land area, but most of this land is "rain-fed, undercapitalized and of poor quality."[25] In Chiapas, he finds a sharp drop in milpa output: 19.6 percent for maize and 18 percent for beans between 1982 and 1987.[26] This drop has occurred despite increases in the area of land dedicated to production (20.6 percent and 10 percent over the same period, respectively) because, Harvey contends, much of this expansion had been into the Lacandón, where "tropical soils are notoriously unsuited for sustainable agriculture once the biomass has been destroyed."[27] There has been no credible long-term study of soil erosion in Chiapas,[28] but by piecing together available data and anecdotal evidence, we can clarify the story of supply-induced scarcities of cropland in the state.

In 1990, the United Nations Environment Program in Nairobi, Kenya, and the International Soil Reference Center in Wageningen, the Netherlands, issued a set of maps of soil degradation around the world.[29] Although the data for any specific region are highly aggregated, the maps do provide provisional soil degradation information for Chiapas. They indicate that moderate topsoil loss due to water erosion affects 20 to 50 percent of the Central Highlands and that 5 to 10 percent of the Highlands suffer from moderate terrain deformation caused by water erosion.[30] This damage is caused by farming and forestry practices, and its severity is increasing rapidly.

The maps further indicate that up to 5 percent of the area of the Eastern Lowlands is moderately degraded by terrain deformation due to water erosion as a result of deforestation. This damage is, in the maps' terminology, increasing at a "medium" rate. In a twenty-kilometer-wide strip along the Soconusco Coast, roughly corresponding to the major coffee-producing area of the state, 10 to 25 percent of the land is moderately degraded by loss of topsoil due to wind erosion, and up to 5 percent is strongly degraded (which means the land is "unreclaimable at the farm level") by waterlogging. The cause of this damage, which is increasing at a medium rate, is farming. Finally, the maps identify a sixty-kilometer-wide strip of land between the coast and the Central Highlands that is affected by conditions similar to those in the Eastern Lowlands.

In a 1975 study of farming techniques in a subregion of the Chiapan Central Highlands, George Collier analyzed the causal links between soil erosion and agricultural production.[31] Land abuse was occurring elsewhere in the Central Highlands, he argued, but the growing population of Chamula (a municipio north of San Cristóbal) particularly tested the ecological limits of highland soils. Collier noted that the region's population grew from 16,010 in 1940 to 22,029 in 1950 and to 26,789 in 1960. Farmers in the region engaged in swidden agriculture: every few seasons, they cut down and burned the forest and brushland to supply fresh fields; once their crop yields fell, farmers fallowed the tired fields or turned them into pastureland. Since the population in Chamula now exceeds 51,000, these degradation processes have probably worsened. Although swidden agriculture is often ecologically sound, if population densities are too high—as they have been now for many decades in Chamula—fallow periods are neglected and the soils do not regenerate adequately. As Collier describes it:

> The water supply in hamlet water holes becomes variable, the soil having lost its capacity to maintain a high water table through the dry winter season. Heavy summer rains erode the edges of trails that crisscross the grasslands, silting in the natural limestone sinks, which alternatively flood and dry as mud flats according to the season. Continued shepherding takes its toll. Because of constant clipping off at the roots, grass gives way to gullies of erosion, which spread out from trails along the hillsides. In a matter of years a hill can erode from grazing land to a heap of rocks devoid of top and subsoil.[32]

Since Collier's 1975 study, Chamula's pattern of declining agricultural production due to environmental scarcities has been replicated, with some variation, in parts of the Eastern Lowlands as structural scarcities have forced hundreds of thousands of people from the Central Highlands and the Soconusco Coast on to the largely unclaimed lands of the Lacandón frontier. This process sharply accelerated in the early 1990s. The new colonizers often use upland swidden agricultural techniques not suited to a tropical ecosystem.[33] The forested land that they clear for subsistence agriculture quickly loses productivity and is converted into pastureland for cattle.

A Model of Soil Erosion in Chiapas

We illustrate the impact of supply-induced scarcity on campesinos and indígenas in the Central Highlands and Eastern Lowlands by adapting a general model of the economic costs of soil erosion developed by David Pimentel and his colleagues.[34] The model begins with several assumptions: seven hundred millimeters of rainfall a year, soil depth of fifteen centimeters, land slope of 5 percent, loamy soil with 4 percent organic matter, and a soil erosion rate of seventeen tons per hectare per year. Under these conditions, the study estimates, the loss of agricultural yield after one year is 8 percent and that after twenty years is 20 percent. The Pimentel study further calculates that in the United States it costs $196 per year per hectare in extra fertilizer and water to replace the soil resources depleted by erosion and thereby to compensate for the yield loss. In developing countries where such funds are not available, the economic cost is paid in lower food production.

Table 2.3 compares the starting assumptions in Pimentel's model with estimates of conditions in the Central Highlands and Eastern Lowlands of Chiapas. This allows us to gauge the relative severity and cost of soil erosion affecting exposed land in these regions. The differences between Pimentel's

TABLE 2.3
Comparison of the Cost of Soil Erosion in the Central Highlands and Eastern Lowlands with Pimentel's Base Projection

Ecological Factor	Pimentel	Central Highlands	Eastern Lowlands
Annual Rainfall	700mm	1500mm	2100mm
Top Soil Depth	15cm	=	-
Slope	5%	++	=
Top Soil Quality	loamy	loamy	fine
Organic Matter	4%	=	++
Erosion Rate on Exposed Land	17 tons/ha/yr	+	+
After 20 years, average annual per hectare			
Yield Loss	20%	+	++
Replacement Costs	US$196	+	++

In this table, " + " means that the factor in question contributes more to erosion than it does in the Pimentel base projection, " − " means the factor contributes less; and " = " means the factor contributes about the same amount to erosion.

Source: Base Projection from Pimentel et al., "Environmental and Economic Costs of Soil Erosion and Conservation Benefits," *Science* 267, no. 5201 (February 24, 1995): 1117–23.

starting assumptions and our estimates for Chiapas suggest that yield loss and resource replacement costs are significantly higher in Chiapas. Not only is annual rainfall two, three, and sometimes four times greater, depending on the location in the state, but the type of rainfall—torrential, heavy tropical rains coupled with high winds—significantly increases soil erosion. The slope of land in the Highlands is often much greater than 5 percent, which means that water runoff is substantial and more likely to carry away the soil. In the Lowlands, the soil is fine. The amount of organic matter in this soil is higher than that of the Highlands, but because of the thinness of lowland soil the extra nutrient content is quickly depleted by successive seasons of production. Taking all these factors into consideration, we estimate that erosion rates in the Central Highlands and the Eastern Lowlands are probably in excess of the baseline rate of 17 tons per hectare per year found by Pimentel et al.[35] Of course, communities that use large amounts of fertilizer may temporarily relieve the effects of erosion, but often at the expense of groundwater pollution and attendant health problems.[36]

The Pimentel model applies to a temperate ecosystem. Although erosion rates may not always be higher in tropical zones than in temperate zones, the consequences for agricultural productivity are often more severe. Rattan Lal notes that "the drastic erosion-caused productivity decline in soils of the tropics is due partly to harsh climate and partly to low-fertility."[37] Because of the shallow topsoil, we estimate in table 2.3 that productivity losses from erosion will be greater in the tropical Eastern Lowlands than the more temperate Central Highlands.

It is also important to distinguish between the rate of soil erosion on exposed land and the total quantity of eroded soil in a given region. Since more land is exposed in the Central Highlands, this region has suffered from more total erosion than the Eastern Lowlands; yet it is not clear that the erosion rates for exposed land in the two regions differ that markedly. So far, soil erosion in the Lacandón is only evident on the steepest slopes at the highest elevations, but given that the population of the Highlands and several other areas is spilling over into the Lacandón, it is likely that erosion there will worsen and will be accompanied by economic consequences of a magnitude suggested by the model in table 2.3.

Structural Scarcity

In Chiapas, the average land endowment for subsistence production is two hectares, while for commercial production it is twenty hectares.[38] This structural scarcity of land for poorer farmers arises from the domination and manipulation of land-tenure arrangements by a wealthy elite of agricultural producers. It is reinforced by the political hegemony of this elite, by the economies of scale and commercial success of large agricultural producers, and by corrupt and inequitable credit and social-spending programs managed by the state. In many areas of the state, prices for agricultural products do not accurately reflect the products' market value, because PRI representatives and caciques control the transportation sector, manage many produce-purchasing programs, and in general manage the market access of smaller producers. This control permits them to secure political support and to enforce the regime of unequal land distribution.

The impact of structural scarcity of land on peasants in Chiapas is magnified by inadequate access to credit and by limited infrastructure. Since the 1980s, access to government and private agricultural credit has increasingly benefited beef producers; on the other hand, small commercial and subsistence farmers have had increasing difficulty getting credit. From 1985 to 1989, almost 80 percent of all agricultural producers in Chiapas had no access at all to government credit. By 1990, the figure was over 87 percent.[39] In addition, economic liberalization has reduced government subsidies for fertilizer, tools, and other inputs. In response, small commercial farmers have set up their own credit agencies, returned to subsistence farming, or left agriculture altogether.

As people spill into the Eastern Lowlands, they move into a situation of deeply institutionalized economic marginalization. Map 2.5 shows the per capita distribution of key infrastructural services on a ten-square-kilometer grid of the state for 1990. The darker the area in the map, the lower the availability of potable water, electricity, and educational and health services. For

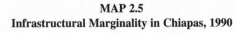

MAP 2.5
Infrastructural Marginality in Chiapas, 1990

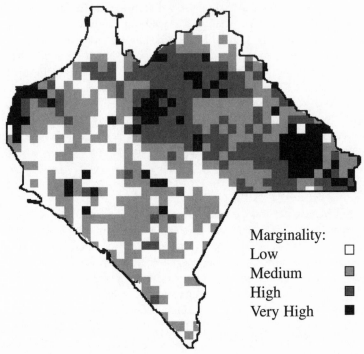

Marginality:
Low   ☐
Medium   ▨
High   ■
Very High ■

Sources: From the GIS system developed by P. Farias, I. March, and M. Fuller at the Centro de Investigaciones Ecologicas del Sureste, San Cristóbal de las Casas, Chiapas, Mexico, 1995. Marginality is determined by data on communities with drainage and piped water and on the use of electricity and cooking fuel, some of which are also presented in appendix 1. The data are provided at the municipio level, generalized into 10 square kilometer quadrants.

the large black region in the Eastern Lowlands, low population density is the main cause for the paucity of infrastructure. However, what is most telling about this map is the strip of "high" marginality (represented by dark gray) that runs from the Central Highlands in the northwest to the Eastern Lowlands in the southeast. This part of Chiapas has a significant and rapidly growing population in areas of marginal infrastructure.

Sixty percent of the productive territory in Mexico is pastureland, producing meat for a population 50 percent of whom never eat meat.[40] The rapid expansion of the economically powerful cattle industry has made structural scarcities of environmental resources worse for many peasants and small farmers. In recent decades in Chiapas, the cattle industry has grown very quickly (see figure 2.2), and it now occupies 30 percent of the state's total

FIGURE 2.2
Growth of Grazing in Chiapas

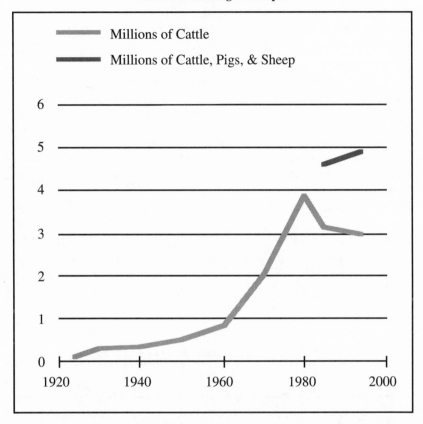

Millions of Cattle

Millions of Cattle, Pigs, & Sheep

Sources: Thomas Benjamin, *A Rich Land A Poor People* (Albuquerque: University of New Mexico Press, 1989), 233, figure 6; Jose Luis Pontigo Sanchez, *La Ganaderia Bovina en Los Regiones de Chiapas: Costa y Norte* (San Cristóbal: CIES, 1988), 11–12; and Maria del Carmen Carmona Lara et al., *Ecologia—Cambio Estructural en Chiapas: Avances y Perspectivas* (Tuxtla Gutiérrez, Mexico: Universidad Autónoma de Chiapas, 1988), 36, and Instituto Nacional de Estadística, Geografía e Informática, *Anuario Estadistico del Estado de Chiapas, Edición 1994* (Mexico, D.F.: Instituto Nacional de Estadística, Geografía e Informática, 1994).

land area. Between 1950 and 1970, the population of grazing animals quadrupled, with 75 percent of the total on private lands.[41] By 1990, the population of grazing animals had doubled again, for the most part still on private lands.

In popular accounts, Latin American beef production for export inevitably causes environmental destruction—especially loss of forests—and various social ills. However, recent scholarship suggests that this "hamburger thesis" is misleading and that it must be heavily qualified by accounts of the specific demand-induced and structural scarcities in each area.[42] In Chiapas, deforestation is only an indirect result of the activities of the rancheros. Particularly in the Highlands and around Palenque, rancheros are responsible for buying, illegally renting, or taking over land that has been cleared of its forest by smallholders and squatters. The slash-and-burn agriculture of these smallholders initially provides rich ground for their crops, but as fields lose productivity, rancheros take over, and their cattle make an already existing erosion problem worse.

Serious structural scarcities can also be found in coffee production. Most of the best land for coffee lies along the Soconusco Coast and is controlled by a small number of large coffee estates. The largest 116 owners control 12 percent of the land devoted to coffee production. As one moves east across the state to land of generally lower quality, farm size drops and the land becomes predominantly public and communal (for example, ejidos) rather than private. The 91 percent of coffee growers in Chiapas who own less than five hectares are mainly located in the Central Highlands and the Eastern Lowlands. Table 2.4 shows that as of 1990, the distribution of coffee land was significantly more skewed toward the wealthy in Chiapas than in Mexico as a whole: Mexico and Chiapas have virtually the same percentage of coffee producers with two hectares or less of land, yet in Chiapas the percentage of coffee growers

TABLE 2.4
Distribution of Coffee Producers by Plot Size, 1990

Hectares	Chiapas	Mexico
up to 2	48,762	194,538
2 - 5	18,248	64,377
5 - 10	5,102	17,881
10 - 20	1,202	4,291
20 - 50	208	808
50 - 100	104	246
over 100	116	178
Total	73,742	282,319

Source: Neil Harvey, "Rural Reforms, Campesino Radicalism and the Limits to Salinismo," in *Transformation of Rural Mexico,* number 5 (La Jolla, Calif.: Ejido Reform Research Project, Center for U.S.-Mexican Studies, University of California at San Diego, 1994), 10, table 2.

with more than fifty hectares is twice as high. Additionally, two-thirds of Mexico's producers with over one hundred hectares operate in Chiapas.

In sum, Chiapas's population—especially its poorest members—has been affected by all three types of environmental scarcity: demand-induced, supply-induced, and structural. Demand-induced and structural scarcities are the most severe; the former are driven by the large increases in the indígena and migrant populations living in the Eastern Lowlands on the frontier with the Central Highlands. The limited evidence available suggests that supply-induced scarcities are sometimes harsh but are generally not as severe or widespread as the other two types. Soil erosion affects the ability of some parts of the Central Highlands to support agriculture; forest resources are particularly taxed near urban areas. The perceived differential between the availability of land and forest resources in the Central Highlands and that in the Eastern Lowlands stimulates the migration of resource-poor peasants into the Lacandón. Unfortunately, the migrants do not escape the impact of the three types of scarcity and of the dislocations caused by economic reform. This is especially true in the Cañadas region of the Eastern Lowlands, the region that spawned the EZLN insurgency.[43]

Resource Capture and Ecological Marginalization

The history of Chiapas is a chain of multiple yet discrete instances of resource capture and ecological marginalization. Resource capture occurs when powerful elites—partly in response to the pressures of population growth and resource depletion—shift in their favor the laws and property rights governing local resources, thereby concentrating ecologically valuable resources under their control. Ecological marginalization occurs when population growth and severely unequal resource distribution in resource-rich regions force poor people to migrate to ecologically fragile areas; as the population density of these migrants increases, they damage local environmental resources, which deepens their poverty.[44]

This chain has most harshly affected the rapidly growing population of indígenas and campesinos. As pressures have mounted on agricultural land in Chiapas, elites and wealthy farmers have often taken control of the best land and have perverted land reform and redistribution policies. Many peasants affected by these degradations have migrated to the periphery of the Lacandón Rain Forest. There they have cleared new land, only to be forced—either by the quick depletion of soil nutrients or by more land seizures by wealthy farmers—to move further into the vulnerable forest.

Period 1: Conquest to Revolution, 1519–1910

From the time of the arrival of the Spanish in the fifteenth century, the indígenas of southern Mexico have fought in countless riots and rebellions against those who would make them slaves and subservient. At the core of each indígena uprising has usually been the demand for land.[45] During this time, the class distinctions that persist to this day began to take shape:

> Within the landscape of haciendas and republics of Indians there stood the cities, the seats of the merchants who supplied both haciendas and mines, of officials who regulated privileges and restrictions, of priests who managed the economy of salvation. From their stores, offices, and churches extended the communal networks which supplied the mines and drew off their ores; the bureaucratic network which regulated life in the hinterland; and the ecclesiastic network which connected parish priests with the hierarchy at the center. In the shadow of palace and cathedral, moreover, there labored the artisans who supplied the affluent with the amenities and luxuries of a baroque colonial world, the army of servants, and the enormous multitude of the urban poor.[46]

During the tumultuous nineteenth century, Mexico City did not firmly establish sovereignty over Chiapas, and the state remained quasi-autonomous because of its isolation. Elites would regularly threaten to alter their allegiances in favor of Guatemala if they received insufficient backing for their plans to manage state resources.

Logging began in the Lacandón in 1859, with the first large cedars and mahoganies felled at the junction of the Usumacinta and Jatate Rivers. In 1880, three large companies cornered the world market for mahogany by controlling the most accessible supplies along the Usumacinta River. Over the next twenty years, other firms joined in, and by the end of the nineteenth century private companies and individuals owned all the shorelines of the major rivers in southern Mexico.[47] By the beginning of this century, four entrepreneurs were allowed to parcel up and purchase much of the remaining 1.2 million hectares of forest at the encouragement of President Porfirio Díaz's investment-hungry regime.

Until the Revolution began in 1910, Díaz also promoted the creation of great latifundios—private agricultural estates varying in size from tens to many thousands of hectares. With the construction of a Pacific railroad, the economic advantage of a strong alliance with Mexico became clear to Chiapan elites, especially to the latifundistas who owned large coffee plantations along the Soconusco Coast.

Period 2: Revolution to Liberalization, 1910–1982

Two motivations strongly influenced the character of the new Mexican Constitution of 1917: first, a need for political stability in a country that had experienced hideous violence since 1910, and, second, a desire to redistribute land to peasants who had lived without secure access to land since the sixteenth century. Article 27 provided clear principles for the redistribution of Mexican territory among the three categories of ejidos, communidades agrarias, and private landholdings. The authors of the Constitution entrenched the right of peasants to petition for legal recognition of their title to land that was being used by their communities, whether the land was formally part of a private holding or an extension of an existing community title. In the following decades, significant parcels of land were expropriated from large estates and redistributed.

In Chiapas, the best lands are around the Grijalva Valley, the Soconusco Coast, and areas of the Central Highlands close to transportation routes, but these areas were seldom subject to redistribution. In fact, the government often met its land reform obligations by promising, usually without actually granting, titles to unused lands in the rain forest with difficult market access. Land reform favored landowners by allowing them to choose which lands to sell and by allowing the owners to retain capital investments in supplies and equipment.[48]

By the late 1950s, the trickle of migrants into the Central Highlands and the Eastern Lowlands had grown to a steady stream from other parts of the state, from neighboring states, and also from Guatemala.[49] People came to participate in the state's logging and agricultural booms. When migrants arrived from outside of Chiapas, they found the PRI's network of caciques strongest in the Highlands and the Soconusco Coast. As population densities rose in the Central Highlands, many people chose to move on to the Lacandón frontier, often with the active encouragement of government officials. They settled in the frontier areas of the Lacandón Rain Forest, occupying lands usually managed by ejido members and coming into conflict with more established communities. This pattern is evident in maps 2.6 and 2.7, which show that the Eastern Lowlands saw most of the state's land redistribution while a large proportion of the agriculturally productive lands between the Soconosco Coast and the Grijalva River basin remained private.

The Lacandón Rain Forest absorbed the high population growth of peasant communities in the state. The rapidly expanding cattle industry in the Eastern Lowlands, however, did not require labor so much as land, and ranchers arriving from the states of Tabasco and Veracruz established large ranches at the northern frontier of the rain forest by clearing new forest or assuming control—by rent or repression—of areas already cleared by migrant farming communities. These communities also competed with state and private logging companies that did not want the forest felled without profit. "By 1971," writes James Nations, "the individuals who controlled these companies realized that the farm families they had pushed into the [Lacandón] were clearing and burning the forests before the commercial hardwoods could be extracted."[50] As competition for land and forest resources increased, the pressure to realign the distribution of resources in the state also grew.[51] In many cases, this realignment occurred under the guise of land reform.

MAP 2.6
Agrarian Reform Over 50 Percent of Municipio Land by 1950

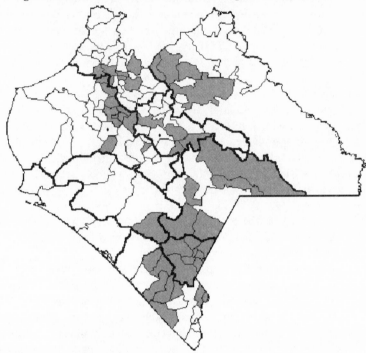

Source: George Collier, *Basta! Land and the Zapatista Rebellion in Chiapas* (Oakland, Calif.: Institute for Food and Development Policy, 1994), 32, fig. 1.3.

Land seizures by indígenas and campesinos became common as communities fought to obtain a basis for subsistence living. The creation of the Montes Azules Bioreserve at the heart of the Lacandón in 1978 did not discourage the flood of people from central and northern Mexico from making their home at the edge of the forest. The government distributed lands that latifundistas were eager to sell off, often giving the same piece of land to several competing peasant communities, creating patchworks of overlapping land titles that still exist around the bioreserve. As populations grew, large landowners were forced to expel squatters, often violently, if only to prevent them from petitioning the federal government for land titles. When the federal government did decree land reform and redistribution, the intended effects were undermined by this resource capture process: special exemptions were issued by the state, landowners surrendered the most marginal lands at high prices, and people were moved into the Lacandón and assigned titles there.

MAP 2.7
Agrarian Reform Over 50 Percent of Municipio Land by 1975

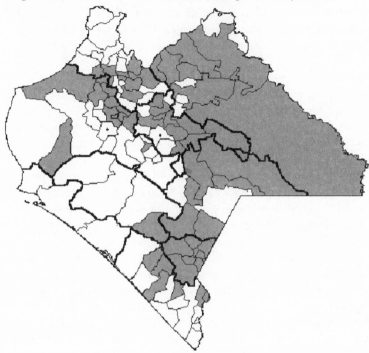

Source: George Collier, *Basta! Land and the Zapatista Rebellion in Chiapas* (Oakland, Calif.: Institute for Food and Development Policy, 1994), 32, fig. 1.3.

In short, the PRI and the elites of Chiapas redistributed just enough land in marginal areas of the state to accommodate a growing population within an inegalitarian resource regime. However, once a community had cleared forest-lands to which they had no legal title, landowners with political clout would buy, rent, or otherwise claim the land for their livestock; by 1983, one hundred thousand campesinos and indígenas were completely landless.[52]

Period 3: Economic Liberalization to Rebellion, 1982–1994

Some analysts believe that Mexico's import substitution industrialization strategy of the 1950s and 1960s had served the nation relatively well and produced a period of stable development during which wages and productivity rose. By the late 1970s, however, wages had begun to lag, and external debt had reached crippling levels. Following the debt rescheduling of 1982, the ruling PRI turned to export-led growth.

In the years following the 1982 debt crisis, Mexico proceeded with economic liberalization by selling its state-owned corporations and by reducing market controls, subsidies, and public credits. These policies shifted power from labor and peasants to private capital, financial institutions, export manufacturers, and multinational corporations. Despite problems of inflation, capital flight, and unstable financial and foreign-exchange markets, the country's economic planners managed to engineer a recovery that continued until the end of 1994 and that was driven by strong private-sector growth.

Many observers argue that the real crisis in Mexico occurred with the erosion of its neocorporatist political system caused by this economic restructuring.[53] Even though the PRI successfully reduced inflation and renewed the interest of foreign investors, economic reform forced the ruling party to reduce its patronage of key client groups—especially labor and peasants—that had reinforced the political system's stability since the Revolution. The PRI has been forced to renegotiate, ignore, or break the economic and political pacts that had maintained relative stability in Mexico since the 1910 Revolution.

Party and class elites at the national, state, and local levels managed the transition in different ways, revealing the remarkable resilience and adaptive power of the PRI's co-optive mechanisms. Restructuring required a speedy capitalization of agriculture, because government farm credits and subsidies for fertilizers, tools, and transport were drying up. In Chiapas, smallholders with significant off-farm earnings could make their agricultural production more capital intensive. Those with little or no capital, however, had to turn to bare subsistence production, or they leased their lands and their labor to wealthier producers.

Furthermore, a massive backlog of land claims had built up within the state bureaucracy as people sought title to lands that they had tilled for decades. Land claims were rarely resolved, and claimants appealing for legal control were often punished and coerced by caciques and private armies.

As peasants found good land increasingly scarce in the Eastern Lowlands of Chiapas, they began to sell their labor as seasonal workers, causing large migrations from the Eastern Lowlands to the great latifundios of the Soconusco Coast. By one estimate, several hundred thousand Chiapan and Guatemalan campesinos and indígenas migrated through the Lacandón each year, destroying over ten thousand hectares annually as they moved through the forest, cleared small plots, gathered fuelwood, and built temporary residential sites along the way.[54] Labor migrants from the Central Highlands and the Eastern Lowlands returned to their communities with money and the expectation that chemical fertilizers and herbicides would coax another season's growth out of tired soils. This was an important step in bringing the economic reforms to the peasants, for, as Collier and his colleagues observe, traditional agricultural methods were supplanted by modern ones or abandoned in favor of microbusinesses.[55]

Because peasants often had to sell their labor to supplement their meager household incomes, latifundistas had a supply of cheap labor. Trapped by indebtedness, peasants frequently settled marginal lands at the edge of great estates. From the 1960s through the 1980s, the PRI regime (often with World Bank funding) used subsidies to encourage peasants to participate in the growing cattle industry. Ultimately, however, large rancheros manipulated smallholders into raising calves, by far the riskiest part of ranching; many smallholders also found it profitable to rent their ejidos illegally for cattle grazing.

At the edge of the Lacandón, severe land scarcities produced fierce competition among farmers, rancheros, squatters, loggers, and indígena communities.[56] Conflict grew increasingly frequent and violent from 1972 on as the pace of expulsions and intercommunity competition quickened. In the 1980s, campesino and indígena communities—often in alliance with church members of all ranks and denominations—were involved in many protests, marches, and riots, mostly against the lack of respect for land rights by state elites. The peasant groups sometimes broke into factions marked by bitter rivalries. To protect private land, particularly land owned by rancheros, the governor issued special *certificados de inafectabilidad* to keep land reform from affecting individual properties. By 1988, 4,714 certificados, 95 percent of the total number distributed in the state since 1934, protected 70 percent of the land used for cattle grazing from agrarian reform.[57] Communities and families continued to be evicted from private and ejido land. As PRI caciques lost their ability to sustain their corporatist obligations with anything other than repression, many communities shifted their political allegiances to opposition parties; however, in doing so, the communities again invited eviction from their land.

As the liberalization policy faltered in the mid-1980s, President Carlos Salinas sought to force its pace in late 1987 with more cuts in the fiscal deficit and tighter monetary policy.[58] He also presented an Economic Solidarity Pact to the labor, agricultural, and business sectors. The pact promised sweeping structural changes in the agricultural sector, including the phased elimination of most food and agricultural subsidies and price controls, the opening of markets by shutting down marketing boards and parastatal purchasing arrangements, and an end to ejidos. In 1991, the PRI amended article 27 of the Mexican Constitution, introducing in 1992 an Agrarian Law that drastically changed the land-tenure system. Campesino and indígena organizations perceived that they were not properly consulted as the Agrarian Law was designed.

Consistent with the government's economic reform program, the new Agrarian Law disbanded the institution of public land titles. Members of the ejidos and the comunidades agrarias were given the legal right to purchase, sell, rent, or mortgage the individual plots and communal lands that constituted each title. If government-endorsed cash crops were grown, private companies of as many as twenty-five individuals could purchase twenty-five times the area allowed by single-land permits. Also, the constitutional mechanism allowing squatters to make land claims was removed.

In Chiapas, the sale and rental of public lands had long occurred illegally in response to environmental scarcities, the pressures of resource capture by elites, and market downturns. By the early 1980s, as a result, a significant portion of the state's ejidos were controlled by latifundistas.[59] Moreover, the original land-redistribution provisions of the Constitution had never been fully enforced, especially with respect to latifundios, which often contained the state's best land.[60] The 1992 changes facilitated further concentration of good land, since it was now possible to buy public land outright. Furthermore, large owners were given a year to sell off excess property that—under the terms of the new Agrarian Law—would eventually be redistributed.[61] The law had a particularly negative impact on the status of women, because the dispersal of family holdings had to be legally approved by the male head of the household, with the wife given the first option to buy released lands.[62] Around this time, EZLN organization began in earnest with the purchase of guns and supplies, the theft of fifteen hundred kilograms of dynamite from PEMEX facilities, and the significant influx of volunteers—almost one-third of whom were women.

In the late 1980s, Mexican and international environmental groups coordinated their actions to lobby for limits to the amount of forestland cleared annually at the edge of the Lacandón. As with many government polices, the limits were unevenly applied, and peasants in the Cañadas region found themselves under a more rigorous regime, enforced by caciques, than that applied to the growing number of rancheros near Palenque. Still, logging of the rain forest continued: between 1983 and 1988, another 143,000 hectares were logged. In total, 665,000 hectares had been logged since the last century, with an astonishing 585,000 hectares logged after 1970.[63]

Map 2.8 shows that in-migration, population growth, and government concession of contradictory and overlapping land titles resulted in serious encroachment on the Montes Azules Bioreserve. This encroachment occurred despite expansion of the bioreserve at various times and efforts by international environmental groups to reduce forest loss. In the lead up to the NAFTA negotiations, the government tightened regulations on community activities in the bioreserve. Severe quotas on deforestation by smallholders were put into effect, and another 81,000 hectares were reclassified as bioreserve lands.

Figure 2.3 summarizes the story outlined in this section. In Chiapas, latifundistas and rancheros invariably captured and controlled the best agricultural land. The land reform initiatives that Mexicans fought so hard to achieve during the Revolution were perverted to marginalize a large portion of the campesino and indígena population on ecologically vulnerable land. These groups

MAP 2.8
Human Settlements and Land Titles Encroaching on the Montes Azules Bioreserve, Eastern Lowlands of Chiapas, Mexico, 1994

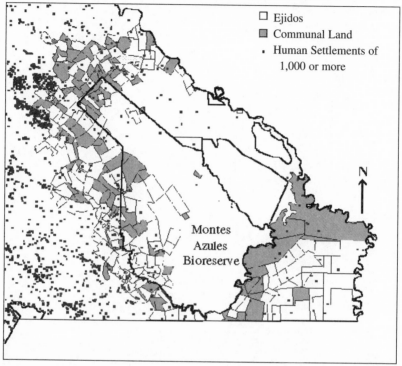

□ Ejidos
▨ Communal Land
▪ Human Settlements of 1,000 or more

Montes
Azules
Bioreserve

N

Source: The GIS system developed by P. Farias, I. March, and M. Fuller at the Centro de Investigaciones Ecologicas del Sureste, San Cristóbal de las Casas, Chiapas, Mexico, 1995.

settled at the periphery of towns on lands or in forests that appeared unclaimed. When local elites needed more land for cash crops, grazing, or industries, the peasants were evicted. Ironically, as the squatters cleared the forests and prepared the land for their crops, they made the land more desirable.

Since the 1950s, rapid population growth compounded the effects of these persistent structural inequalities to force more poor people into ecologically, socially, and economically marginal areas, particularly in the Cañadas at the frontier of the Lacandón. In the Central Highlands, supply-induced scarcities of soil resources also provoked migration to the forest. Moreover, recent policies of economic liberalization reinforced structural inequalities, because the PRI regime embraced the interests of private capital and largely removed economic support for peasant agriculture.

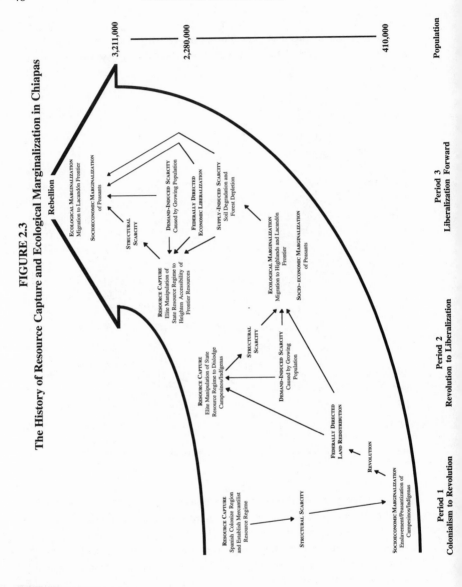

FIGURE 2.3
The History of Resource Capture and Ecological Marginalization in Chiapas

Violent Conflict

Civil strife is a function of both the level of unredressed grievance motivating challenger groups and the opportunities available to these groups to act on their grievances. The probability of civil strife is greatest when multiple pressures at different levels in society interact to increase grievance and opportunity simultaneously.[64] Drawing on the above analysis, figure 2.4 shows how changes in grievance and opportunity occurred in Chiapas.

Population growth among peasants dependent on subsistence agriculture coupled with the expansion of land-intensive activities—such as ranching—increased the demand for cropland. A political economy deeply rooted in the region's colonial past combined with unstable property rights to produce persistent structural scarcities. In a context of limited land resources and a closing of the agricultural frontier (partly because of ever-greater restrictions on expansion into the Lacandón), these factors caused higher demand-induced scarcity of cropland, especially for marginal indígenas and campesinos. High population densities and lack of agricultural capital contributed to land degradation in parts of the Central Highlands.

Demand-induced, supply-induced, and structural scarcities interacted to generate processes of resource capture and ecological marginalization of peasants. During the period of economic reform in the 1980s, these processes combined with the loss of agricultural subsidies and credits for small producers to sharply aggravate economic hardship and, in turn, the grievances of poor peasants. Economic reform also weakened the PRI's political control within the state, changing the structure of political opportunities facing potential challengers to the regime. Independent peasant organizations and segments of the church promoted the "cognitive liberation" of peasants, which heightened their perceptions of grievance and opportunity. Eventually, the simultaneous rise in grievance and opportunity produced the EZLN insurgency.

Rising Grievances

We have shown above that in the years preceding the rebellion, demand-induced and structural scarcities of cropland were increasing for indígenas and campesinos in Chiapas, and these scarcities strongly contributed to chronic economic hardship for peasants dependent upon subsistence food production. We have also noted that the economic liberalization that occurred in the 1980s eviscerated the agricultural subsidies and credits upon which many of these smallholders depended. Unfortunately, peasants affected by acute land scarcity had only limited economic alternatives in the state economy, in part because the economic adjustments of the 1980s reduced labor absorption in key industries, such as oil, and also because new agricultural technologies reduced labor intensity on many latifundios.

These factors harshly affected indígenas and campesinos, causing sporadic outbreaks of violence. But harsh poverty did not, by itself, make the coordinated insurgency of the EZLN inevitable. Contrary to common belief, there is no clear correlation between poverty (or economic inequality) and social conflict.[65] Whether or not people become aggrieved and violent when they find

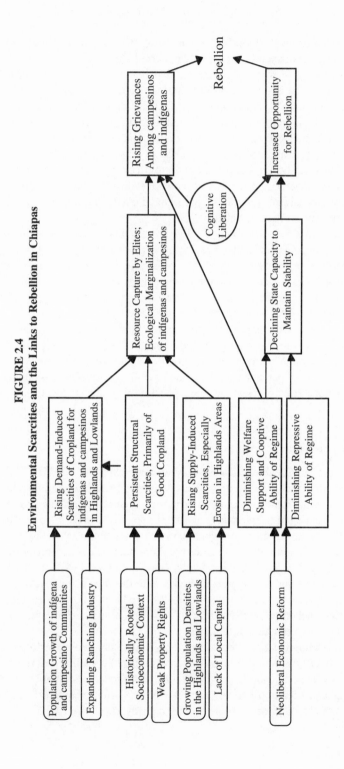

FIGURE 2.4
Environmental Scarcities and the Links to Rebellion in Chiapas

themselves increasingly poor depends, in part, upon their notion of economic justice. For grievances to become severe, people must perceive that there is a substantial and widening gap between the level of satisfaction they have achieved and the level they believe they deserve.[66] The church and independent peasant organizations played a critical role in shaping the Chiapan peasants' shared conception of justice.[67]

To cause civil strife, economic crisis must be severe, persistent, and pervasive enough to erode the legitimacy or moral authority of the dominant social order and system of governance. System legitimacy is therefore a critical intervening variable between rising poverty and civil conflict. The Zapatista leadership articulated and channeled peasant grievances so as to focus blame for the peasants' hardship on the PRI regime.

Article 27 of the Mexican Constitution entrenched a commitment to land reform and redistribution. The PRI tied its legitimacy, in part, to these revolutionary principles, and through corporatist practices it has tried to channel opposition into political consensus and regime support.[68] However, economic reform made both adherence to constitutionally mandated agrarian policy and corporatist politics too costly. The Zapatistas argued that the changes to Article 27 and the new Agrarian Law signaled that the PRI would never honor its land reform and redistribution commitments. The goal of the insurgency, therefore, was to force the government to renew its land redistribution efforts with greater honesty; it also hoped to force the government to reform the electoral process so that democracy could provide an outlet for peasant grievances.

In important ways, the EZLN insurgency is different from other Latin American guerrilla movements. Unlike, for example, the Sendero Luminoso in Peru, the EZLN's leaders do not espouse a revolutionary dogma, they have not evoked in their followers a religious fervor, and they do not plan to seize control of the state. Instead, Zapatista demands are fundamentally local. The most important items on their agenda are relief from environmental scarcities and local democracy.

Changing Opportunity Structure and Declining State Capacity

In Chiapas, the Zapatistas have exploited long-standing social and class cleavages. They have explicitly mobilized the indígenas and campesinos against the elite classes of landowners, rancheros, and capitalists. Although peasant groups have had a long and unfortunate history of squabbling among themselves, the Zapatistas have successfully evoked class- and ethnicity-based collective identities. Furthermore, the weakening of the PRI has significantly influenced the structure of political opportunities for challenger groups. Economic reforms under way for almost a decade have eroded the regime's ability to bribe and co-opt opposition groups within the state. The national and state

PRI governments have had less money to spend on maintaining political consensus, and in the absence of political consensus, groups negatively affected by economic reform have found it easier to organize ever more vociferous and violent opposition.

The PRI regime, however, has some powerful weapons in its fight to retain its legitimacy and social control. Mexicans have a deep desire for civil stability; they widely agree that the violence of revolution should never again be allowed to consume Mexican society. This desire for stability is often said to be the bedrock of the PRI's legitimacy. Indeed, during the most recent national election campaign, the PRI effectively played on the danger of social instability.[69] Zedillo won the election by equating the opposition parties with uncertainty and instability and by convincing the electorate that no party other than the PRI would be able to guide the country through its economic and social turmoil.

Chiapas and other southern states are a crucial power base for the PRI's national political strategy. In past presidential elections, the PRI has been able to claim that solid votes in its favor by southern peasant constituencies legitimized the entire country's electoral result, despite serious fraud in urban centers, such as Mexico City, and in the industrial northern states. In Chiapas, the PRI has used co-optive methods, and sometimes outright coercion, to secure voter support: caciques establish political ties with influential landowners, business people, and union bosses that guarantee votes from the people they oversee, commercial and transportation licenses are granted and removed according to political allegiance, and even basic judicial procedures, such as divorce, can be used to isolate community members who support opposition parties.[70] But economic reforms have weakened this structure of co-option and coercion, and there are indications that the regime has had to rely more and more on outright electoral fraud to maintain its political control of the state.[71]

In adjusting to liberalization in the 1980s and 1990s, the PRI has tolerated a more open dialogue throughout Mexico about the country's ailments, and it has even conceded some high-level electoral victories to the center-right party, the National Action Party (PAN). It has conceded few victories, however, to the center-left party, the Democratic Revolutionary Party (PRD), a party that has never fully recovered from its loss in the 1988 presidential election. Even though the PRD has been the main opposition voice in Chiapas for a long time, it has had less and less to offer its supporters, and for many aggrieved groups—such as the EZLN—it has not been radical enough. These aggrieved groups long ago gave up on the state's democratic institutions, and they perceive no peaceful opportunities to express their rising dissatisfaction.

Cognitive Liberation

The Catholic and Protestant churches have provided key venues for the discussion of political repression in Chiapas. Relations between the Catholic

Church and the Mexican state have been strained since before the Revolution, because the state expropriated church lands and enforced a separation of responsibilities in such areas as education. However, the Catholic Church remains a tremendously powerful social institution for many rural communities. The Diocese of San Cristóbal (which includes all municipios east of San Cristóbal), led by Bishop Ruiz, has drawn heavily on liberation theology to inspire the faith of the region's peasants. Liberation theology emphasizes the basic material needs of the poor, including adequate food and shelter; it argues that peasants must be free from exploitation. The Protestant evangelicalism that has taken root in some communities in the Eastern Lowlands has similar principles. However, it has more seriously strained relations with caciques, by disavowing the need for the alcohol and festival tithes that are used to keep campesinos indebted to the caciques and to reinforce PRI loyalties. In response, the caciques drive Protestant families and communities from their land when they refuse to participate in traditional religious and cultural practices. In the end, the effect of the activities of both the Protestant and the Catholic churches has been to create networks of lay preachers and catechists with parishes that cooperate remarkably well across denominations.[72]

There has been a large rise in Protestant affiliation among Chiapan peasants. Many municipalities, especially in the indígena communities of the Eastern Lowlands, have over 20 percent of their population in evangelical parishes.[73] Protestantism and liberation theology have encouraged indígenas and campesinos to set up non-PRI social organs. The Emiliano Zapata Peasant Organization (OCEZ), the Independent Confederation of Agricultural Workers and Peasants (CIOAC), and the Union of Ejido Unions of Chiapas (UU) are the most active and independent organizations working for land reform, labor rights, and fair credit programs. Such grassroots organizations experiment with community development, create networks among different ethnic groups, and foster regional and class identities.[74] Since the mid-1970s, these peasant groups have become increasingly radical.[75]

President Echeverría's attempt in 1972 to expel occupants from the Lacandón turned the sympathies of many peasants in the Eastern Lowlands toward liberation theology and the Protestant churches. It also encouraged land claims and provoked radical new groups to form and resist co-option by the PRI. Twenty years later, in 1992, the Salinas government gave a decisive push to the cognitive liberation of the campesinos and indígenas when it abolished the institution of ejido land titles. Not only did the radical peasant groups see the last legal safeguards for their property fall to economic liberalization, but some realized that rebellion was necessary. The EZLN was formed and began quietly acquiring weapons, medical supplies, uniforms, and members. Subcommandante Marcos writes:

> It strikes me that what most radicalized our companions were the changes to Article 27. That was the door that was shut on the Indian people's ability to

survive in a legal and peaceful manner. That was the reason they decided to take up arms, so that they could be heard, because they were tired of paying such a high blood tax.[76]

The intellectual leadership provided by such figures as Subcommandante Marcos gave the peasants an insurgent consciousness. They acquired an interpretation of the economic, social, and ecological forces that entrapped them. Many peasants who support the EZLN have intimate ties to local resources and have long lived with inadequate, marginal lands. Their awareness of "environmental scarcities" is shown by their repeated demand for healthy land and their refusal to accept land titles in state bioreserves.[77] Zapatista leaders have built on this ecological awareness by explaining to the peasants not only why the best lands in the state have gone to the elites, but also how the economic reforms have damaged the "ecological bases" of indígena and campesino culture.[78]

Conclusions

Two central conclusions can be drawn from our analysis of environmental scarcities and the EZLN rebellion. First, the situation in Chiapas in the early 1990s represented a particularly explosive combination of factors: a rapidly growing peasant population, structural imbalances in resource distribution that were deeply embedded in the social and economic character of the society, and weak property rights that were easily abused by powerful interest groups. Throughout the state's long history, elites regularly violated constitutional and statutory property rights by capturing the best resources for themselves and marginalizing others to ecologically fragile areas. Elites circumvented land redistribution and hindered efforts by local communities to organize crop production for subsistence and export. Without clear and vigorously enforced property rights, resource capture was easy.

It is not easy, however, to improve this situation. Clear and enforced property rights are not enough. If the distribution of resources is not changed, strong property institutions will simply reinforce the dominance of predatory elites. Land redistribution must therefore play a major role in any future development strategy that hopes to gain support from campesinos and indígenas. Indeed, most developmental models recognize that land redistribution and strong property laws are together essential to the success of late industrializing countries.[79] So far in Chiapas, however, the PRI's spasmodic and halfhearted efforts at land redistribution have only produced chaos.

Second, EZLN activities are part of a larger "wedge" splitting open the authoritarian character of Mexico's corporatist regime. This wedge includes diverse social groups working on issues ranging from human rights to the environment, external and internal investors concerned about Mexican political stability, and PRI technocrats who hope to promote meritocracy and democracy within Mexican society in order to salvage a future for their party.

The EZLN insurgency has had a profound impact on the PRI corporatist regime, catching it at a particularly sensitive moment of transition. Movements such as the EZLN disrupt "traditional patterns of presidentialism, official-party dominance, patrimonialism, clientelism, and corporatism across the whole terrain of government urban planning and policy."[80] Even though the EZLN's demands are mainly focused on issues in Chiapas, the insurgents have successfully coaxed out similar demands in other parts of the country.[81] Moreover, the PRI executive that ruthlessly crushed violent uprisings in the past is now more sensitive to national and international opinion. George Phillip notes that the international community is not always willing to isolate the economic prospects of a society "from the nature of its political system or the willingness of its rulers to respect human rights."[82] The regime finds itself scrutinized by multiple external and internal groups, each with access to different pressure points and each pursuing diverse, but not always opposed, agendas.

The uprising has brought new hope for democracy in Mexico, though Chiapas remains a highly militarized zone. The EZLN and other grassroots organizations held a national plebiscite on issues of justice and land reform; they have used modern communication technologies to encourage widespread public dialogue; and they are offering the policy alternatives necessary for a healthy democracy. However, there are still victims of "passive military engagement" by the Mexican and private armies—sexual assaults, assassinations, disappearances, and kidnappings are tactics of this engagement.[83]

Zedillo has chosen to negotiate with the EZLN and, for the most part, has kept the dialogue open. His regime confronts a growing internal meritocracy, an ever-better-educated and -informed polity, and a restructuring international economy. As a result, the pressures on the Mexican regime for real democracy and an adequate livelihood for the poor will only grow stronger. For the indígenas and campesinos of Chiapas, this livelihood requires sustainable access to healthy environmental resources.

APPENDIX 1

Relative Social Marginality: Comparative Statistics on Indigenous Population of Mexico, Total Population of Chiapas, and Indigenous Population of Chiapas

	Indigenous Population of Mexico	Total Population of Chiapas	Indigenous Population of Chiapas
Population			
1970	3,111,415	1,569,053	287,836
1990	5,282,347	3,210,496	716,012
Annual Growth Rate	2.6%	3.6%	4.6%
Literate Population over 15 years		Percentage	
	59.0	69.6	45.6
Instruction of Population over 15 years			
No Instruction	37.0	29.0	49.2
Primary incomplete	32.8	31.0	28.3
Primary completed	13.8	13.8	10.7
Post Primary	12.3	22.8	6.9
Religious Population over 5 years			
Catholic	81.4	67.6	61.5
Protestant	10.4	16.3	22.6
Other	1.1	1.9	2.2
None	5.6	12.7	11.6
Homes by Infrastructure			
Without Drainage	72.2	55.7	80.7
Without Piped Water	46.5	40.5	49.6
Without Electricity	37.0	33.1	61.3
With No Services	25.5	20.5	36.5
With 1 Service	28.1	24.4	32.1
With 2 Services	24.8	20.9	19.8
With 3 Services	20.7	33.4	10.4
Homes by cooking fuels			
Firewood	69.8	60.9	90.9
Gas	28.3	36.9	7.6
Electricity or oil	0.9	1.1	0.6
Infant Mortality			
Official	39/1000	39/1000	
Independent			54.7/1000

Sources: Compiled from Instituto Nacional de Estadística, Geografía e Informatíca, *Chiapas: Hablantes de Lengua Indígena* (Aguascalientes, Ags., Mexico: INEGI, 1993). The independent measure of indígena infant mortality is cited in Roger Burbach and Peter Rosset, *Chiapas and the Crisis of Mexican Agriculture* (Oakland, Calif.: Institute for Food and Development Policy, 1994), 2.

APPENDIX 2

Relative Economic Marginality: Comparative Statistics on Indigenous Population of Mexico, Total Population of Chiapas, and Indigenous Population of Chiapas

	Indigenous Population of Mexico	Total Population of Chiapas	Indigenous Population of Chiapas
Population			
1970	3,111,415	1,569,053	287,836
1990	5,282,347	3,210,496	716,012
Annual Growth Rate	2.6%	3.6%	4.6%
Population by Minimum Wage Level		Percentage	
Unwaged labor	21.0	19.0	32.5
1 minimum wage or less	38.7	40.0	49.1
Between 1 and 2 minimum wage	22.9	21.1	7.9
Between 2 and 3 minimum wage	6.8	8.0	2.9
Between 3 and 5 minimum wage	3.2	4.1	1.2
More than 5 minimum wage	2.3	3.6	1.3
No specific wage	5.1	4.2	5.2
Population by Economic Sector			
Primary Sector	59.6	58.3	83.0
Secondary Sector	15.6	11.1	5.5
Tertiary Sector	21.9	27.4	8.6
No Specific Sector	2.9	3.1	2.9
Working Population by 5 Main Groups			
Agricultural Workers	59.9	58.1	83.7
Educational Workers	2.8	3.7	2.5
Artisans	11.6	8.8	3.9
Commercial clerks	4.6	5.2	1.8
No Specific	2.4	2.2	2.6
Women over 12 "inactive" economically			
	86.8	86.4	89.7
Economically Inactive Population Over 12 Years By Category			
Household work	71.3	66.6	75.5
Students	15.6	24.3	18.3
Retirement Home	1.4	0.7	0.3
Handicapped	1.7	1.2	0.8
Other	10.0	7.2	5.1

Source: Compiled from Instituto Nacional de Estadística, Geografía e Informatíca, *Chiapas: Hablantes de Lengua Indigena* (Aguascalientes, Ags., Mexico: INEGI, 1993).

Notes

An earlier version of this chapter was published as Philip Howard and Thomas Homer-Dixon, *Environmental Scarcity and Violent Conflict: The Case of Chiapas, Mexico*, Occasional Paper of the Project on Environment, Population, and Security (Washington, D.C.: American Association for the Advancement of Science and the University of Toronto, 1995). For their valuable help, the authors thank Patricia Atristan-Monserrat, George Collier, Richard Enthoven, Pable Farias Campero, Michael Fuller, Neusa Hidalgo-Monroy, Declan and Patrick Hill, Ken Mitchell, James Nations, Ron Nigh, Karen O'Brian, Aimee Robinson, Dick Roman, Peter Rosset, Ian Rowlands, Druscilla Scribner, Evon Vogt, and Phil Wheaton.

1. The recent Zapatista uprising takes its name from Emiliano Zapata, a leader of poor peasants at the turn of the century who led the Mexican Revolution from the south. The insurgency has invoked his memory to focus the minds of today's peasants in Chiapas on decades of oppression by large landowners and ranchers.

2. To achieve this goal, land availability and electoral reform have remained the key demands of the EZLN from the beginning of the insurgency. In one of his "declarations," Zapatista spokesperson Subcomandante Marcos presented a clear set of demands to President Ernesto Zedillo in twelve words: "work, land, shelter, bread, health, education, democracy, liberty, peace, independence, and justice."

3. See Andrew Reding, "Chiapas Is Mexico," *World Policy Journal* 11, no. 1 (spring 1994): 11–24, and Joseph Whitmeyer and Rosemary Hopcroft, "Community, Capitalism, and Rebellion in Chiapas," draft paper, Department of Sociology, University of North Carolina, December 1995.

4. See Hilary French, "Forging a New Global Partnership," chap. 10 in *State of the World 1995*, ed. Lester Brown et al. (New York: Worldwatch Institute, 1995), and Greenpeace reports and popular discussion on the World Wide Web; for the argument that environmental degradation in Chiapas seriously affected agricultural production between 1982 and 1987, see Maria del Carmen Carmona Lara et al., *Ecología— Cambio Estructural en Chiapas: Avances y Perspectivas* (Tuxtla Gutiérrez, Mexico: Universidad Autónoma de Chiapas, 1988).

5. See George Collier, *Basta! Land and the Zapatista Rebellion in Chiapas* (Oakland, Calif.: Institute for Food and Development Policy, 1994); Neil Harvey, "Rural Reforms, Campesino Radicalism and the Limits to Salinismo," in *Transformation of Rural Mexico*, number 5 (La Jolla, Calif.: Ejido Reform Research Project, Center for U.S.-Mexican Studies, University of California at San Diego, 1994); and "Chiapas: Challenging History," *Akwe:kon—Journal of Indigenous Issues* 11, no. 2 (summer 1994).

6. The latter growth rate is a conservative estimate, yet it is astonishingly high compared with other population growth rates around the world. Demographers generally accept a 4 percent annual growth rate as near the upper bounds of biologically possible human reproduction.

7. Luis Raul Salvado, *The Other Refugees: A Study of Nonrecognized Guatemalan Refugees in Chiapas, Mexico* (Washington, D.C.: Hemispheric Migration Project, Georgetown University, 1988), 13.

8. Ron Nigh and Felipe Vallagran, private communication, 25 May 1995.

9. World Bank, *Mexico: Second Decentralization and Regional Development Project Report* (Washington, D.C.: World Bank, 19 August 1994), 1.

10. Harry Patrinos and Alexis Panagides, "Poverty and Indigenous People in Mexico," *Akwe:kon—Journal of Indigenous Issues* 11, no. 2 (summer 1994): 73.

11. The drilling activities of the national oil monopoly, Petróleos Mexicanos (PEMEX), in the northern municipio of Reforma have drawn people from neighboring municipios and from out of state. The region has seen its population increase from 6,136 in 1960 to 30,875 in 1990. Many of the most accessible oil reserves in Mexico are beneath the soils of Reforma and the Lacandón; consequently, the Lacandón will support a growing number of drilling sites and an expanding population of labor in coming years. See Roberto Thompson, *Problemática Agraria y Política Petrolera en Chiapas* (Tuxtla Gutiérrez, Chiapas: Centro de Investigaciones Ecológicas del Sureste, 1983); Instituto Nacional de Estadística, Geografía e Informática, *Anuario Estadístico del Estado de Chiapas, Edición 1994* (Mexico, D.F.: Instituto Nacional de Estadística, Geografía e Informática, 1994), 35; and Steven E. Sanderson, "Mexico's Environmental Future," *Current History* 92, no. 571 (February 1993): 76.

12. See Thomas Homer-Dixon, "Environmental Scarcities and Violent Conflict: Evidence from Cases," *International Security* 19, no. 1 (summer 1994): 8–9.

13. Jeffrey Wollock, "Globalizing Corn," *Akwe:kon—Journal of Indigenous Issues* 11, no. 2 (summer 1994): 57.

14. Hydroelectric energy from the Grijalva River is captured by a system of dams from Lake Angostura to its delta in the state of Tabasco. The dams have been responsible for the flooding of over one hundred thousand hectares of prime land in the basin. Further expansion of the dam system has not been possible, since peasant communities have increasingly anticipated relocation and mobilized opposition in time.

15. Salvado, *The Other Refugees*, 13.

16. In this study, "marginal" land is land that is ecologically vulnerable; it is relatively susceptible to rapid degradation by erosion and overuse. It may be fertile and productive in the short term, but this productivity is difficult to maintain for more than a few years.

17. Analysts often inappropriately assemble and compare government census data in an effort to identify trends. Particularly in the case of Chiapas, marginal areas are often inadequately represented in these data or are given characteristics of neighboring communities. Political manipulation of municipio boundaries by the PRI hinders calculation of time-series data on environmental scarcity. In general, Chiapas data cover only some four million of the state's seven million hectares, or around 60 percent of the total. Thus, we stress trends in proportions and ratios; where census data must be used, we present as many alternative data sources as possible.

18. Rodrigo Medellin, "Mammal Diversity and Conservation in the Selva Lacandón, Chiapas, Mexico," *Conservation Biology* 8, no. 3 (September 1994): 780–99.

19. O. Mazera et al., "Carbon Emissions from Deforestation in Mexico," manuscript, Centro de Ecología, Universidad Autónoma de México, Mexico, D.F., 1990; Secretaría de Agricultura y Recursos Hidráulicos, as cited in Ronald Nigh, "Consecuencias de la Colonización Agropecuaria para las Selvas Tropicales del Sureste de Mexico: Implicaciones Regionales y Globales," working paper for the Centro de Investigaciones y Estudios Superiores en Antropología Social del Sureste, 1994, 15.

Some of the best evidence on the impact of deforestation is subjective. A recent study showed that a large majority of Chiapans believe that campesinos and indígenas are more seriously affected by deforestation than rancheros, the Mexican government, or people in other nations. See Lourdes Arizpe et al., *Cultura y Cambio Global: Percepciones Sociales sobre la Desforestación en la Selva Lacandóna* (Mexico, D.F.: Centro Regional de Investigaciones Multidisciplinarias, 1993).

20. A. Cortez Ortiz, *Estudio Preliminar sobre Desforestación en la Region Fronteriza del Río Usamacinta* (Mexico, D.F.: Informe Técnico, Instituto Nacional de Estadística, Geografía e Informática, 1990), as cited in Nigh, "Consecuencias de la Colonización Agropecuaria," 15.

21. A. Cuaron, "Conservación de los Primates y Sus Habitats en el Sur de México," master's thesis, Universidad Nacional de Costa Rica, Heredia, 1991, as cited in Nigh, "Consecuencias de la Colonización Agropecuaria," 15.

22. See J. Conrad, "Maximo Lopez, Firewood Gatherer," *American Forests*, November/December 1988, 38, for anecdotal evidence of the impact of receding forests.

23. See Rattan Lal, *Soil Erosion in the Tropics* (New York: McGraw-Hill, 1990).

24. Olaf Erenstein, Centro Internacional de Mejoramiento de Maiz y Trigo, private communication, 30 May 1995.

25. Neil Harvey, "Playing with Fire, the Implications of Ejido Reform," *Akwe:kon—Journal of Indigenous Issues* 11, no. 2 (summer 1994): 22.

26. Milpa agriculture is a traditional method of crop rotation among maize, beans or coffee, and fallow. In the Eastern Lowlands, despite the fallow period allowed by milpa production, land is still exhausted quickly.

27. Harvey, "Rural Reforms," 11.

28. A 1981 publication used LANDSAT images to generate soil erosion data for Chiapas; however, because of a typographical error, it is impossible to determine which year the data were collected. See Secretaría de Agricultura y Recursos Hidráulicos, *Inventario de Erosión en el Estado de Chiapas mediante Imágenes del Satélite Landsat* (Secretaría de Agricultura y Recursos Hidráulicos, Dirección General de Conservación del Suelo y Agua, 6 March 1981). One study suggests that declining agricultural yields in Chiapas between 1982 and 1987 were caused by environmental degradation. However, this five-year period was marked by low rainfall, high currency inflation, and radical adjustment programs that better explain the sharp decline in yields, especially for small producers. The study neglected the effects of liberalized agricultural policy and structural scarcities; it is a good example of the hazards of not placing the analysis of environmental degradation in a political and economic context. See Carmona Lara et al., *Ecología*.

29. Global Assessment of Soil Degradation, *World Map on Status of Human-Induced Soil Degradation*, Sheet 1, North and South America (Nairobi, Kenya/Wageningen, The Netherlands: United Nations Environment Programme/International Soil Reference Center, 1990).

30. According to the maps, "moderate" degradation causes "greatly reduced agricultural productivity."

31. See George Collier, "Soil Erosion in Chamula," in *Fields of the Tzotzil: The Ecological Bases of Tradition in Highland Chiapas* (Austin: University of Texas Press, 1975), 121. See also Raul García-Barrios and Luis García-Barrios, "Environmental

and Technological Degradation in Peasant Agriculture: A Consequence of Development in Mexico," *World Development* 18, no. 11 (1990): 1572.

32. Collier, *Fields of the Tzotzil*, 115.

33. Pablo Farias Campero, ECOSUR, Chiapas, Mexico, private communication, May 1995.

34. See David Pimentel et al., "Environmental and Economic Costs of Soil Erosion and Conservation Benefits," *Science* 267, no. 5201 (24 February 1995): 1117–23, for an excellent review of the effects of soil erosion and its consequences for agricultural sustainability.

35. There are clear limitations to this use of the analysis of Pimentel et al. The most obvious is that they assume homogeneous terrain, whereas the Central Highlands and the Eastern Lowlands of Chiapas are extremely heterogeneous in elevation and soil type.

36. Pimentel et al., "Environmental and Economic Costs," 119; Maximiliano Huerta Cisneros et al., *Características Generales de la Vegetación y Su Utilización en 25 Municipios de Chiapas* (Chiapas, Mexico: Fomento de Corporación de Chiapas, 1986), 16; Carmona Lara et al., *Ecología*, 28, 29; Olaf Erenstein, Centro Internacional de Mejoramiento de Maíz y Trigo, private communication, 30 May 1995.

37. Lal, *Soil Erosion in the Tropics*, 16.

38. Nigh, "Consecuencias de la Colonización Agropecuaria," 27.

39. Secretaría de Agricultura y Recursos Hidráulicos and Comisión Económica para América Latina y el Caribe, *Primer Informe Nacional sobre Tipología de Productores del Sector Social* (Mexico, D.F.: Subsecretaría de Política Sectorial y Concertación, 1992), 19.

40. Nigh, "Consecuencias de la Colonización Agropecuaria," 14.

41. Ibid., 12.

42. Marc Edelman, "Rethinking the Hamburger Thesis: Deforestation and the Crisis of Central America's Beef Exports," in *The Social Causes of Environmental Destruction in Latin America*, ed. Michael Painter and William Durham (Ann Arbor: University of Michigan Press, 1995).

43. Average coffee yields in Cañadas are under 300 kilograms per hectare, compared with the state average of over 500. Similarly, the average maize yield for the Cañadas region is about 1,300 kilograms per hectare, but for the state it is over 2,000. A. Carlos Santos, "Development and Conservation of Natural Resources in the Las Cañadas Region of the Lacandóna Rain Forest" ("Population/Environment Equation: Implications for Future Security," Third Conference on Environmental Security, 31 May–4 June 1994).

44. Homer-Dixon, "Environmental Scarcities and Violent Conflict," 5–40, especially 8–16.

45. "Land hunger propelled the Chamulas [indígenas] forward as much as did their talking stones and living Saints. The *criollos* of San Cristóbal so dominated cultivable land in these high pine mountains that the holdings of Chamulas—much as they still are today—were measured in rows and not hectares." John Ross, *Rebellion from the Roots* (Monroe, Maine: Common Courage Press, 1994), 67. Pages 251–67 provide an excellent account of the role of the jungle for Mayan and Chiapan history.

46. Eric Wolf, *Peasant Revolutions of the Twentieth Century* (New York: Harper and Row, 1969), 5.

47. Felipe Vallagran, "Forest Policies in Chiapas," public communication to Oscar Gonzalez Rodriguez, Subsecretary of Natural Resources, Secretariat of Environment, 10 May 1995.

48. In 1974, a quasi-official committee of indígenas called the Indigenous Congress complained about injustices throughout the state: "We have problems with ranchers who invade our lands. . . . We need land, we don't have enough of it, so we have to rent it, or go away to work. The lands we have been given are infertile. We need to be taught our rights under the Agrarian Laws." Collier, *Basta!*, 63. For more on how state elites disrupted the land reform efforts of the Revolution, see Antonio García de León, *Resistencia y Utopía* (Mexico, D.F.: Ediciones Era, 1985).

49. Ross writes: "The first wave of settlers were, like the 'new' Lacandónes before them, Chol refugees pushed out of Palenque. They were soon joined by highland Tzotziles, squeezed off the undernourished soils of Chamula. . . . Non-Mayan Indians from Oaxaca, forced off their communal lands by government dams, arrived in the Desert of Ocosingo; *indígenas* [were] dislodged by the White Guards of southern Veracruz's murderous cattle kings, a regional industry sustained by World Bank credits; landless mestizo farmers from as far away as Guerrero and Michoacán joined the flow in pursuit of a patch on which to grow a little corn." Ross, *Rebellion from the Roots*, 255–56.

50. James Nations, "The Ecology of the Zapatista Revolt," *Cultural Survival Quarterly* 18, no. 1 (spring 1994): 32.

51. Logging interests have strong historical ties to state and PRI elites. When demand increased substantially after World War II, entrepreneurial effort was channeled into buying up land and working around the rules established by the Constitution. For example, by 1949 the firm Vancouver Plywood had pasted together a territory of 600,000 hectares by a system of name lending between families and contractors. In 1957 and 1961, presidential decrees granted various privileges to logging companies to facilitate the removal of precious hardwoods, such as mahogany, tropical cedar, oak, madrone, and pine. Then, in 1972, President Luis Echeverría Álvarez granted the small community of Maya Lacandón of the Eastern Lowlands—comprising only sixty-six families—communal title to a vast tract of over 600,000 hectares of the Lowlands containing much of the remaining Lacandón Rain Forest. The president and the state elites knew that this Mayan community would easily relinquish control of substantial portions of this land to rancheros and logging companies. He ordered the area's other occupants—campesinos and indígenas—to relocate to several larger communities or to move out entirely. Only after major protest by these occupants, who suddenly found themselves declared squatters, were some of their land titles recognized. Government relocation programs continued, however, and private loggers easily secured rights to extract the remaining hardwoods. In 1974, the Lacandóna Forestal Company and Palenque Triplay Company were granted a concession of 1.3 million hectares of virgin, secondary, and fragmented forest lands with permission to continue operations until 1986. Logging companies operating in the Lacandón were nationalized later that year, and operations were significantly expanded with public capital. Road construction into the forest increased again with a PEMEX study of the area's oil reserves. Although the Montes Azules Bioreserve was created in 1978, campesinos, rancheros, and commercial loggers continued to push in to the rain forest. Thus, in the decades leading up to economic liberalization, competition for forest resources grew fierce as firms were

forced to work further up the Usumacinta River and cut deeper into the forests: between 1970 and 1975, 314,000 hectares was logged; another 128,000 hectares was lost between 1976 and 1980. Ross, *Rebellion from the Roots*, 255; Vallagran, "Forest Policies in Chiapas."

52. Roger Burbach and Peter Rosset, *Chiapas and the Crisis of Mexican Agriculture* (Oakland, Calif.: Institute for Food and Development Policy, 1994), 6.

53. Corporatism is the state's practice of absorbing social movements into its bureaucracy or party apparatus before they organize independently. Opposition is thereby confined to local and marginal political spaces, if it poses little threat, or it is eliminated entirely if it seriously challenges elites. In the current Mexican context, neocorporatism means the PRI's practice of negotiating with various opposition groups and economic sectors—especially labor, peasants, and private capital—to produce economic and political pacts that maintain social stability; importantly, the regime is not assured of getting everything it wants from this process. Neocorporatism is a process of co-opting sectoral and opposition leaders into the policy process and opening up a little political space for groups not aligned with the PRI. The concession is offered in exchange for support of the PRI's policies, and the arrangement is managed by commissions, committees, and other political institutions designed to contain political dissent at a high level and dissuade local protest. However, both economic sectors and opposition groups may still be subjected to repression, including harassment, imprisonment, and assassination by the police, army, and private armed forces. Groups are thus paralyzed by threats, by diminishing resources, and by a lack of leadership during crucial moments of political action. See Neil Harvey, "The Difficult Transition: Neoliberalism and Neocorporatism in Mexico," in *Mexico: Dilemmas of Transition*, ed. Neil Harvey (London: Institute for Latin American Studies, 1993); Denise Dresser, *Neopopulist Solutions to Neoliberal Problems: Mexico's National Solidarity Program* (La Jolla: Center for U.S.-Mexican Studies, University of California at San Diego, 1991); Judith Adler Hellman, *Mexico in Crisis* (New York: Holmes and Meier Publishers, 1988), chap. 5; Frederick C. Deyo, "Economic Policy and the Popular Sector," in *Manufacturing Miracles, Paths of Industrialization in Latin America and East Asia*, ed. Gary Gerefii and David L. Wyman (Princeton: Princeton University Press, 1990); and Wayne Cornelius, Judith Gentleman, and Peter Smith, eds., *Mexico's Alternative Political Futures*, Monograph Series, no. 30 (La Jolla: Center for U.S.-Mexican Studies, University of California at San Diego).

54. Allan de Janvry and Raul Garcia, "Rural Poverty and Environmental Degradation in Latin America," manuscript, Department of Agricultural and Resource Economics, University of California at Berkeley, 1988, 7; see also Salvado, *The Other Refugees*.

55. George Collier, Daniel Mountjoy, and Ron Nigh, "Peasant Agriculture and Global Change: A Maya Response to Energy Development in Southeastern Mexico," *Bioscience* 44, no. 6 (June 1994): 406; Collier, "The Toll of Restructuring on Lives and Communities," in *Basta!*, 107–24.

56. See Patricia Gomez Cruz and Christina Maria Kovic, *Con un Pueblo Vivo en Tierra Negada* (San Cristóbal, Chiapas: Centro de Derechos Humanos, 1994), for a detailed account of the marches, land occupations, detentions, assassinations, demands for state assistance, and conflict among campesinos generated from agricultural con-

flicts; see Carlos Heredia and Mary Purcell, *The Polarization of Mexican Society* (Mexico, D.F.: Equipo Pueblo, 1994), for a general account of social friction in Mexican agriculture; see the epilogue of Thomas Benjamin, *A Rich Land a Poor People* (Albuquerque: University of New Mexico Press, 1989), on how the PRI and landowning elites cooperate against peasants in Chiapas.

57. Harvey, "Rural Reforms," 22.

58. See Nora Lustig, *Mexico: The Remaking of an Economy* (Washington, D.C.: Brookings Institution, 1992).

59. Burbach and Rosset estimate that by 1983, 30 percent of the state's ejidos were controlled by large landowners. Burbach and Rosset, *Chiapas and the Crisis of Mexican Agriculture*, 6.

60. Statewide, a significant amount of land has been redistributed since the Revolution. Although this redistribution has produced a large statistical reduction in the level of land concentration, as we have noted in this chapter, the majority of the land distributed has been of inferior quality, allowing persistently high concentrations of the most ecologically robust land.

61. In response to widespread peasant opposition to the new Agrarian Law, the PRI regime compromised, first, by permitting some further land redistribution and, second, by keeping the existing land appeals process in place for an interim period. As of 1994, almost two thousand unresolved land claims—30 percent of those filed in all of Mexico—were for tracts of land in Chiapas.

62. Harvey, "Playing with Fire," 23.

63. Vallagran, "Forest Policies in Chiapas." Calculating deforestation rates is often difficult, because definitions of what is meant by a "logged" region vary and because the contribution of forest regeneration to overall forest size is rarely taken into account.

64. Homer-Dixon, "Environmental Scarcities and Violent Conflict," 25, 27.

65. See William Ford and John Moore, "Additional Evidence on the Social Characteristics of Riot Cities," *Social Science Quarterly* 51, no. 2 (September 1970): 339–48, and Robert Jiobu, "City Characteristics and Racial Violence," *Social Science Quarterly* 55, no. 1 (June 1974): 52–64.

66. See Ted Gurr, *Why Men Rebel* (Princeton: Princeton University Press, 1970).

67. See James Scott, *The Moral Economy of the Peasant: Rebellion and Subsistence in Southeast Asia* (New Haven: Yale University Press, 1976), 1–11.

68. See Roberto Newell and Luis Rubio, *Mexico's Dilemma: The Political Origins of Economic Crisis* (Boulder, Colo.: Westview Press, 1984).

69. See María Luisa Tarrés, "Middle-Class Associations and Electoral Opposition," in *Popular Movements and Political Change in Mexico*, ed. Ann Craig and Joe Foweraker (Boulder, Colo.: Lynne Rienner Publishers, 1990).

70. George Collier, "The New Politics of Exclusion: Antecedents to the Rebellion in Mexico," *Dialectical Anthropology* 19, no. 1 (1994): 1–44.

71. See Christian Anglade and Carlos Fortin, "Accumulation, Adjustment and the Autonomy of the State in Latin America," in *State and Capital Accumulation* (Pittsburgh: Pittsburgh University Press, 1985).

72. Father Pablo Romo Cedano, Diocese of San Cristóbal, private communication, 4 April 1995.

73. See Collier, "Protestant Evangelization," in *Basta!*.

74. Harvey, "Playing with Fire," 21.

75. On the radicalization of peasants in eastern Chiapas, see Collier, "The Building of Social Movements," in *Basta!* and Harvey, "Rural Reforms," and on the growth of social movements on rural reform, see Jonathan Fox, *The Politics of Food in Mexico* (Ithaca, N.Y.: Cornell University Press, 1993).

76. Subcomandante Marcos, *La Jornada*, 7 February 1994.

77. In some places in the Lacandón, indígenas and campesinos, with the support of local nongovernmental organizations, have successfully maintained the rain forest and generated some income for their communities through agroforestry projects that cultivate organic crops within secondary forests. Agricultura Orgánica and A.C. Dana, "Productive Reforestation: A Cooperative Project with the Lacandón Rainforest Community," Chiapas, Mexico, 1995.

78. See Collier, *Fields of the Tzotzil*; Nations, "The Ecology of the Zapatista Revolt," 31–33; and Victor M. Toledo, "The Ecology of Indian Campesinos," *Akwe:kon—Journal of Indigenous Issues* 11, no. 2 (summer 1994): 41–46.

79. For a survey of the literature supporting this claim, see Anglade and Fortin, "Accumulation, Adjustment and the Autonomy of the State," 211–26.

80. See Juan M. R. Siaz, "Urban Struggles and Their Political Consequences," in *Popular Movements and Political Change in Mexico*, ed. Ann Craig and Joe Foweraker (Boulder, Colo.: Lynne Rienner Publishers, 1990).

81. If "Chiapas is Mexico," as some have argued, in that environmental scarcities are appearing in other southern states, such as Oaxaca and Guerrero, and in that vast portions of central Mexico, including Puebla, Veracruz, Hidalgo, and Michoacán suffer similar neglect, the PRI can expect to receive demands from insurgent groups similar to those of the EZLN (see Reding, "Chiapas Is Mexico"). As in Chiapas, ejido titles throughout Mexico are often to land that is "marginal, hilly, eroded or otherwise not suitable for permanent agriculture" (Billie Dewalt et al., "The End of the Agrarian Reform in Mexico: Past Lessons, Future Prospects," Transformation of Rural Mexico, number 3 [La Jolla, Calif.: Ejido Reform Research Project, Center for U.S.-Mexican Studies, University of California at San Diego, 1994], 45). For studies of environmental scarcities in Chiapas and the prospects for other parts of Mexico, see Sanderson, "Mexico's Environmental Future"; Dewalt et al., "The End of the Agrarian Reform in Mexico"; and Burbach and Rosset, *Chiapas and the Crisis of Mexican Agriculture*.

82. George Phillip, *The Presidency in Mexican Politics* (Basingstoke, U.K.: Macmillan, 1992), 174.

83. The plebiscite, run entirely by volunteers in local committees, collected almost 1 million votes from around Mexico and over 80,000 votes internationally. A strong majority encouraged the EZLN to become an independent political party, a transition that is just beginning.

3

The Case of Gaza

Kimberley Kelly and Thomas Homer-Dixon

Overview

As the first source of fresh water north of the Sinai Desert, the area currently known as the Gaza Strip was once considered to have great strategic value. However, a massive influx of refugees to the area in 1948 placed tremendous stress on its fragile resources. By the time of Israeli occupation in 1967, Gaza hovered on the verge of a water supply crisis. Today, sapped by further years of strain on limited resources, Gaza has become "the most horrifying case of all"[1] in the notoriously water-scarce Middle East region. Rapid decline in both the quality and the quantity of water supplies, frequent outbreaks of waterborne disease, increased alkalinity and salinity of the soil, and the almost total absence of proper sewage disposal or reasonable domestic hygiene have made Gaza "an area which even the most fervent Zionists recognize as a drain on the state that should be off-loaded [to] any Arab country willing to accept it."[2]

In August 1993, Israel did indeed "off-load" Gaza, ceding partial power to a Palestinian administration. Amid much ceremony on the White House lawn, Israeli prime minister Yitzhak Rabin and Palestine Liberation Organization (PLO) chairman Yasir Arafat shared a reluctant handshake as U.S. president Bill Clinton bid them "shalom, salaam, peace." However, the transition to Palestinian self-government in Gaza has proved anything but peaceful. As of mid-1995, Israeli security forces continued to clash with Palestinians on the edges of the autonomous areas; within Gaza, confrontations between the new Palestinian administration and its Islamic opposition have sometimes turned violent; and Islamic militants have launched suicide bomb attacks against Israeli targets in an attempt to derail the peace talks. In the two years since the "Gaza-Jericho first" accord, hundreds have been killed in continuing violence.[3]

The Western media usually explain this conflict as a result of the spread of fanatical Islamic fundamentalism in the Territories. Yet this focus often distorts rather than clarifies the roots of violence, by giving insufficient consideration to underlying political, economic, and ecological conditions.

In the case of Gaza, years of occupation and resistance have interacted with severe resource scarcities to produce a dismal socioeconomic environment, which has raised the probability of seemingly "irrational" violence. Where opportunities for peaceful expression of deep grievances appear inadequate and living conditions are desperately poor, violent self-sacrifice may take on its own peculiar logic. As Mustafa al-Masri, a psychiatrist at Gaza's only community mental health program, says: "In the hopelessness and helplessness of this world, there is the bright promise of the next life."[4]

While the links between environmental scarcity and conflict in Gaza are complex, it is clear that over the years water scarcity has worsened socioeconomic conditions. These conditions, in turn, have contributed to the grievances behind ongoing violence against Israel and tensions among Palestinians in Gaza. To describe this relationship, we provide an overview of Gaza's recent political history and then analyze the current state of water scarcity and its impact on economic and political stability.

We must note, however, that our analysis has been hindered by a critical shortage of good data.[5] Any information on water is politically sensitive. No figure on population, water supply, or consumption stands uncontested. The situation is further complicated by the fact that resources and population in Gaza are administered by several authorities, including the UN Relief Works Agency (UNRWA), the Israeli military government, and the Palestinian Authority (PA). The PA took over the administration of Gaza's agricultural water supply in May 1994. The Gaza Agricultural Department, while staffed with experienced Palestinian water professionals, had been deprived of resources, staff, equipment, and training throughout the occupation.[6] The lack of sufficient institutions for water management under the PA further limits the availability of accurate data. Despite data problems, however, few deny that the water situation in Gaza is now desperate.

Background

From 1917 to 1948, Gaza was a part of Palestine under the British mandate. The current boundaries of the Gaza Strip are a product of the Arab-Israeli War of 1948, which incorporated two-thirds of mandate Gaza into Israel. An armistice between Israel and Egypt brought the remaining one-third of Gaza's most marginal land—the 365 square kilometers now referred to as the Gaza Strip—under Egyptian military administration. The 1948 war displaced approximately 900,000 Palestinians; 250,000 of these refugees fled to the Gaza Strip, increasing the population of the area by more than 300 percent. The huge influx, combined with the loss of resources and disruption of domestic trade, created an unstable economic situation. The Egyptian administration did little to promote economic self-sufficiency in Gaza or to increase ties with its own economy, assuming instead that Gaza's future would rest on an economic relationship with Israel. By the time of the Israeli occupation of 1967, Gaza's economy remained "fragile and underdeveloped," dominated by its service sector, and heavily dependent on citrus agriculture.[7]

The Six-Day War in June 1967 brought both the West Bank and the Gaza Strip under Israeli occupation. Israel fostered economic dependence in order to keep a hostile Palestinian state from being established on its vulnerable borders. Israeli policy exhibited two overriding priorities: absolute control over land and water resources in the Occupied Territories and suppression of any form of independent political or economic organization.[8] In Gaza, these aims were embodied in a range of policies, including the expropriation of land and water resources, restrictions on research and training, low levels of investment in infrastructure, the absence of financial support or credit facilities for Palestinians, the prohibition of land- and water-use planning, severe restrictions on travel, and restrictions on exports.[9] A large percentage of the Gaza workforce became incorporated into the lower echelons of Israel's economy, especially in construction and as unskilled labor. The net effects of these policies have been the economic and political isolation of the Palestinian population in Gaza and the further weakening of already fragile local economic structures.[10]

From the outset, the occupation was resisted within both the Occupied Territories and throughout the Palestinian diaspora. Internationally, it brought the PLO to prominence. Formed in 1964 by a summit of Arab leaders, the PLO served as an umbrella organization for various groups supporting the cause of disenfranchised and displaced Palestinians. In the early years of the occupation, the PLO became notorious for airplane hijackings and attacks on Israeli civilians. Although these activities did much to undermine the international legitimacy of the PLO, they did not extinguish concern for Palestinian rights. In 1974, the United Nations (UN) granted the PLO observer status as "the sole legitimate representative of the Palestinian people." The PLO has undeniably served as a locus of unity for Palestinian nationalism. However, its history is primarily that of a representative body in exile—a symbol of struggle with little hand in the day-to-day lives of Palestinians in the Territories. This gap between the powerful symbolism of the PLO and its efficacy in the Territories was thrown into sharp relief by the outbreak of the intifadah in late 1987.

The intifadah caught Israel, the world, and the PLO by surprise. A sustained and largely grassroots uprising that began in Gaza's Jabalya refugee camp (which residents now refer to as the "camp of the revolution"), the intifadah was the culmination of years of sporadic resistance. On 8 December 1987, funeral services for four Palestinians killed by an Israeli army tank transport became a massive rally of ten thousand protesters. Within days, similar protests erupted throughout Gaza and the West Bank. The Israeli government immediately took military action to suppress what it dismissed as "riots." Anita Vitullo, an observer in Gaza at the time, noted, however, that the protests exhibited a "sense of community, purposeful resistance."[11] The acts of civil disobedience that characterized the intifadah were not in themselves significantly different from those preceding them. What differentiated the intifadah was its duration and its scope. Prior resistance had been commonplace, yet widely dispersed and therefore containable; the intifadah, despite its spontaneous origins, rapidly became organized, widespread, and sustained, rendering the Occupied Territories largely ungovernable.[12]

The uprising drew massive media coverage and shifted international attention from Palestinian terrorism to the nature of the Israeli occupation. It put a face on the people whom the PLO ostensibly represented, which increased the organization's international legitimacy,[13] but it did so at a considerable cost. It also resulted in large loss of life, declining living conditions, and intra-Palestinian violence, including the killings of suspected collaborators. Israel's imposition of prolonged curfews and closures of the Territories in response to the uprising cut off Palestinians from their livelihoods.[14]

The Persian Gulf War brought an already precarious situation to the point of total collapse. As a result of the Iraqi occupation of Kuwait and PLO support for Iraq, remittances from Palestinians employed in the Persian Gulf states fell sharply. Moreover, direct aid to the PLO from Saudi Arabia was cut off and transfer payments to the Territories from the PLO declined precipitously. Palestinian employment in Israel fell to its lowest level since the occupation of the West Bank and Gaza in 1967. Gaza was also cut off from its principal export markets in the Persian Gulf, resulting in a crisis for citrus agriculture.

Violence in the Territories rose as conditions deteriorated. In March 1993, Yitzhak Rabin's newly elected Labor government responded by sealing off the Territories, cutting off 130,000 Palestinians from their jobs in Israel. In time, Israel allowed some workers back into Israel and promoted local job creation within Gaza. However, the number of unemployed far outstripped the capacity of Gaza's economy to absorb labor.[15]

As conditions in Gaza deteriorated, Arafat attempted to shore up his eroding position by renouncing violence and calling for an end to the uprising. Eventually, secret talks culminated in mutual recognition by Rabin's government and the PLO. This recognition, in turn, set the stage for the signing of the Gaza-Jericho First Accord (the Accord) that provided limited autonomy for Gaza Palestinians. The signing ceremony sparked celebrations among Israelis and Palestinians who hoped that the agreement would be the beginning of a lasting peace in the region, but the stability of a semiautonomous Gaza was almost immediately in jeopardy. By the time the agreement was signed, the economic crisis had fractured the once-strong nationalist unity in Gaza, and "growing inter- and intra-factional rivalries for . . . scarce resources were increasingly apparent."[16]

The Accord has transferred responsibility for a resource-poor, overpopulated, and politically unstable region—a region frequently referred to under Israeli occupation as a time bomb—from Israel to the newly formed PA. The future of the peace process has been made conditional on the authority's success in creating a stable political entity in Gaza, and yet the limited autonomy under which this is to be achieved has proven to be more restrictive than many had anticipated.

Because of its size and position between Israel and the Sinai Desert, the Gaza Strip can be easily sealed off and isolated. Outside and on the edges of the autonomous area, many policies of occupation have continued unabated.[17] Freedom of movement for Palestinians has actually been reduced; travel between Gaza and the West Bank is all but impossible. Within Gaza, Israeli troop levels have not declined. As of January 1996, the Israeli military remains in control of all main roads[18] and of the areas around the Jewish settlements, which, while small, are dispersed throughout Gaza.[19] Overall, the Israeli military still controls over one-third of Gaza's territory.

Within the autonomous areas, the optimism engendered by Arafat in July 1994 gave way to a more cautious view of the future. The political freedom thought to have been promised by the agreement failed to quickly materialize and some of Arafat's actions have been perceived as autocratic and biased. He has kept his PLO patronage network firmly in place, installing formerly exiled old-guard Fatah officials in positions of power, at the expense of Gaza's younger activists. These actions have cost the PA the substantial grassroots support enjoyed by the local Fatah activists, who are seen as having paid their dues by organizing within Gaza under the pressures and dangers of the occupation, and who often served jail terms for their activities. Furthermore, many of Arafat's appointees "lack credibility or legitimacy within the community [and] are distrusted or hated, and, in some instances, even perceived as collaborators."[20] The conspicuous consumption of many appointees in the face of Gaza's extreme poverty has further undermined the image of the new administration.

The most significant issue for the majority of Gazans is whether or not the PA can improve economic conditions. Since the implementation of limited autonomy, there have been visible signs of improvement—wealthy returnees have financed a construction boom. Nonetheless, unemployment has risen, and the grim living conditions of most Palestinians have not markedly im-

MAP 3.1

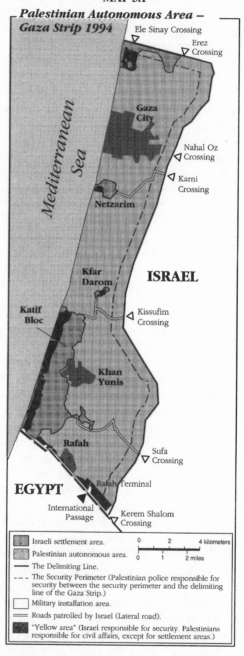

Palestinian Autonomous Area — Gaza Strip 1994

Ele Sinay Crossing

Erez Crossing

Gaza City

Mediterranean Sea

Nahal Oz Crossing

Karni Crossing

Netzarim

Kfar Darom

ISRAEL

Katif Bloc

Kissufim Crossing

Khan Yunis

Rafah

Sufa Crossing

Rafah Terminal

EGYPT

International Passage

Kerem Shalom Crossing

Israeli settlement area.

Palestinian autonomous area.

0   2   4 kilometers

0   1   2 miles

—— The Delimiting Line.

- - - The Security Perimeter (Palestinian police responsible for security between the security perimeter and the delimiting line of the Gaza Strip.)

Military installation area.

═══ Roads patrolled by Israel (Lateral road).

"Yellow area" (Israel responsible for security. Palestinians responsible for civil affairs, except for settlement areas.)

Source: Foundation for Middle East Peace. Reprinted by permission.

proved.[21] The PA has come under fire for relying on its police force to maintain control.[22] Arafat himself has staked his position on the success of the peace process, yet since negotiations began, support for the process among Palestinians has fluctuated greatly, both within the Territories and in the diaspora. While most Palestinians remain supportive of Arafat, opponents of the process have been vocal: Arafat has on occasion been accused of losing sight of the goals of Palestinian nationalism, ignoring the Territories for which he is now responsible, trading away the gains of the intifadah, and tying himself to an Israeli agenda.

At first, disenchantment with the PA within Gaza was accompanied by vocal support for Islamist groups, such as Hamas and Islamic Jihad.[23] In November 1994, thousands protested at the funeral of an assassinated Islamic Jihad leader, and Arafat was roughed up by protesters and forced to leave the ceremony. The media described the protest as a reaction to declining conditions, the slow pace of reform, and Arafat's "hounding" of Islamic leaders in the Territories.[24] While Hamas's leaders immediately issued an apology and called for unity, the incident illustrated increasing intra-Palestinian tensions within Gaza.

Initially, Arafat responded by adopting increasingly authoritarian measures, requiring that permits be issued for public gatherings and delaying the distribution of newspapers that allegedly exaggerated the number of people involved in pro-Hamas demonstrations. Numerous petitions for Arafat to reform his methods and increase his accountability to his constituents have had little effect. Shortly after the Accord was signed Edward Said wrote that "the leadership has so misunderstood its people that there is now simmering—and frequently open—revolt more or less everywhere that Palestinians gather and live."[25]

Since then, however, Palestinian support for Islamic radicals has fallen. Every time a bomb explodes in Israel—and Israel responds by closing its borders to Palestinian workers and trade—there is a popular reaction against Hamas and Islamic Jihad within Gaza. The result of Palestinian disillusionment with both the PLO and the Islamists has been rising political apathy and disengagement.

Environmental Scarcity

Sandra Postel calls the Middle East the "region of the most concentrated water scarcity in the world," with nine out of fourteen countries facing water-scarce conditions.[26] In Gaza, the water crisis is a function of population growth, an agriculturally intensive economy, a fragile water ecosystem, and a highly inequitable distribution of resources (see figure 3.1).

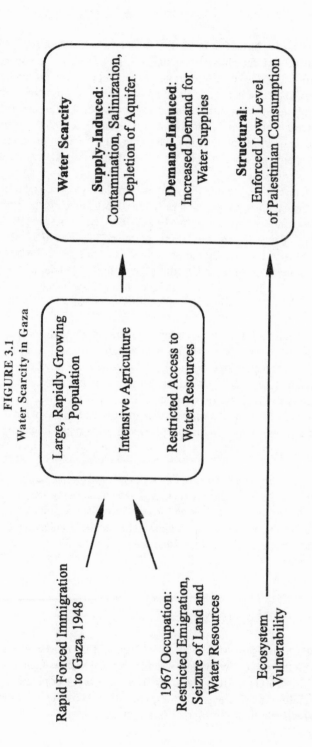

FIGURE 3.1
Water Scarcity in Gaza

Ecosystem Vulnerability and Overall Availability

Gaza's climate ranges from semiarid in the north to arid in the south. The warm climate causes high potential enviro-transpiration,[27] between 1,040 and 1,900 millimeters per year (mm/year) for Gaza as a whole.[28] Of the average annual rainfall in Gaza (200–400 mm/year, which amounts to 117 million cubic meters [mcm] of total water from precipitation in Gaza's catchment area), only 40 percent is estimated to recharge the single freshwater aquifer underlying the territory, while the remainder is lost through surface runoff to the Mediterranean or to evaporation.[29] Another 30 mcm of recharge comes from agricultural return flow, wastewater infiltration, and groundwater flow from the east,[30] though the last may have decreased over the years due to a number of wells drawing reservoir water beyond the Green Line.

For its freshwater supply, Gaza relies almost entirely on groundwater drawn from its aquifer, with minimal amounts obtained from other sources, such as rooftop rainwater catchments.[31] Gaza's aquifer is often only a few meters from the surface. It is also shallow, ranging in thickness from 120 meters near the coast to 10 meters in the east.[32] Since it is near the Mediterranean and a deeper, highly saline aquifer,[33] it is vulnerable to declining water levels, saltwater intrusion, and contamination from agricultural and industrial activity. Estimates of the aquifer's renewable yield vary widely, ranging from 25 to 80 mcm per year, with around 65 mcm the most frequently quoted figure.[34]

Some analysts of the region suggest that the water crisis in Israel and the Occupied Territories is solely a consequence of structural scarcity—rather than of demand or supply pressures.[35] This argument may be valid if one considers the water inventory of Israel and the Occupied Territories as a whole. However, Gaza's aquifer is relatively self-contained, which means that its water inventory can be considered independently. Moreover, although the water resources in the entire region are sparse, on a per capita basis they are nonetheless relatively abundant compared with those in Gaza. Although there are serious distribution problems in Gaza, high population growth and years of heavy extraction have produced a crisis of absolute water availability.

Structural Scarcity

Discriminatory water allocation and pricing structures have significantly contributed to the present crisis in Gaza. Throughout the occupation, Israel restricted Palestinian water consumption in both Gaza and the West Bank. In 1967, Israel declared all water resources in the Territories to be state owned and under the jurisdiction of the military. Strict quotas were placed on Palestinian consumption. To preserve Gaza's aquifer under the occupation, Military Order 158 (which applied only to the Arab population of Gaza, and not to Israeli settlers) prohibited the drilling of new wells or the rehabilitation of existing wells for any purpose without a permit.[36] While restrictions applied to both Territories, limits may have been more difficult to enforce in Gaza, where the aquifer is close to the surface and relatively easy to access.

With the exception of allowances for increased drinking-water demand, Palestinian pumping quotas were effectively frozen at 1967 levels.[37] Measures to limit Palestinian water consumption included the uprooting of thousands of citrus trees, demolition of cisterns, and the blockage of natural springs and existing wells. Extended curfews often prevented Palestinians from having normal access to water for domestic and agricultural purposes.[38] As a result of a one-month curfew imposed on both Gaza and the West Bank in early 1991,

> some 2,500 dunums [250 hectares] of squash and additional dunums of fava beans were lost because farmers were not able to spray their crops at the appropriate times. Greenhouse agriculture on 10,000 dunums [1,000 hectares] in the Tulkarm region and in Gaza were also severely affected. The loss of grazing, brought on by drought conditions and exacerbated by the curfew has caused in one month estimated financial losses of $6 million.[39]

Conversely, Israelis in the Territories and in Israel proper face fewer restrictions on water drawn from the same sources, and they consume on average eight to ten times more than the Palestinians.[40] These inequities have been a persistent source of tension. A UN report quotes a Palestinian farmer in Gaza:

> Israeli authorities have forbidden anyone to dig a well to irrigate his citrus groves because "Gaza has no water." But at the same time, ten meters away on the other side of the 1967 border, they will dig not one well but ten. I myself have a farm and they have prevented me from digging a well on my own land, on the pretext that there is not enough water.[41]

Israel has also allocated resources in its favor through the selective appropriation of agricultural land, placing settlements in the most favorable areas in terms of groundwater quantity and quality and in terms of underground flow.[42] In addition, several Israeli wells have been drilled in the catchment area of the coastal aquifer, which is inside Israel but along the border of Gaza. Palestinian water experts argue that these wells have reduced the flow of groundwater to Gaza.[43] This has, however, been a point of contention among hydrologists. Israeli sources argue that these wells are blocking the flow of saline water which could damage the aquifer. Others contend that these wells draw on a separate part of the coastal aquifer system and do not affect Gaza's aquifer at all.[44]

Uneven pricing schemes are another cause of structural scarcity. Although weak institutions and deteriorating infrastructure provide barely adequate quantity and quality of water, Gaza Palestinians pay much higher prices than do residents in Israel and Israeli settlers in the Territories. Settlers receive significant subsidies, paying $0.10 per cubic meter (/m³) for water that costs $0.34/m³; Palestinians, who receive no subsidies, can pay up to $1.20/m³ for water from local Arab authorities.[45] Relative to per capita income, Palestinians pay as much as twenty times what Israeli settlers pay for water.[46]

This pricing system does not reflect the vulnerability of the region's water resources: the heavy subsidization of Israeli farmers, especially in the Territories, promotes waste and overconsumption. Surprisingly, a large price differential also exists between the West Bank and Gaza for both Israelis and Palestinians; water is much cheaper in Gaza, yet the crisis there is far more severe.

The net effect of Israel's policies in Gaza is to buffer Israelis from the effects of declining levels of water quality and quantity, while Palestinians bear the brunt of water scarcity. This imbalance has contributed to a prosperous Israeli settler economy co-existing directly alongside a stagnant Palestinian economy. The consumption restrictions imposed on Palestinians and the widening water gap generate serious friction between these communities.

Demand-induced Scarcity

Population size is possibly the most contested statistic for Gaza. As no proper census has been taken since 1967, available figures are approximate at best, and they tend to vary markedly, depending on the source and the purpose of the data.

The size of Gaza's current population is largely the result of the original refugee influx from the 1948 war. Approximately 70 percent of Gaza's population is made up of these refugees and their descendants.[47] Most contemporary sources place Gaza's current Palestinian population at 700,000 to 800,000, but these figures may underestimate the total by as much as 16 percent.[48] Most estimates of the present Palestinian population growth rate range between 5.2 and 6 percent,[49] among the highest rates identified for any group in the world. (Official Israeli estimates tend to be slightly lower; see table 3.1). Fertility tends to be higher for refugees than for residents, which means the fastest population growth is in the refugee camps—the areas that are also under greatest environmental stress.

Estimates of average population density range from 1,936 people per square kilometer (/km²) to 2,055 people/km².[50] Densities are, again, much higher in the refugee camps; Jabalya camp, where the intifadah originated, has one of the highest population densities in the world at 100,000 people/km² in extremely poor living conditions.[51]

Gaza's growing population and limited water resources are driving down per capita water availability. The Swedish hydrologist Malin Falkenmark has identified one thousand cubic meters per person per year as a "water barrier" for agricultural and industrial development. She defines this barrier as "the

TABLE 3.1

Estimated Palestinian Population of the Gaza Strip, 1945, 1967–1992

Year	Population (Thousands)	Natural Increase (%)	Net Emigration (%)	Year	Population (Thousands)	Natural Increase (%)	Net Emigration (%)
1945	72	-	-	1980	445	3.80	1.15
1967	390	0.85	3.13	1981	457	3.88	1.16
1968	381	2.18	8.48	1982	470	3.79	0.66
1969	357	2.80	0.81	1983	477	3.81	0.21
1970	364	2.58	0.91	1984	495	4.08	0.97
1971	370	3.03	0.65	1985	510	3.90	0.57
1972	379	3.22	1.06	1986	527	4.10	0.68
1973	387	3.31	-0.44	1987	545	4.33	0.61
1974	402	3.56	0.45	1988	566	4.53	0.48
1975	414	3.62	0.85	1989	589	4.88	1.16
1976	426	3.78	0.99	1990	610	5.05	-0.25
1977	437	3.73	0.66	1991	643	5.12	-0.06
1978	451	3.75	1.04	1992	676	5.03	-1.01
1979	463	3.56	1.04	1993	717	-	-

Sources: 1945 figure from Sara Roy, *The Gaza Strip: The Political Economy of De-Development* (Washington, D.C.: Institute for Palestine Studies, 1995), 49. Figures from 1967 (time of census) onward are from Israel's Central Bureau of Statistics, cited in World Bank, *Developing the Occupied Territories: An Investment in Peace*, vol. 6 (Washington, D.C.: The World Bank, 1993), 6.

level of water availability below which serious constraints to development will arise."[52] The ratio in Gaza—even using low population estimates and optimistic estimates of sustainable water supply—is considerably less than one hundred cubic meters per person per year.

Gaza's limited resource base also supports a number of Israeli settlements, which occupy an estimated 10 percent of Gaza's cultivated area.[53] Their residents are generally not incorporated in recent population figures. In 1993, the World Bank estimated that the Israeli population of Gaza was 4,000 to 5,000.[54] Surprisingly, this number may still be increasing, despite the autonomy agreement. The American Foundation for Peace in the Middle East has reported a 20 percent increase in the number of settlers in Gaza.

The lack of water for agriculture and industry has hamstrung economic development in Gaza for years, and it is especially burdensome now because of pressure on the PA to improve living standards. Gaza's economy relies heavily on agriculture, and particularly citrus agriculture, which is water intensive. Although steadily declining due to limits on water use, today citrus still makes up 55 percent of the total irrigated area, consuming roughly half of Gaza's agricultural water supply.[55]

Consumption of groundwater in Gaza consistently outstrips the sustainable supply of around 65 mcm per year. Estimates of present consumption for Gaza Palestinians range from 100 to 140 mcm per year[56] (85 to 100 mcm for agricultural purposes). Israeli consumption from Gaza's aquifer is a small fraction of total withdrawal; most sources estimate an average of between 4 and 10 mcm per year.[57] Yet average per capita domestic water consumption by Palestinians is less than one-tenth that of settlers: 137 compared with 2,000 cubic meters per person per year.[58] In general, consumption by settlements, promoted in part by subsidization, is thought to be excessive[59] in the context of the local water supply.

However, once again, data on the size of the Gaza groundwater deficit are soft. Of the 3,000 wells thought to exist in Gaza, some 500 to 700 have been illegally drilled (many since autonomy was implemented) and are drawing unknown amounts.[60] Decentralization of control makes accurate estimates of consumption almost impossible. In Gaza, administration of the water supply is the responsibility of a confusing hodgepodge of entities: individual operators of wells, Mekorot (an Israeli water company), the Gaza Agriculture Department, utilities, municipal and village councils, and the UNRWA, which supplies water to 20 percent of the population in the refugee camps.[61]

Some scholars suggest that with rapid population growth in Gaza, demand for drinking water alone may soon outstrip safe supply. It is also possible that Israeli settler demand will increase even if settlement population remains stable, due to "increasing per capita demands for both irrigated acreage and domestic amenities, such as grass and swimming pools."[62] Even if demand remains stable, Gaza's present water inventory may be in far worse shape than is implied by official figures: some experts suggest that pumping rates in Gaza are 1.5 to 2 times officially declared levels.[63]

Supply-induced Scarcity

Gaza's limited water supply has been overexploited (mined) since the early 1970s, and probably since the period of Egyptian control.[64] The continuous mining of the Gaza aquifer, on average by an estimated 60 to 65 mcm per year, has caused falling water tables, salt intrusion, and chemical contamination.[65]

In its natural state, the top of the Israeli coastal aquifer, which is analogous to the neighboring Gaza aquifer, is 3 to 5 meters above sea level. Overpumping has reduced the Gaza aquifer to well below sea level and continues to draw it down by 15 to 20 centimeters per year.[66] This decline reduces the aquifer's hydrostatic pressure, allowing the infiltration of saltwater from the Mediterranean and from saline aquifers below and to the east. Saltwater intrusion has already been detected as far as 1.5 kilometers inland. While levels of salinity vary geographically, Gaza's groundwater is generally classified as very saline, ranging from 650 to 3,600 parts per million (ppm).[67] Salinity increases an average of 15 to 20 parts per million per year.[68] This rapid increase has led some to predict the total salinization of the aquifer, if there is insufficient additional water to replace that lost to overpumping.[69]

Agricultural activity has resulted in chemical contamination of Gaza's groundwater.[70] Unregulated use of pesticides, herbicides, and fertilizers contributes to severe pollution, especially since the aquifer is close to the surface. Chemicals banned from use in Israel and elsewhere, such as DDT, are often used in Gaza—and often misused because there are no Arabic labels on their containers.

As a result, Gaza's groundwater is often unsuitable for irrigation, as it can damage the soil and lower crop yields.[71] Salinity is the greatest concern and in Gaza most groundwater is suitable only for use on highly salt-tolerant crops and highly permeable soil. Yet citrus is a significant agricultural crop and, in addition to being water intensive, citrus cannot tolerate high salinity. Farmers are already seeing declining crop yields and declining quality in many areas due to the use of high salinity irrigation water.[72]

Experience elsewhere shows that farmers can adapt to such contamination by shifting to more salt-tolerant crops, adding gypsum and organic matter to the soil, and applying excess clean irrigation water to flush the soil of salt.[73] However, with current limits on water consumption and a chronic lack of capital for the farming sector, these measures may not be feasible.

Inadequate disposal of waste matter has also contributed to the contamination of Gaza's aquifer. Ten percent of Gaza's population is not served by any wastewater management system and is simply dumping raw sewage onto sand dunes.[74] What systems are in place remain inadequate, particularly in the refugee camps (see table 3.2). Public latrines are still widely in use, and the majority of the population throughout Gaza relies on septic tanks and soaking pits. These frequently overflow into lanes, streets, and homes and pose a significant health hazard.[75] Furthermore, only one-third of Gazans outside of the refugee camps are served by solid waste collection; and while all of the refugee camps do have collection services, proper sanitary landfill sites have not been con-

TABLE 3.2
Wastewater Situation in Selected Gaza Localities, 1993–1994[76]

Locality	Estimated Population	Water-works Staff	Percentage of Population Served	Treatment Facility	Disposal Site or Method
Gaza City and Beach Camp	344,999	26	85	Aeration and stabilization	Wadi Gaza and into the sea
Jabalya	94,710	18	70	Oxidization ponds	Sand dunes
Beit Lahia	20,000	7	15	None	Sand dunes
Beit Hanoun	17,000	4	Unknown	None	Outside
Rafah	101,926	21	20	Oxidization ponds	Pumped to the sea
Khan Yunis	160,463	23	30	None	Cesspools
Deir-El-Balah	38,000	5	Unknown	None	Cesspools
Abasan	12,000	6	Unknown	None	Cesspools
Khuza'a	4,500	2	Unknown	None	Cesspools
Bani Suhaila	20,000	3	Unknown	None	Cesspools
Nuseirat Camp	35,500	1	Unknown	None	Cesspools
Bureij Camp	22,500	2	Unknown	None	Cesspools
Maghazi Camp	15,000	3	Unknown	None	Cesspools

Sources: Population figures from Sara Roy, *The Gaza Strip: The Political Economy of De-development* (Washington, D.C.: Institute for Palestine Studies, 1995), 15–16. Wastewater capacity figures from Ramzi Sansur, *Environment and Development Prospects in the West Bank and Gaza Strip* (New York: UN Conference on Trade and Development, 1995).

structed anywhere in Gaza.[77] As a result of inadequate infrastructure, both sewage seepage and leachate from solid waste disposal have contaminated the aquifer.

According to one relatively optimistic analyst, 50 percent of Gaza's drinking-water supply is "murky," and 23 percent is not potable at all.[78] The Applied Research Institute in Jerusalem (ARIJ) is far more pessimistic, maintaining that Gaza groundwater is simply not fit for human consumption. A water quality survey conducted by ARIJ in 1992 identifies concentrations of several key substances that far exceed what are generally regarded as acceptable levels for potability (see table 3.3). A similar study conducted between 1987 and 1994 by UNRWA and the Palestinian Health Authority determined that every one of Gaza's 60 drinking water wells exceeded acceptable levels for at least two tested contaminants (see table 3.4).[79] While extensive testing for many toxins has not been conducted, several analysts have expressed concern about the infiltration of heavy metals, fuels, toxic organic compounds, fertilizers,

TABLE 3.3
Potability of Groundwater in the Gaza Strip

Dissolved Substances	Acceptable Concentration* (ppm)	Gaza Concentration (ppm)
Total Dissolved Solids	500	1,200 – 3,200
Sodium (Na^+)	20	300 – 1,100
Chloride (Cl^-)	250	400 – 1,500
Calcium (Ca^{+2})	36	40 – 120
Sulfate (SO_4^{-2})	250	50 – 400
Magnesium (Mg^{+2})	30	40 – 120
Bicarbonate (HCO_3^-)	225	300 – 700
Potassium (K^+)	4	6 – 10
Nitrate (NO_3^-)	45	40 – 140
Fluoride $(F)^{**}$	1.5	0.4 – 2.9

*World Health Organization standard levels.
**Fluoride figures drawn from Zaher Kuhail and Zaki Zoarob, *Potable Groundwater Crisis in the Gaza Strip, 1987–1994* (Gaza: UNRWA and Palestinian Health Authority, 194), 11.

Source: Hisham Zarour, Jad Isaac, and Violet Qumsieh, "Hydrochemical Indicators of the Severe Water Crisis in the Gaza Strip," in *Final Report on the Project Water Resources in the West Bank and Gaza Strip: Current Situation and Future Prospects* (Jerusalem: Applied Research Institute in Jerusalem, 1994).

TABLE 3.4
Suitability of Drinking Water Wells in the Gaza Strip

Material	Suitable Wells*	Percentage of All Wells
Total Dissolved Solids	23	39.7
Sodium	27	46.6
Chloride	24	41.3
Calcium	46	79.3
Sulfate	52	90.0
Magnesium	57	98.3
Potassium	32	55.2
Nitrate	0	0
Fluoride	47	80.0
Hardness	6	10.3
Alkalinity	0	0

*Out of a total of 60 drinking water wells in Gaza.
Source: Zaher Kuhail and Zaki Zoarob, *Potable Ground Water Crisis in the Gaza Strip, 1987–1994* (Gaza: UNRWA and the Palestinian Health Authority, 1994), 31.

pesticides, and herbicides into Gaza's drinking water supply.[80] Some analysts estimate that the contamination is already irreversible and that Gaza's population—including both Palestinians and Israeli settlers—will soon have to find alternate sources of drinking water. At present, however, there are few other sources.[81] Overall, contamination and salinization have been costly—politically, economically, and in terms of public health.

Social Effects of Environmental Scarcity

Health Impacts

Anthropologist Anna Bellisari argues that the routine consumption of contaminated or saline water by Gaza Palestinians contributes to deterioration of the overall health of the population:

The water crisis is very costly to Palestinians not only in the agricultural and industrial sectors, but especially in terms of public health, which depends largely upon adequate, safe supplies of domestic water. Water shortages and pollution are responsible for a major portion of the acute and chronic infections widespread throughout the Occupied Territories, and are likely to cause permanent health damage to a large segment of the population.[82]

This conclusion is supported by a recent World Bank report, which suggests that inadequate and contaminated water supplies contribute to the high incidence of gastrointestinal and parasitic infections found in Gaza. There are no studies that provide decisive proof, but preliminary evidence suggests a causal link between scarce and contaminated drinking water and Gaza's high levels of infant mortality, infectious disease, hypertension, and other health-related problems.

If the salinity of Gaza's aquifer continues to rise, eventually its water will be undrinkable. Salinity levels of Gaza groundwater range from 650–3,600 ppm. The U.S. standard for drinking water is 500 ppm, and water over 1,000 ppm is considered saline. Sea water has a salt concentration of 35,000 ppm. A maximum physiologically tolerable level of salinity in drinking water cannot be identified; sodium intake in water must be considered as a component of overall dietary intake. Ten grams per day is the maximum recommended salt intake for adults who are healthy, well-nourished, and not predisposed to hypertension or other salt-sensitive disorders. This level is also based on the presumption that the individual has access to sufficient fresh water to flush excess sodium: at best, human kidneys can concentrate urine to 6 grams of sodium per liter of water. Sodium intake in excess of this level must be flushed in order to keep plasma sodium levels normal. It is recommended that people with hypertension or cardiovascular disorders (both of which are common in Gaza) should not exceed 20 ppm sodium in their drinking water. Anything above that level is considered a major salt component of their diet.[83]

Some experts think that high salt concentrations are already producing adverse health effects: "Gaza physicians are convinced that salty water is responsible for the high incidence of kidney and liver complaints among Gaza residents."[84] Salinity has also been linked to hypernatremia,[85] thought to be responsible for a large percentage of "crib deaths" and early brain damage.[86] In recent years, nitrate contamination of Gaza's drinking water has increased rapidly: in 1987, 84 percent of Gaza's drinking water wells were considered suitable for drinking in terms of nitrate levels; by 1994, not a single safe well remained.[87] Elevated nitrate levels are also suspected of contributing to infant mortality by causing acute anemia or "blue baby disease."[88] Severe cases can result in anoxia (oxygen deprivation) and death. Nitrates have also been linked to cancer and to increased incidence of spontaneous abortion, both in humans and in animals.[89]

Gaza Palestinians are exposed to high fluoride concentrations in their groundwater and also in the fish and the tea that are staple foods. When consumed in large amounts, fluoride is toxic and contributes to ulcers, kidney failure, soft-tissue calcification, and skeletal and dental fluorosis.[90] The effects in Gaza of groundwater chemical pollution from fertilizers, pesticides, and herbicides are hard to establish, because data on concentrations and health impacts are not available. However, studies in the West Bank show that absorption through the skin or ingestion of such chemicals can damage the nervous system.[91] Similar products and practices are used in Gaza, so it follows that similar impacts may be present there. While aquifer concentrations are probably not high enough to produce extreme results, we should not rule out serious health effects because of sustained low-level exposures.

The most prevalent and serious health problem in Gaza is infectious disease caused by waterborne bacteria, viruses, and parasites. These diseases largely result from poor personal hygiene and inadequate sewage disposal, which are, in turn, exacerbated by insufficient water for washing and waste removal.[92] Moreover, open sewers are common in urban areas. Thus in November 1994, heavy rains caused sewage to mix with freshwater supplies, producing an outbreak of cholera in Gaza City, with fifty cases and one death in a week.[93]

Although this outbreak received widespread attention, infectious disease is common in Gaza: "The Union of Palestinian Medical Relief Committees, which operates clinics in the Gaza Strip and in the West Bank, reported that three-quarters of all clinic patients suffered from infectious diseases, which were responsible for 74 percent of all childhood deaths."[94] Intestinal parasites are prevalent. Researchers at Birzeit University found that 50 percent of Gaza children suffered from roundworms. However, according to Bellisari, these infections are often considered to be a fact of life rather than a pressing health concern, so many people may not seek treatment. Fungal infections and various other skin conditions due to poor personal hygiene are also common. These diseases are worst in refugee camps, where poor sanitation is magnified by overcrowding.[95]

The World Bank estimates that 7 percent of Gaza's GNP is allocated to health concerns, but there is little sign of improvement in overall population health.[96] According to Bellisari, without clean and ample water supplies, disease will recur as fast as it is treated, and resources will remain focused on symptoms and not on prevention.[97] Thus, Gaza's health care system will remain overburdened, producing strain on the limited resources of the PA and frustration among patients and health care workers.[98]

Agricultural Decline

Agriculture is key to Gaza's economy but has been in relative decline since the middle of the 1970s.[99] The percentage of the total workforce employed in agriculture dropped from 31.8 in 1968 to 18.3 in 1988. Between 1981 and 1991, per capita agricultural GDP dropped from approximately $5,235 to $4,330.[100] When considered by themselves, these figures could be interpreted as signs of economic growth: the decline of agriculture relative to other sectors of the economy, such as industry and services, is often a hallmark of a developing economy. However, in the case of Gaza, other economic sectors grew too slowly to absorb any significant percentage of labor moving out of agriculture. The overall result of agricultural decline in Gaza has not been economic development, but rather increased poverty and economic dependence on Israel.

Agricultural decline in Gaza is in part a result of water scarcity. The contraction and degradation of the water supply and discriminatory allocation policies interact to produce significant reductions in crop yields. During the occupation, Israeli policy not only limited Palestinian water consumption for agriculture but also restricted the cultivation of water-intensive crops. In some cases, Israeli authorities even uprooted Palestinian fruit trees: between 1973 and 1987, for example, about 700 hectares of citrus trees were uprooted in the Territories. To protect Israeli production from competition, exports from Gaza were heavily restricted; furthermore, water resources were allocated to Palestinians on the basis of soil conditions and type of crop.[101] Today, production is heavily influenced by trade imbalances that have their roots in the occupation. While Israel restricts imports of Gaza crops that compete with Israeli produce, Israel sells freely in the Occupied Territories.[102] Israel exports "substantial quantities of fruits and vegetables at prices with which Gazan farmers have been unable to compete."[103] Previously a net exporter of agricultural produce, Gaza has been a net importer since 1984 (see table 3.5).

Water scarcity and imbalanced trade have affected citrus production. The area under citrus cultivation contracted steadily from the early 1970s to the mid-1980s. Productivity per hectare also appears to have declined (see table 3.6).[104] In the late 1980s, citrus production accounted for only 20 percent of the value of agricultural output, down from 50 percent in the previous decade.[105] This drop in production has affected other sectors of Gaza's economy, such as processing. "Many orchards lie abandoned because water salinity is too high for the crop. Today it is uncertain whether Gaza citrus production can utilize the full capacity of a newly constructed orange juice production plant."[106]

Israel maintains that agriculture in Gaza expanded under the occupation. The Israeli claim is likely based on a steady increase in the area used for vegetable production: from 300 hectares in 1967 to 4,800 in 1985–86. While the output of all fruits, including citrus, has declined from a 63 percent share of total agricultural value in 1969 to 27 percent in 1990, vegetables have increased from 14 to 50 percent in the same period. Vegetable crops are less water intensive and more salt tolerant, but they are also less productive (particularly in rain-fed areas) and more labor intensive. Profitability of vegetables has suffered because some export markets (for instance, Jordan) have imposed annual quotas, and competition has increased.[107]

TABLE 3.5
Surplus Agricultural Exports Over Imports in Gaza

Year	Value (Millions of Dollars)
1972	10.7
1973	10.5
1974	11.9
1975	18.5
1976	17.1
1977	29.1
1978	13.0
1979	27.9
1980	25.4
1981	19.1
1982	13.3
1983	1.8
1984	−14.3
1985	−10.3

Source: Israel Central Bureau of Statistics, cited in David Kahan, *Agriculture and Water Resources in the West Bank and Gaza, 1967–1987* (Boulder, Colo.: Westview Press, 1987), 162.

Water scarcity has also adversely affected grazing areas and animal husbandry. Although livestock increased its share of total agricultural value from 21 percent in 1969 to 30 percent in 1990,[108] military constraints on land use and overgrazed rangeland have combined with water scarcity to limit real growth in this sector.[109] The greatest growth has occurred in the area of poultry production; more profitable types of livestock, such as cattle and sheep, have remained comparatively limited (see table 3.7).

In sum, water scarcity has hampered agriculture in Gaza, discouraged investment and forced many Gazans to look for off-farm work. Hydrologist Gwyn Rowley writes, "The net effect [of water scarcity] is that carrying capacities and herd sizes are diminished and crop outputs are reduced or fail and the population has to 'move on,' for example, with younger elements seeking employment elsewhere as in urban areas."[110]

Economic Decline

Industry now accounts for a larger share of Gaza's GDP than prior to the occupation, rising from 4.4 percent in 1965 and 1966 to 12.2 percent in 1990.

TABLE 3.6
Citrus Branch Changes—Gaza

Year	Area Under Production (Hectares)	Total Yield (Tons)	Yield/Hectare (Tons)
1967/68	3,500	91,000	26.0
1971/72	6,300	176,400	28.0
1973/74	7,200	197,000	27.4
1974/75	7,000	210,000	30.0
1975/76	7,000	243,000	34.7
1977/78	7,000	186,000	26.6
1978/79	7,000	189,000	27.0
1979/80	7,000	172,100	24.6
1980/81	7,158	179,300	25.0
1981/82	7,147	201,300	28.2
1982/83	6,920	166,500	24.1
1983/84	6,671	159,500	23.9
1984/85	6,600	175,700	26.6
1985/86	6,534	137,000	21.0
1990/91	NA	134,000	NA
1991/92	NA	119,300	NA
1992/93	NA	109,900	NA

Source: Judea, Samaria, and Gaza Area Statistics: Agricultural Branch Accounts, Central Bureau of Statistics. Cited in David Kahan, *Agriculture and Water Resources in the West Bank and Gaza 1967–1987* (Boulder, Colo.: Westview Press, 1987), 144. Figures from 1990 onward from Central Bureau of Statistics, Statistical Abstract of Israel, 1994.

But overall industrial growth in Gaza has been slow, well behind the pace of "similar" cases, according to the World Bank.[111] As a result, labor has moved from agriculture to wage employment in Israel rather than into other sectors of Gaza's economy (see table 3.8).

A recent World Bank report says that the increase in migrant labor during the occupation was simply a function of "pull" factors in Israel: "Following the occupation, major changes took place; Occupied Territories workers were

TABLE 3.7
Composition of the Livestock Branch in Gaza

Year	Cattle (Head)	Sheep (Head)	Poultry (Units)
1966	10,000	10,000	10,000
1972/73	5,500	50,000	508,000
1973/74	5,300	45,000	510,000
1974/75	5,500	40,000	420,000
1979/80	6,000	40,000	125,000
1982/83	3,600	33,000	2,046,000
1984/85	3,618	28,900	2,045,000
1985/86	3,200	25,374	2,500,000

Source: Statistical Abstract of Israel 1986, cited in David Kahan, *Agriculture and Water Resources in the West Bank and Gaza 1967–1987* (Boulder, Colo.: Westview Press, 1987), 146.

allowed to seek employment across the 'Green Line' which ultimately created a massive drain of people out of the agricultural sector."[112] This perspective neglects the "push" side of the process. While it is likely that the prospect of wage labor in Israel is attractive to some Palestinians,[113] the lack of economic opportunities in Gaza also contributes to the movement of labor.

An exclusive focus on pull motivations also ignores the role that Israeli policy in Gaza played in creating the migrant labor economy. Policies that enforced low levels of water consumption made agriculture "a burden rather than a source of income and jobs." Restrictions on development in other sectors of the economy contributed to general stagnation. As a result, local job opportunities were rare, and by 1994 more than 140,000 out of 2 million Palestinians in the Occupied Territories had, at some point, worked in Israel.[114]

The dependence on wage labor in Israel, coupled with Israeli border closures, are strong contributors to the current economic crisis in Gaza. In 1994 alone, closures produced an estimated loss of $400 million in earnings in the Occupied Territories.[115] The impact has been proportionately greater in Gaza, which is much poorer than the West Bank. Prior to the intifadah, close to 70 percent of Gaza's workforce was employed in Israel. In January 1994, this number was 11 percent (see table 3.9).[116] Not only has the migrant labor economy collapsed, so too have the support services that grew out of it. The remainder of Gaza's economy has been unable to absorb this new wave of job-

TABLE 3.8

Gaza GDP by Sector and Percentage of GNP from Foreign Sources, 1966 and 1987

Sector	Percentage of GDP 1966	Percentage of GDP 1987
Agriculture	34.4	17.3
Industry	4.2	13.7
Construction	6.2	69.0
Services	55.2	-

	Percentage of GNP 1966	Percentage of GNP 1987
Net Factor Income from Abroad		
Remittances from Abroad and Transfer Payments from UNRWA	24	7
Employment in Israel	-	42

Sources: Fawzi Gharabibeh, *The Economics of the West Bank and Gaza Strip* (Boulder, Colo.: Westview Press, 1985), 17; and Sara Roy, *The Gaza Strip: The Political Economy of De-development* (Washington, D.C.: Institute for Palestine Studies, 1995), 223, 237, 251.

TABLE 3.9
Estimated Number of Gazans Employed in Israel, 1987–1995

Date	Number Employed
December 1987	80,000
January 1993*	32,200
January 1994	15,400
February 1994	13,900
April 1995	8,000-10,000

*Prior to the March 1993 closure.
Sources: Sara Roy, "The Seed of Chaos, and of Night: The Gaza Strip after the Agreement," *Journal of Palestine Studies* 23, no. 3 (spring 1994), and Sara Roy, "Alienation or Accommodation?" *Journal of Palestine Studies* 24, no. 4 (summer 1995).

less Palestinians. Unemployment is currently estimated at 60 percent;[117] among working males, underemployment is around 38 percent.[118]

Faced with the task of creating a stable political structure within a territory that has been in upheaval for decades, the PA found itself woefully ill equipped to deal with the additional burdens of an exploding population and a shrinking resource base. A little over a year after the signing of the Accord, initial elation had faded. "We can now go freely to the beach," one resident said, "but we have also never been so badly off in economic terms."[119] The hardship faced by Gazans perpetuated the long-standing resentment of Israel; it also contributed to the emergence of dissatisfaction with Arafat's regime.

Legitimacy and Control

The 1990s have been years of rapid change in the Middle East. Elements of the following analysis may therefore be quickly superseded by events. Yet it remains likely that unless an alternate source of fresh water is developed, water scarcity in Gaza will continue to place real constraints on economic development and threaten political and social stability. The Gazan case appears to support the hypothesis that environmental scarcity can simultaneously increase economic deprivation and disrupt key social institutions, leading to civil strife and insurgency.[120]

To cause civil strife, economic crisis must be severe, persistent, and pervasive enough to erode the legitimacy or moral authority of the dominant social order and system of governance. System legitimacy is therefore a critical intervening variable between rising poverty and civil conflict. It is influenced by the aggrieved actors' subjective blame system, which consists of their beliefs about who or what is responsible for their plight.[121]

While the majority of Gazans continue to hold Israel accountable for the conditions under which they live, it is clear that Arafat's administration is being held accountable as well (see figure 3.2). The survival of the PA in Gaza ultimately rests on its ability to balance the dual objectives of achieving legitimacy in the eyes of Gazans and achieving the control of terrorist attacks demanded by Israel. Currently, Arafat's authority derives more from his police force as popular support for his administration wavers.

In major population centers, Palestinian police have replaced Israeli soldiers as the immediate source of authority. Arafat's ability to serve simultaneously as an effective administrator and as a nationalist icon is in question. Diaspora Palestinians see Arafat as a distant local leader who has lost the ability to represent their interests internationally; many Gaza Palestinians see him as an autocrat committed to a peace process that ignores their immediate economic needs. Arafat risks becoming a "Mr. Palestine increasingly disowned by Palestinians."[122]

Opposition in the Diaspora

As the prominent Palestinian poet Mamoud Darwish has written: "The irony of history is that Israel has adopted the old Palestinian formula— namely, that no solution is possible without the PLO."[123] But the more loudly the Israeli government proclaims Arafat and Fatah to be its partners in the peace process, the more dissension arises within the ranks of the Palestinian nationalist movement as to whether the peace process legitimately represents the movement's interests. Certainly, as an umbrella organization, the PLO has always contained opposition groups; these include the left-wing splinter groups the Popular Front for the Liberation of Palestine (PFLP), the Democratic Front for the Liberation of Palestine (DFLP), and the People's Party (PPP) (formerly the Communist Party). Prior to the Accord, none of these groups questioned Arafat's legitimacy. Today, however, these parties, and even members of Fatah, are calling for a rehabilitation of the image of the PLO within the nationalist movement. Some believe this rehabilitation requires the movement to distance itself from Arafat.

Arafat's autocratic methods are one significant source of intraparty friction. He has continually delayed adopting a more democratic structure within Fatah. Party elections in Gaza were postponed after similar elections in Ramallah, West Bank, resulted in the defeat of almost all Arafat appointees. Arafat has since overturned these results.[124] A 1994 meeting of the PLO exec-

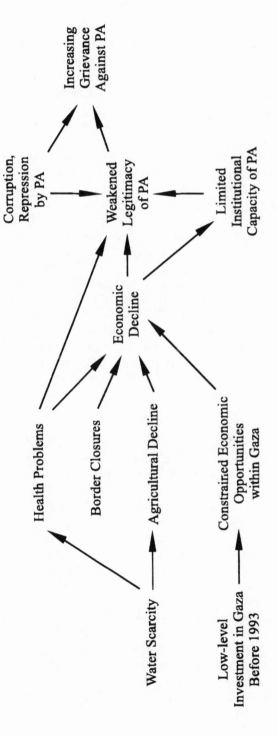

FIGURE 3.2
Threatened Government Legitimacy in Gaza

utive became a protest against his leadership when only eight of eighteen members participated.[125] Shafiq al-Hout, PLO ambassador to Lebanon, who resigned from the executive shortly after the Accord was signed, is a member of a newly formed opposition group called the National Coalition. "Arafat is simply irreformable," he says. "There is no alternative to the PLO. But how can we rescue this organization now hostage to Arafat and Gaza? We think that the way out is to get Arafat to choose between leading his National Authority in Gaza and Jericho or leading the PLO."[126]

The direction of the ongoing peace talks with Israel is another cause of opposition. Many Palestinians fear that the power imbalance between Israel and the PLO at the bargaining table has translated into a series of agreements that protects Israeli interests without producing commensurable gains for Palestinians. The recent agreement on limited autonomy for the West Bank is a significant step forward; however, opposition groups within the PLO immediately labeled the agreement "a disaster" and expressed concern that the terms of transfer are flawed and heavily biased toward Israel.[127] Skepticism surrounds the upcoming talks on the "difficult" issues of the right of return for Palestinian refugees, water, the future of Israeli settlements, and the fate of Jerusalem. From the perspective of some Palestinian nationalists, Arafat appears to be bargaining from a position of tremendous weakness: having recognized Israel and renounced the Palestinian use of violence, he is seen as having given up the main source of Palestinian bargaining power. For many, Arafat has traded away the PLO's overriding goal of an independent state for all Palestinians in order to ensure that he maintains leadership in Gaza.

Opposition In Gaza

The dissension within the PLO has significant implications for politics within Gaza, as the organization no longer serves in any meaningful respect as a source of unity. Parties once united under the PLO represent themselves separately in Gaza, and popular support for the PLO is split among them (see table 3.10). Palestinian allegiance to the PLO has translated into widespread support for Arafat; most Gazans still express great affection for Arafat as the unquestioned leader of the nationalist cause. This affection does not, however extend to the PA as a whole and, as a result, Arafat's position in Gaza is not secure. From the outset, many Gazans, especially those who fought in the intifadah, saw Arafat's administration as "outsiders." The years of PLO exile resulted in a leadership with weak ties to its constituents, as illustrated by the comments of one of Arafat's aides regarding the "uneasy" return of the PLO to Gaza: "We're scared. . . . We don't know those people and they don't know us."[128] Some of the policies pursued by the PA since the transfer of authority have done little to bridge this gulf.

Arafat's patronage system has created suspicion that international aid is

TABLE 3.10
Political Factions and Support, West Bank and Gaza, 1994

Affiliation	Party	Support (Percentage)
	Fatah	40
PLO	Popular Front for the Liberation of Palestine	7 - 8
	Democratic Front for the Liberation of Palestine	
	People's Party	5
Islamists	Hamas	15 - 20
	Islamic Jihad	
No Affiliation		30

Source: Adapted from Dan Connell, "Palestine on the Edge: Crisis in the National Movement," *Middle East Report* 25, no. 3/4 (May–June/July–August 1995).

being misallocated. The PA says that less than 20 percent of a promised $2.1 billion in aid has actually reached Arafat's administration. Of this sum, the majority has undoubtedly gone to meet the payroll of the PA's vast bureaucracy of 20,000 soldiers[129] and 28,000 civil servants,[130] with the result that little remains for investment in infrastructure and development. There is widespread resentment of the PA's financial agenda: "We know that Arafat gets money, but we don't know where it goes, into his pocket or to his friends. We don't see any of it."[131]

The exclusion of the majority of Gazans, and especially veterans of the intifadah, from political structures has exacerbated these grievances. The transition to limited self-government has only slowly provided a nonviolent channel through which Gazans can express their political will. The achievements of the peace process, significant as they are, do not in themselves provide a stable long-term basis of support for Arafat's government.

Violent Conflict

While Fatah maintains majority support within Gaza and the West Bank, significant elements of opposition are evident. The PA's weakened legitimacy at first appeared to increase support for "radical" Islamist groups. Tensions between the PA and Islamists came to a head in November 1994, when sixteen died and two hundred were wounded in an eruption of hostilities between Arafat's police and supporters of Hamas and Islamic Jihad.[132] In August 1995, an estimated one thousand protesters again violently confronted Palestinian police who were trying to arrest suspected Hamas leaders.

Incidents of this scale are not regular occurrences in Gaza, but political unity under the PLO has disintegrated; factionalism is rife as the realities of life under limited autonomy take shape. A major factor producing support for the Islamists is the ongoing economic crisis of the territory. It is simplistic and misleading to ascribe popular support for Islamist groups to the religious fervor of Palestinians within the territories or to a "global" expansion of Islam.

Three main Islamist groups operate in the Occupied Territories: Hamas, Islamic Jihad, and Tahrir. An elitist, ideologically oriented sect, Tahrir is not significantly involved in Palestinian politics. Islamic Jihad is notorious for several recent terrorist attacks. It focuses almost exclusively on violent action rather than on expanding its popular base in Gaza and the West Bank. Thus it is Hamas that is the major political threat to Arafat's PA.[133]

Like Islamic Jihad, Hamas has become notorious since the Accord was signed for a series of suicide bombings against Israelis in both Israel and Gaza. Western media coverage has focused exclusively on these activities, which were conducted by the organization's military wing, 'Izz al-Din al-Qassam. The media have not acknowledged what some have called the "other face of Hamas." There is a tangible basis for the group's popularity: it tries to provide some social and economic support for Gaza's population. Islamic groups are, by most accounts, relatively wealthy. In addition to significant contributions from the diaspora,[134] they are still able to obtain funds from Arab regimes in the Persian Gulf states that cut off support to the PLO.[135] In some communities, Hamas provides monthly allowances to poorer families and loans for medical expenses, education, and businesses. It has put in place a network of charities to support free hospitals, schools, orphanages, and clinics.[136] While Arafat's political achievements have won him considerable acclaim, within Gaza, Hamas's social activities may have a more immediate impact on an impoverished population.

At one point in mid-1994, almost one-third of Gaza's population claimed to support Hamas.[137] While that percentage has since diminished considerably, Arafat recognizes the power of Hamas and keeps open a line of communication with the organization's moderate political wing. Some say this wing is adapting itself to become a legitimate party in future elections.[138]

'Izz al-Din al-Qassam, however, has shown little interest in adapting to politics under the PA. The horrific and much-publicized terrorist bombings for which Hamas has openly claimed responsibility initially garnered considerable popular support in the Territories. The first few attacks were followed by massive rallies to commemorate the suicide bombers, who were held up as role models. Gazan children traded and collected pictures of the bombers like baseball cards. But such popular public endorsement has all but disappeared. The militants' activities are undermining support for Hamas as a whole: Israel's total closure of the Territories after each attack cuts off thousands of Palestinians from their livelihood, exacerbates poverty, and turns many Palestinians against the Islamists. This has not, however, translated into greater support for the PA; the fastest-growing percentage of Gazans is that which claims disillusion with *all* political parties.

In the long run, however, an Israeli policy of tight border restrictions may actually reduce Israeli security. By weakening Gaza's economic base further, increasing frustration, and undermining Arafat's legitimacy, such a policy will exacerbate grievances within Gaza, grievances that could eventually catalyze even greater violence against Israel.[139]

Even if Israel were to completely close off Gaza, radical Palestinians would still have opportunities for violence against Israeli targets because of the continuing presence of settlements. These settlements occupy a significant amount of territory, and as the quantity and quality of Gaza's natural resources deteriorate, they may become the focus of additional violence. The relative luxury of the settlements provides an immediate comparison point and a powerful source of resentment in light of the poor conditions faced by most Gazans.

Threats to the security of Israelis may, however, be less direct. As the presence of Israeli soldiers declines in autonomous areas of Gaza, the high levels of social frustration in Palestinian society may instead be focused on internal Palestinian targets, leading to more intra-Palestinian violence in the Territories (see figure 3.3). Israel's insistence that Arafat suppress the Islamist movement in Gaza already is a major source of intra-Palestinian friction. Israel is suspicious of the mass arrests of Hamas's supporters after each terrorist incident, as charges are rarely laid and as Arafat refuses to extradite suspects. Nonetheless, the sweeps—which often result in gun battles between the police and the Islamists—have damaged Arafat's image in Gaza, and there have been calls for him to stop "hounding Hamas's holy fighters."[140] Recent accusations of human rights abuses and torture of Palestinians by the PA's secret services in Gaza and Jericho have further undermined the image of the administration.[141]

Grievance has not, at present, been redirected from Israeli targets toward the Palestinian police on a significant scale. However, many young people in Gaza, having grown up under the occupation, have an entirely negative perception of authority.[142] The authoritarian actions and conspicuous consumption of the PA have done little to alter this perception. The PA risks being seen—especially among Palestinian youth—as the continuation of Israeli occupation.

At present, most Palestinians oppose the ascendancy of conservative Islamists. The lack of a widely acceptable alternative to Arafat's government has

FIGURE 3.3
Dynamics of Violence in Gaza

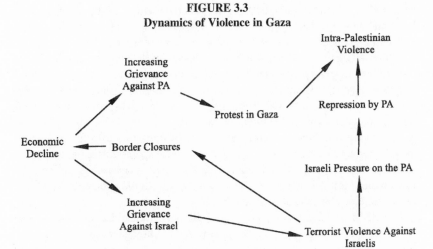

resulted in political apathy rather than political revolt. Now that the nationalist unity that endured for so long under the PLO has largely evaporated, many Palestinians are left with a sense of hopelessness. Dr. al-Masri writes:

> Our own society is somehow committing suicide. . . . Look at our streets—we are neglectful of everything. There is a depression in this country. At social gatherings you hear people talking about basic needs, political and economic problems, but there is no mention whatsoever of the future.[143]

Conclusions

Early 1996 provided a break in this atmosphere of political apathy in Gaza. On January 20, Palestinians in Gaza, West Bank, Jericho, and East Jerusalem voted in the first Palestinian general elections. Turnout in Gaza was extremely high, estimated at 85 percent of registered voters. This showing was interpreted as a rebuff against Hamas, who had called for a boycott of the election process. Arafat, as expected, won an overwhelming majority—88 percent of the vote for the presidency—and Fatah is expected to dominate the 88-member legislative council.[144]

Amid the excitement surrounding the elections, several observers were cautiously optimistic about the difficult transition from authoritarianism to democracy now facing Arafat's government.[145] The elections will provide the PA with greater legitimacy if the legislative council provides an effective forum for open political expression and increased participation in the political process. If, conversely, the council is an inadequate mechanism to balance the power of the leadership, and opportunities for participation remained limited in the absence of improvements in living conditions, what once appeared to be unshakable Palestinian faith in Arafat will likely crumble.

Rapid population growth and intense agricultural activity in a region of scarce resources have combined with Israel's policies throughout the occupation to produce a potentially volatile political environment in Gaza. Today, the monumental task of achieving political stability is further complicated by the PA's authoritarian tendencies and Israeli policies of economic disengagement.

The interaction of severe supply, demand, and structural scarcities has constrained development and has contributed to the impoverishment of Gaza's population. Deteriorating economic and social conditions have produced collective grievance and violence against Israel and, more recently, against the PA. Solutions to the water crisis in Gaza will not in themselves solve the conflict. Nonetheless, steps toward the conservation and rehabilitation of the aquifer and the more equitable apportionment of the water that is available will be essential elements of a stable peace.

Notes

An earlier version of this chapter was published as Kimberley Kelly and Thomas Homer-Dixon, *Environmental Scarcity and Violent Conflict: The Case of Gaza*, Occasional Paper of the Project on Environment, Population, and Security (Washington, D.C.: American Association for the Advancement of Science and the University of Toronto, 1995). For their valuable help, the authors thank David Brooks, Peter Gleick, James Graff, Philip Howard, Jad Isaac, David Kelly, James Moore, Stephanie Nolen, Leah Patry, Valerie Percival, John Sigler, and Jill Tansley.

1. John Bulloch and Adel Darwish, *Water Wars: Coming Conflicts in the Middle East* (London: Victor Gollancz, 1993), 36.

2. Ibid.

3. See *The Jerusalem Post*, 24 September 1994, international edition, 24, and Serge Schmemann, "Bus Bomb Kills 5 in Jerusalem," *New York Times*, 22 August 1995, p. A6.

4. Joel Greenberg, "Palestinian 'Martyrs' Defiant and So Willing," *New York Times*, 25 January 1995, p. A6.

5. David Brooks and Stephen Lonergan, *Watershed: The Role of Fresh Water in the Israeli-Palestinian Conflict* (Ottawa: International Development Research Centre, 1994), 8–10.

6. Water Resources Action Program (WRAP), *Palestinian Water Resources* (Jerusalem: WRAP, 1994), 9.

7. Sara Roy, *The Gaza Strip: The Political Economy of De-Development* (Washington, D.C.: The Institute for Palestine Studies, 1995), 31–99.

8. Ibid., 110.

9. Conversely, there are no restrictions on Israeli imports to Gaza and the West Bank.

10. Roy, *The Gaza Strip: The Political Economy of De-Development*, 131.

11. Anita Vitullo, "Uprising in Gaza," *Middle East Report* 18, no. 3 (May–June 1988): 22.

12. Salim Tamari, "What the Uprising Means," *Middle East Report* 18, no. 3 (May–June 1988): 27.

13. Barry Rubin, *Revolution Until Victory? The Politics and History of the PLO* (Cambridge: Harvard University Press, 1994), 86.

14. Roy, *The Gaza Strip: The Political Economy of De-Development*, 303.

15. Ibid., 309–16.

16. Sara Roy, "The Seed of Chaos, and of Night: The Gaza Strip After the Agreement," *Journal of Palestine Studies* 23, no. 3 (spring 1994): 86.

17. These allegedly include house demolition, curfew, and assassinations by undercover Israeli security forces. Stanley Cohen, "Justice in Transition?" *Middle East Report* 25, no. 3/4 (May–August 1995): 4. Amnesty International reported in 1995 that human rights abuses in the form of illegal detentions and the torture of detainees (through beating, sleep deprivation, hooding, and binding in painful positions) continue under both the Israeli Defense Forces and the Palestinian Authority. Amnesty International, *Country Report: Israel and the Occupied Territories: Human Rights: A Year of Shattered Hopes* (AI index: MDE 15/07/95).

18. After implementation of the Accord, Raji Sourani of the Gaza Centre for Rights and Law estimated that there were some fifty-two checkpoints monitoring Palestinian movement within Gaza.

19. Derek Brown, "Disillusion Sours Hopes in Gaza," *Manchester Guardian Weekly*, 27 November 1994, 3. The pattern of settlement reflects the objectives of settlement policy following the Camp David accords of 1979: to create a strong Israeli presence that would make it difficult to form an independent Palestinian state in Gaza and to physically isolate Arab communities from one another, decreasing the possibility of unified autonomy. See Sara Roy, *The Gaza Strip: A Demographic, Economic, Social and Legal Survey* (Boulder, Colo.: Westview Press, 1986), 137.

20. Roy, "The Seed of Chaos," 86.

21. There are notable exceptions to this downward trend; a recent article profiled several Gaza Palestinians who have benefited greatly under autonomy. However, the examples chosen are all people with outside sources of financial support or with close ties to Arafat and Fatah's power elite. The article notes that "most Gazans still live in dire poverty." See Isabel Kershner, "Signs of Life in Gaza," *Jerusalem Report*, 13 July 1995.

22. Arafat's Authority employs an estimated twenty thousand policemen—one for every fifty residents in the autonomous areas.

23. See Greenberg, "Palestinian 'Martyrs' Defiant and So Willing," p. A6.

24. *The Jerusalem Post*, 12 November 1994, international edition, 1.

25. Edward Said, *The Politics of Dispossession* (London: Chatto and Windus, 1994), 414.

26. Sandra Postel, *The Last Oasis: Facing Water Scarcity* (London: Earthscan Publications, 1992), 29.

27. Enviro-transpiration, or evapo-transpiration, is the loss of water an ecosystem experiences through evaporation from plant life and soil.

28. H. J. Bruins, A. Tuinhof, and R. Keller, *Water in the Gaza Strip,* Hydrology Study, Final Report (Netherlands: Government of Netherlands, Ministry of Foreign Affairs, Directorate General for International Cooperation, 1991), 6, and WRAP, *Palestinian Water Resources*, 4.

29. WRAP, *Palestinian Water Resources*, 4.

30. Jad Isaac, Applied Research Institute in Jerusalem, personal communication, 23 September 1995.

31. The Wadi Gaza, the area's only source of surface water, is impounded by Israel before it enters Gaza. Some piped water is supplied to Gaza from the Israeli Water Carrier (about 5 mcm, according to Jad Isaac of the Applied Research Institute in Jerusalem). However, "it is not clear whether Israel is actually supplying water to the Gaza Strip or is simply putting Gaza water into the Carrier." David Brooks and Stephen Lonergan, *Economic, Ecological and Geopolitical Dimensions of Water in Israel* (Victoria, B.C.: Centre for Sustainable Regional Development, 1992), 77.

32. Bruins, Tuinhof, and Keller, *Water in the Gaza Strip*, 8.

33. The salinity of the deeper aquifer is estimated to reach 60,000 ppm in some areas, almost double the salinity of sea water. Zaher Kuhail and Zaki Zoarob, *Potable Ground Water Crisis in the Gaza Strip, 1987–1994* (Gaza: UNRWA and the Palestinian Health Authority, 1994).

34. See Natasha Beschorner, *Water and Instability in the Middle East* (London: International Institute for Strategic Studies, 1992), 14, and Bruins, Tuinhof, and Keller, *Water in the Gaza Strip*, 9.

35. See A. A. Kubursi and H. A. Amery, "Water Scarcity in the Middle East: Misallocation or Real Shortages?" (paper presented at the conference, "The Middle East Water Crisis: Creative Perspectives and Solutions," University of Waterloo, Waterloo, Ontario, 1992).

36. Roy, *The Gaza Strip: The Political Economy of De-Development*, 165.

37. Adnan Shqueir, "The Environment in the West Bank and Gaza Strip," *Palestine-Israel Journal* 2, no. 5 (winter 1995): 90.

38. United Nations (UN), Committee on the Exercise of the Unalienable Rights of the Palestinian People, *Water Resources of the Occupied Palestinian Territory* (New York: United Nations, 1992), 52–53.

39. Ibid., 53.

40. Brooks and Lonergan, *Watershed*, 92.

41. UN, *Water Resources of the Occupied Palestinian Territory*, 27.

42. Ibid., 31–32.

43. Taher Nassereddin, "Institutional Aspects of Joint Management of Aquifers by Israel and the Occupied Territories," in *Joint Management of Shared Aquifers: the First Workshop*, ed. Eran Feitelson and Marwan Haddad (Jerusalem: Palestine Consultancy Group and Harry Truman Institute, 1994), 60.

44. Brooks and Lonergan, *Watershed*, 134–35.

45. Ibid., 131.

46. Sharif Elmusa, "The Israeli-Palestinian Water Dispute Can Be Resolved," *Palestine-Israel Journal* 1, no. 3 (summer 1994): 26.

47. Roy, *The Gaza Strip: The Political Economy of De-Development*, 15.

48. Brooks and Lonergan, *Watershed*, 40.

49. From the Statistical Abstract of Israel, 1992, cited in *Israel Water Study for the World Bank*, draft study, Ben Gurion University and Tahal Consulting Engineers, Beersheba, Israel, 1993, and WRAP, *Palestinian Water Resources*, 2.

50. WRAP, *Palestinian Water Resources*, 3, and Bruins, Tuinhof, and Keller, *Water in the Gaza Strip*, 2.

51. When he visited Gaza in 1992, Said wrote: "Jabalya Camp is the most appalling place I have ever seen. . . . There is no sewage system, the stench tears at your gut. . . . The statistics are nightmarish: the worst infant mortality rates, the worst unemployment, the lowest per capita income, the most days of curfew, the least medical services, and on and on." Said, *The Politics of Dispossession*, 195.

52. Peter Gleick, "Water and Conflict: Fresh Water Resources and National Security," *International Security* 18, no. 1 (summer 1993): 90.

53. World Bank, *Developing the Occupied Territories: An Investment in Peace*, vol. 2 (Washington, D.C.: The World Bank, 1993), 35. In 1989, the Gaza Agriculture Department estimated that a total of 20,500 hectares were under cultivation (by both Palestinians and Israelis) in Gaza. Using these figures, the per capita figure for cultivated land for Israeli settlers in Gaza is 0.41–0.51 hectares, compared with 0.023–0.026 hectares for Palestinians.

54. World Bank, *Developing the Occupied Territories: An Investment in Peace*, vol. 1 (Washington, D.C.: The World Bank, 1993), 10.

55. World Bank, *Developing the Occupied Territories: An Investment in Peace*, vol. 4 (Washington, D.C.: The World Bank, 1993), 53.

56. Beschorner, *Water and Instability*, 14.

57. Nassereddin, "Institutional Aspects of Joint Management of Aquifers," 64, and Isaac, personal communication. While the majority of sources concur on these estimates for Israeli settlers, some sources suggest that settlers' withdrawals are considerably higher. One recent study estimated a total of thirty Israeli wells in Gaza in 1992, drawing approximately 20 mcm a year. Palestinian Committee for Peace and Afro-Asian Solidarity, "The Water Problem in Gaza and Proposed Solutions," *Development and Socio-Economic Progress*, no. 53 (1992).

58. Isaac, personal communication. "Consumption" refers to the amount of water *actually* withdrawn from the aquifer, as opposed to "sustainable supply," which refers to the amount that can *safely* be withdrawn without exceeding renewable yield.

59. The definition of "excessive" in this case is extremely subjective. Thomas Naff (quoted in Brooks and Lonergan, *Watershed*, 88) notes that, compared with Canada and the United States, Middle Eastern nations, including Israel, are "remarkably efficient," but "not as efficient as the crisis and the scarcity requires them to be." The key issue regarding efficiency in this context is that settlers' consumption may be perceived as unreasonable relative to the strict limits placed on Palestinian consumption.

60. WRAP, *Palestinian Water Resources*, 13.

61. Ibid., 9.

62. Brooks and Lonergan, *Watershed*, 39.

63. David Brooks, *Summary Trip Report: Toronto, Israel, Gaza and Egypt* (Ottawa: Environment and Natural Resources Division, International Development Research Centre, December 1994), 4.

64. Official Israeli sources tend to blame the state of Gaza's water supply on the Egyptian administration that preceded them. Overexploitation almost certainly occurred prior to the annexation of Gaza in 1967. Under the Egyptian authorities, water consumption was not regulated, and the massive influx of refugees after 1948 put tremendous strain on the area's resources. Nonetheless, while the Israeli authority introduced regulations that may arguably have slowed down the rate of consumption, the resources continue to be overexploited. One commentator writes that "the water system in Gaza has been managed by Israel for twenty-seven years; it cannot wash its hands of the problem by blaming it, as it does on the Egyptian administration." Elmusa, "The Israeli-Palestinian Water Dispute," 20.

65. This figure represents the differential between estimates of safe renewable yield and actual consumption. Safe renewable yield is estimated at 60–65 mcm; consumption is estimated at 100–140 mcm. If we subtract a midpoint estimate of 120–125 mcm from the 60–65 mcm available, we are left with a deficit in the area of 60 mcm per year. Some sources, including the Israeli Defense Forces and the UN Conference on Trade and Development, estimate this deficit to be much lower, approximately 30 mcm per year. The balance of evidence from all sources, however, appears to support the higher estimates cited here.

66. Brooks and Lonergan, *Economic, Ecological and Geopolitical Dimensions of Water in Israel*, 77.

67. Hisham Zarour, Jad Isaac, and Violet Qumsieh, "Hydrochemical Indicators of the Severe Water Crisis in the Gaza Strip," in *Final Report on the Project Water Resources in the West Bank and Gaza Strip: Current Situation and Future Prospects* (Jerusalem: Applied Research Institute in Jerusalem, 1994), 9.

68. Beschorner, *Water and Instability*, 15.

69. K. Assaf, N. al-Khatib, E. Kally, and H. Shuval, "Water in the Israeli-Arab Conflict," *Palestine-Israel Journal* 1, no. 3 (summer 1994): 14.

70. Anna Bellisari, "Public Health and the Water Crisis in the Occupied Palestinian Territories," *Journal of Palestine Studies* 23, no. 2 (winter 1994).

71. Zarour, Isaac, and Qumsieh, "Hydrochemical Indicators of the Severe Water Crisis," 13.

72. Highly saline water is regularly used for irrigation, with damage to crop yields already in evidence in many cases. Water sources in Gaza that fall below salinity levels of 600 ppm chloride are considered acceptable for irrigation; in Israel, levels between 200 and 300 ppm chloride are considered dangerous to citrus. Roy, *The Gaza Strip: The Political Economy of De-Development*, 163.

73. Zarour, Isaac, and Qumsieh, "Hydrochemical Indicators of the Severe Water Crisis," 20.

74. Roy, *The Gaza Strip: The Political Economy of De-Development*, 164.

75. Sameer A. Abu-Eisheh, *Public Utilities in the West Bank and Gaza Strip* (New York: UN Conference on Trade and Development, 1994), 39.

76. Rafah's treatment capacity has been severely reduced since its construction in 1987 due to poor maintenance and excessive input of waste. See Abu-Eisheh, *Public Utilities in the West Bank and Gaza Strip*, 39. At the time of publication of these figures, expansion of the Rafah network was underway, and upgrading of its treatment facility was under consideration. The expansion of the Jabalya sewage network was

also under consideration; see Ramzi Sansur, *Environment and Development Prospects in the West Bank and Gaza Strip* (New York: UN Conference on Trade and Development, 1995).

77. World Bank, *Developing the Occupied Territories: An Investment in Peace*, vol. 6 (Washington, D.C.: The World Bank, 1993), 19.

78. Beschorner, *Water and Instability*, 15.

79. Kuhail and Zoarob, *Potable Ground Water Crisis*, 40.

80. Bellisari, "Public Health and the Water Crisis," 55–57, Kuhail and Zoarob, *Potable Ground Water Crisis*, 40.

81. There is one small desalinization plant operating on the Gaza coast, and several studies suggest that this is the best alternative for future water supply in Gaza. However, desalinization on a large enough scale to provide a viable alternative drinking-water source would involve prohibitive capital and operating costs given the current state of Gaza's economy. "Palestinians are skeptical of this mega-project approach, in part for fear that they will get stuck with expensive sources of supply, and in part because it diverts attention from the inequitable distribution of existing supplies." Brooks and Lonergan, *Watershed*, 136.

82. Bellisari, "Public Health and the Water Crisis," 61.

83. Kingston Frontenac and Lennox and Addington Health Unit, personal communication, 10 November 1995.

84. Bellisari, "Public Health and Water Crisis," 56.

85. Hypernatremia is a maldistribution of body water caused by a sodium imbalance. High concentrations of sodium in blood plasma draw water out of the red blood cells, causing them to collapse and consequently inhibiting gas exchange. The thirst mechanism is the body's primary defense against such an imbalance. Vulnerable individuals include infants or unconscious patients whose thirst mechanism is faulty or who cannot access water as needed. Vulnerability is also increased by high environmental temperatures, low humidity, and small size. See Lawrence Finberg, "Hypernatremia," in *Sodium: Its Biologic Significance*, ed. Solomon Papper (Boca Raton, Fla.: CRC Press Inc., 1982), 266–76.

86. National Research Council, *Drinking Water and Health* (Washington, D.C.: National Academy of Sciences, 1977), 403.

87. Kuhail and Zoarob, *Potable Ground Water Crisis*, 34–35.

88. National Research Council, *Drinking Water and Health*, 403.

89. Ibid., 411–25, and Bellisari, "Public Health and the Water Crisis," 56–57. Spontaneous abortion may have impacts for animal husbandry, but the incidence and economic implications of this phenomenon in Gaza have not been examined.

90. "Skeletal fluorosis is manifested in brittle bones, increased rates of bone fractures and crippling deformities. Dental fluorosis...not health threatening itself, [is] indicative of enamel brittleness and potential damage to teeth." Bellisari, "Public Health and the Water Crisis," 56.

91. See Ramzi Sansur, S. Kuttab, and S. Abu al-Haj, *Evaluation of the Extent of Exposure of Farm Workers to Organiphosphate Pesticides in the Jordan Valley, West Bank* (Birzeit: Birzeit University Center for Environmental and Occupational Health Science, 1990).

92. Bellisari, "Public Health and the Water Crisis," 57–60.

93. While immediate testing of the water supply determined that the pollution was limited to one Gaza City neighborhood, Israel reacted by imposing a ban on all food imports from Gaza. *The Jerusalem Post*, 19 November 1994, international edition, 24.

94. Bellisari, "Public Health and the Water Crisis," 60.

95. Ibid., 57–60.

96. World Bank, *Developing the Occupied Territories*, vol. 1, 10. This expenditure is comparable to Israel's as a percentage; according to the Statistical Abstract of Israel for 1993, Israel's 1990 expenditure accounted for 7.8 percent of GNP. Of course, Israel's GNP is considerably greater than Gaza's in terms of dollar value. Seven percent of Gaza's GNP for 1990 ($825 million) amounts to approximately $58 million. Israel's health expenditure for 1990 amounted to approximately $3.8 billion.

97. Bellisari, "Public Health and the Water Crisis," 61.

98. For example, in January 1995 workers at a private clinic in Gaza City went on strike, demanding higher wages, social benefits, and the right to organize. The strike, which was not publicly acknowledged by the PA, was surprising, given massive unemployment in Gaza. See Amira Hass, "Gaza Workers and the Palestinian Authority," *Middle East Report* 25, no. 3/4 (May–August 1995): 25–26.

99. Roy, *The Gaza Strip: The Political Economy of De-Development*, 223.

100. World Bank, *Developing the Occupied Territories*, vol. 4, 85–86.

101. UN, *Water Resources of the Occupied Palestinian Territory*, 60.

102. Anne Mosely Lesch, *Transition to Palestinian Self-Government* (Bloomington, Ind.: Indiana University Press, 1992), 104.

103. Roy, *The Gaza Strip: The Political Economy of De-Development*, 233.

104. The average yield per hectare for other fruit crops also declined slightly, from 4.2 tons/hectare in 1967–68 to 3.8 in 1985–86. David Kahan, *Agriculture and Water Resources in the West Bank and Gaza 1967–1987* (Boulder, Colo.: Westview Press, 1987), 43, 145.

105. Ibid., 38.

106. WRAP, *Palestinian Water Resources*, 16.

107. World Bank, *Developing the Occupied Territories*, vol. 4, 38–39.

108. Ibid., 5.

109. Ibid., 42–43.

110. UN, Water Resources of the Occupied Palestinian Territory, 48–49.

111. According to the World Bank, "similar cases" include Mauritius, with 33 percent industrial share of GDP for 1990, and Lesotho, with 30 percent. World Bank, *Developing the Occupied Territories: An Investment in Peace*, vol. 3 (Washington, D.C.: The World Bank, 1993), 27.

112. World Bank, *Developing the Occupied Territories*, vol. 4, 22.

113. A semiskilled construction worker can earn up to $71 a day, whereas in Gaza that same worker would earn only $14. Roy, "The Seed of Chaos," 93.

114. Ali Wihaidi, "The Economic Aspects of Joint Management of Shared Aquifers: A Palestinian Perspective," in *Joint Management of Shared Aquifers; the First Workshop*, ed. Eran Feitelson and Marwan Haddad (Jerusalem: Palestine Consultancy Group and Harry Truman Institute, 1994), 124.

115. Derek Brown, "Gaza Awards No Prizes for Peace," *Manchester Guardian Weekly*, 18 December 1994, 4. While GDP figures for 1994 are not available, 1992

figures provide a point of comparison. The Central Bureau of Statistics in Israel estimates the GDP of the Occupied Territories at between $2.4 and $2.5 billion for 1992. A $400 million loss would represent approximately 16 percent of GDP for 1992.

116. Roy, "The Seed of Chaos," 92.

117. Patrice Claude, "Year of 'Peace' Proves Disappointing for Palestinians," *Manchester Guardian Weekly*, 13 May 1995, 13.

118. Roy, "The Seed of Chaos," 90.

119. Claude, "Year of 'Peace'," 13.

120. Homer-Dixon, "Environmental Scarcities and Violent Conflict: Evidence from Cases," *International Security* 19, no. 1 (summer 1994): 23–24.

121. Ibid., 26.

122. David Hirst, "Asking Arafat to Do the Unthinkable," *Manchester Guardian Weekly*, 11 December 1994, 3.

123. Mona Naim, interview with Mamoud Darwish, *Middle East Report* 25, no. 3/4 (May–August 1995): 18.

124. Dan Connell, "Palestine on the Edge," *Middle East Report* 25, no. 3/4 (May–August 1995): 8.

125. Anat Cygielman, ed., "Chronology of Events," *Palestine-Israel Journal* 2, no. 4 (autumn 1995), 127.

126. David Hirst, "Arafat's Foes Wait to Pounce on Their Prey," *Manchester Guardian Weekly*, 11 June 1995, 12.

127. The Israeli Right also came out in immediate opposition to the agreement, calling it a "black day in the history of Israel." Derek Brown, "Israel Agrees to Quit West Bank," *Manchester Guardian Weekly*, 1 October 1995, 1.

128. "Palestinians Feel the Stress of Change," *The Economist* 330, no. 4847 (22 January 1994): 43.

129. Claude, "Year of 'Peace,' " 13.

130. *Foreign Reports*, 18 May 1995.

131. Brown, "Gaza Awards No Prizes for Peace," 4.

132. Brown, "Disillusion Sours Hopes in Gaza," 1.

133. Lisa Hajjar, "The Islamist Movements in the Occupied Territories: An Interview with Iyad Barghouti," *MERIP Reports* 23, no. 4 (July–August 1993): 10.

134. James Brooke and Elaine Sciolino, "U.S. Muslims Say Their Aid Pays for Charity, Not Terror," *New York Times*, 16 August 1995, pp. A1, A6.

135. Hajjar, "The Islamist Movements in the Occupied Territories," 11.

136. Brooke and Sciolino, "U.S. Muslims Say Their Aid Pays for Charity, Not Terror," p. A1.

137. *Foreign Reports*, 18 May 1995.

138. Ahmad S. Khalidi, "Security in a Final Middle East Settlement: Some Components of Palestinian National Security," *International Affairs* 71, no. 1 (January 1995): 16.

139. In August 1995, the leader of Israel's Likud party, Binyamin Netanyahu, estimated that 170 Israelis have been killed in the two years since the Accord was signed; this figure reveals a marked increase from the 49 Israeli deaths in the year preceding the Accord. See Serge Schmemann, "Bus Bombing Kills 5 in Jerusalem," *New York Times*, 22 August 1995, p. A6, and Cygielman, "Chronology of Events," 10.

140. *The Jerusalem Post*, 12 November 1994, international edition, 1.

141. Shyam Bhatia, "Arafat's Torturers Shock Palestinians," *Manchester Guardian Weekly*, 24 September 1995, 13.

142. Roy, "The Seed of Chaos."

143. Cited in Greenberg, "Palestinian 'Martyrs' Defiant and So Willing," p. A6.

144. Serge Schmemann, "Big Vote Turnout for Palestinians," *New York Times*, 21 January 1996, p. A1.

145. Martin Cohn, "Warnings Amid the Euphoria," *Toronto Star*, 22 January 1996, p. A3.

4

The Case of South Africa

Valerie Percival and Thomas Homer-Dixon

Overview

Scholars have overlooked the role of environmental scarcity—the scarcity of renewable resources—as a contributor to social instability in South Africa. The severe environmental problems confronting the country have been eclipsed by the negative social impacts of apartheid, opposition to minority rule, and the effort to build a post-apartheid political order. The transition to democracy was an astonishing achievement, the culmination of decades of struggle. Even so, apartheid has left behind a grim ecological legacy that will influence political, social, and economic conditions for decades.

Although the linkages between environmental scarcity and violence in South Africa are complex, this chapter traces the causal role of environmental scarcity in the recent civil strife. In the context of apartheid, environmental scarcity contributed to reduced agricultural productivity in the homelands, migrations to and within urban areas, and the deterioration of the local urban environment. These pressures undermined the ability of the state to provide for the needs of society. The level of grievances within society rose, and the transition from minority rule provided opportunities for the violent expression of these grievances. After the election of Nelson Mandela, violence subsided in most areas of the country. Yet, as of October 1995, civil strife continues in the KwaZulu-Natal region, an indication that underlying stressors—such as environmental scarcity—remain.

We begin the description of the South African case by outlining the effects of apartheid and the process of transition from apartheid rule. We then provide an overview of environmental scarcity in South Africa, its social effects, and its relationship to violence, with a specific focus on the KwaZulu-Natal region. We conclude by discussing what our analysis means for social stability in post-apartheid South Africa.

The context specific to each case determines the precise relationship between environmental scarcity and outbreaks of violent conflict. The quantity and vulnerability of environmental resources influence the activities of a society's population and determine the environmental impacts of these activities. Contextual factors also include the balance of political power, patterns of interaction, and the structure of economic relations among social groups. These factors affect how resources will be used, the social impact of environmental scarcities, the grievances arising from these scarcities, and whether grievances will contribute to violence. The particular relationship between state and society is crucially important to the character of the links between environmental scarcity and violence.

Our analysis faced serious limitations in data quality and quantity. Therefore, rather than providing definitive conclusions, this chapter offers suggestive findings and provides a framework for further research on South Africa. Analysts need to identify the key social and political factors intervening between environmental scarcity and violent conflict. They must also generate good data on agricultural productivity, soil erosion, and fuelwood availability within the former homelands and on migration rates to urban settings. For urban areas, researchers need to establish the degree of dependence of the local population on renewable resources, and they must determine how access to these resources is manipulated by local leaders. Such information is essential to competent policy formation and implementation in the post-apartheid period.

Background

South Africa is one of the few countries that has experienced a relatively smooth transition to democracy. The apartheid regime, dominated by the National Party, voluntarily agreed to democratic elections in which it had little chance of victory. The election outcome allowed the African National Congress (ANC) majority to form the Government of National Unity (GNU) in cooperation with Inkatha and the National Party. The GNU will rule the country for five years, until new constitutional arrangements for South Africa are finalized. Scholars and policy makers perceive South Africa as a model for democratic transition in ethnically divided societies. However, prospects for a prosperous, peaceful, and democratic South Africa look very different when the contributions of environmental scarcity to the country's social instability are better understood.

MAP 4.1
Apartheid South Africa

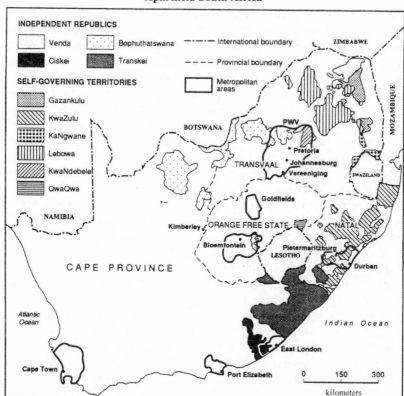

Source: David M. Smith, "Introduction," *The Apartheid City and Beyond: Urbanization and Social Change in South Africa,* ed. David M. Smith (London: Routledge, 1992), 3. Reprinted by permission.

Apartheid and the Political Geography of African Communities

Although British colonial rule gradually dispossessed the original Africans of their land, racial separation was entrenched with the 1948 victory of the National Party, which slowly began to implement apartheid (apartness). Apartheid provided whites with 87 percent of the land, while blacks—almost 75 percent of the country's population—lived within the 10 Bantustans or homelands, which accounted for only 13 percent of the land. The black people in these areas sustained themselves through agriculture, local service industries, and as migrant labor in white-owned mines and industry.

The homelands became a dumping ground for the black South African population. From 1960 to 1980, the government forced 1.75 million people into the homelands to clear what it called "black spots"—squatter settlements in urban areas and rural villages consisting of blacks whose labor-tenant contracts on white farms had been canceled. The population density of the homelands increased dramatically as a result. Quasi-urban communities emerged on homeland borders as the labor force commuting to neighboring cities, mines, and industries grew rapidly in the 1970s. Other black workers lived in single-sex hostels near industries too far from the homelands for daily commuting. The remainder of the black population was restricted to legally defined "townships" lying outside white urban areas and was employed in industry and mines or as domestic laborers.[1]

A recognizable apartheid city emerged—and it remains largely in existence today. Natural features, such as rivers, steep valleys, and escarpments, or human-made barriers, such as industrial areas, commercial belts, and railways, separate racial groups. Urban land is inequitably distributed: the township areas allocated for black South Africans are not sufficient for the numbers of people living there. These communities are also found on the periphery of the city, in the least attractive sectors—downwind from dirty industries, on poor land, and far from the city center. Informal settlements, which emerged first within the townships and then on public land throughout the major cities, continue to grow.[2] Both townships and settlements receive few services and lack infrastructure. The inadequacy of the infrastructure, such as sewage systems, water supplies, and energy sources, means that the urban black population relies extensively for its day-to-day needs on the local environment— including small vegetable plots and local streams, trees, and brush. Because many of these communities are located in fragile environments close to hillsides and river valleys, the environment quickly deteriorates.

The Struggle Against Apartheid

The ANC, originally formed in 1912, escalated its activities in the 1950s as the National Party established the institutions of apartheid. With the escalating protest came increased government repression. The government banned the ANC and other opposition groups in 1960. Forced underground, the ANC established the military wing Umkhonto we Sizwe ("Spear of the Nation"), which began violent attacks against the government. Nelson Mandela, one of the leaders of the ANC, was arrested in 1961 and received a life sentence for treason in 1964.

Incremental reform began when P. W. Botha became prime minister in 1978. The political openings provided by reform stimulated increased opposition activities; in response, the government—concerned about losing control of the pace of change—heightened its repression. The main opposition group, the United Democratic Front (UDF), the exiled ANC's ally within South Africa, fiercely opposed the limited character of these reform measures and worked to make the country ungovernable. The government declared a nation-wide state of emergency in 1986, while pressing on with limited reforms aimed at desegregating transportation and education. International companies began to divest, and many countries imposed sanctions on South African goods.

F. W. de Klerk was sworn in as state president on 20 September 1989. In the words of his foreign minister, Pik Botha, "The government began to shift away from apartheid when it realized that it was impossible to stem the tide of Africans moving to the urban areas in search of employment, signaling that the homeland system did not work."[3] On 1 February 1990, de Klerk lifted the thirty-year ban on the ANC and several other political organizations and allowed the return of political exiles. He released Nelson Mandela on 11 February 1990. With this watershed event, the process of dismantling apartheid became irreversible.

Negotiating Democracy

Almost immediately after Mandela's release, the incidence of violence sky-rocketed. Both the ANC and Inkatha became officially recognized political parties engaged in the struggle for control of the state. Clashes between their supporters gripped the KwaZulu-Natal region and the townships surrounding Johannesburg. Despite calls by all sides for an end to the bloodshed, it persisted until national elections established a multiracial democracy in April 1994.

Economic problems complicated the pre-election period. The South African economy stagnated in the late 1980s and early 1990s, debilitated by economic sanctions, low commodity prices, labor unrest, rural-urban migration, and wars in Namibia, Angola, and Mozambique. Annual real growth dropped from 3.4 percent in the 1970s to 1.5 percent in the 1980s; in 1990, the economy actually shrank. "Meanwhile [the total South African population in 1990] was swelling by 2.5 percent a year, adding around one thousand newcomers to the work force each day. According to the best available estimates, more than one in three workers had no formal job, and half the unemployed did not even have unofficial work in the subsistence economy."[4]

In December 1991, the government, the ANC, the National Party, and most other political parties, with the exception of Inkatha and the radical Pan-African Congress, participated in CODESA—the Convention for a Democratic South Africa. After many false starts and difficult negotiations, CODESA produced a draft postapartheid constitution and set 27 April 1994 as the date for the country's first multiracial election. The ANC won a majority but was constitutionally obligated to form a Government of National Unity from all parties winning twenty or more seats. Both the National Party and Inkatha obtained the required twenty seats, and, with the ANC, formed the Government of National Unity. Nelson Mandela, once the South African regime's most reviled political prisoner, now presides as its president.

Mandela's Presidency

The transition from apartheid to post-apartheid South Africa is being guided by the Reconstruction and Development Program [RDP], which has as its goal the mobilization of "our people and our country's resources toward the final eradication of apartheid and the building of a democratic, non-racial and non-sexist future."[5]

Initially, the international and domestic business communities were concerned that the RDP was an inflationary social-spending program intended to rectify the years of apartheid injustices. Instead, the Mandela government put into place austere measures aimed at promoting both foreign and domestic investment. After years of near zero growth, the economy grew at a rate of 6.4 percent in the fourth quarter of 1994, which brought 1994 growth to 2.3 percent.[6]

The government's economic policies, coupled with its so-far-successful management of the political transition to majority rule, have bolstered confidence in its ability to transform South Africa from a conflict-ridden apartheid society to a prosperous democratic success story. Many commentators believe that the liberalization of markets and strict fiscal discipline are quickly addressing the development priorities of South Africa. However, the social and ecological legacies of apartheid will continue to affect the ability of both state and society to meet the goals of the RDP.

Environmental Scarcity

This chapter analyzes environment-conflict linkages in South Africa as a whole. Moreover, we make specific reference to KwaZulu-Natal because it is one of the most populous and poverty stricken provinces in South Africa, and since the mid-1980s, it has also been one of the most violent.[7] It is a valuable case for understanding environment-conflict linkages for two reasons. First, the University of Natal has carefully conducted research on the causes of violence within the region and has developed a useful database on migration, growth of informal settlements, and violent deaths. Second, because much of the black population in the region is Zulu, explanations of violence cannot be reduced to ethnicity. Intra-ethnic divisions—caused in part by the effects of environmental scarcity—produced levels of violence in the region akin to civil war. We outline below the environmental situation in South Africa in general, with particular attention to KwaZulu-Natal.

Physical Geography

The South African ecosystem is characterized by low rainfall, water scarcity, and soils susceptible to erosion. Approximately 65 percent of the country receives less than 500 millimeters (mm) of annual precipitation, a threshold that is widely regarded by experts as the minimum required for rain-fed cropping.[8] About 60 percent of South African cropland is characterized by low organic matter content. After repeated cultivation, organic matter is rapidly lost and the soil is easily eroded.[9] Other factors affecting erosion include climate, slope, plant cover, and land-use management. Plant cover is especially critical for controlling soil erosion: in one study in the Mflozi catchment in northern KwaZulu-Natal, only 2 percent of the land receiving 900 to 1,000 mm of rain was eroded, compared with 13.5 percent of land receiving less than this amount. The reason for this curious differential was found to be the extensive plant cover within the former region.[10]

Low rainfall and fragile soils limit agriculture potential. Only 16 percent (about 16 million hectares) of the total amount of land used for crops and pasture is considered suitable for crops, while the rest is used for pasture. About 4 percent is high-potential agricultural land. Of the total area of cropland, 13 million hectares fall within commercial farming areas, while only 2.5 million are in small-scale farming areas in the former homelands.[11] This imbalance, combined with other natural resource limits—including weak soils and poor rains—has resulted in extensive environmental scarcities in the homelands.

Structural Scarcity Under Apartheid

The apartheid system institutionalized the uneven social distribution of environmental resources in South Africa, which caused serious structural scarcity for blacks.[12] Land ownership by black South Africans was tightly restricted in both rural and urban areas, curtailing economic advancement. Unequal access to land affected 15 million blacks living in the homelands or as tenants and laborers on "white" land.[13] In the 1980s, 95 percent of the black population earned less than 100 dollars per month, whereas 89 percent of the white population earned more. With an average disposable income of only 150 dollars a year—one-sixteenth the white average—homeland farmers in particular could not make the long-term investments necessary to protect their land.[14]

Table 4.1 uses differences in per capita availability of farmland to illustrate the structural land scarcities affecting blacks in South Africa.

Not only did blacks suffer from an imbalanced distribution of the quantity of land, but they also often received the most marginally productive land. Moreover, under the apartheid regime, structural scarcities of land were often

TABLE 4.1
Comparison of Population Densities Within Rural South Africa, 1991

| | Population Density (Hectares/Person) | | | | |
	South Africa	White Areas	Former Homelands	Natal	KwaZulu
Cropland & Pastureland	4.70	16.22	0.92	5.36	0.68
Cropland	0.75	2.54	0.16	1.10	0.08

Source: Adapted from Development Bank of South Africa, *South Africa's Nine Provinces: A Human Development Profile* (Halfway House, South Africa: Development Bank of South Africa, April 1994), 99.

reinforced by stark shortfalls in agricultural inputs, such as capital, fertilizer, veterinary services, and new agricultural technologies. Tables 4.2 and 4.3 compare statistics for crop yields and cattle performance in Natal and Kwa-Zulu.

Structural scarcities of land also existed *within* the former homelands. Rights to communal land were unevenly distributed among homeland populations: up to 80 percent of production came from 20 percent of the farmers who controlled most of the land, and in some areas three or four landholders owned 80 percent of the livestock grazing on communal land. Widespread landlessness existed even in Transkei, the homeland with the best land, where fewer than 50 percent of villagers were allocated a field, and 60 percent had no cattle.[15] In urban areas, black townships were built on sites not useful to the white community. They were often overcrowded, short of housing, and

TABLE 4.2
Comparison of Yields in Crop Agriculture, Natal and KwaZulu, 1983–84

Crop	Yield (Tons/Hectare)	
	Natal	KwaZulu
Cereals (maize)	2.088	0.826
Legumes (dry beans)	1.011	0.337
Roots (potatoes)	24.015	5.006
Sugarcane	53.814	28.795

Source: Norman Bromberger and Francis Antonie, "Black Small Farmers in the Homelands," in *State and Market in Post Apartheid South Africa,* ed. Merle Lipton and Charles Simkins (Johannesburg: Witwatersrand University Press, 1993), 421.

TABLE 4.3
Comparison of Statistics of Cattle Performance, Natal and KwaZulu, 1987

	Performance (Percentage)	
	Natal (Private Land Tenure)	KwaZulu (Communal Grazing)
Herd Mortality	3.9	7.4
Calving Rate	80.0	32.0
Slaughter and Export Rate	25.0	5.0

Source: Norman Bromberger and Francis Antonie, "Black Small Farmers in the Homelands," in *State and Market in Post Apartheid South Africa,* ed. Merle Lipton and Charles Simkins (Johannesburg: Witwatersrand University Press, 1993), 422.

located downwind from dirty industries. Infrastructure was inferior, with few services such as electricity and running water.[16] Overcrowding and poverty meant that new residents built their houses from nonconventional materials scavenged from local dumps and public buildings; they used mud, grass, and straw from nearby streams, fields, and hillsides, which tended to increase local erosion and flooding damage.

In sum, the black population, with little political or economic power in South Africa, was forced to subsist on a severely restricted and eroded land base. Because of the particular vulnerabilities of the South African ecosystem, this structural scarcity interacted with and exacerbated demand- and supply-induced scarcities.

Demand-induced Scarcity

The estimated population of South Africa in 1995 is 42.6 million, with an annual increase of 970,000. About 28 million people—over 66 percent of the population—live within towns and cities, while 15 million reside strictly within urban areas.[17] The black population is expected to grow at a 3 percent rate from its current 32 million to 37.2 million people by the year 2000, which will be 78.3 percent (up from 74.8 percent in 1991) of the anticipated total population of 47.5 million. Conversely, the white population will stay constant at approximately 5 million, and its proportion of the total population will drop from 14.1 to 11.4 percent.[18]

The growth of the black population results in more severe scarcity of land and exacerbates the differentials in land availability per capita shown in table 4.1. Under apartheid, the average population density of the former homelands was ten times the density of rural "white" South Africa. When labor requirements in commercial agriculture declined, apartheid ensured that black South Africans could not move to cities when they were expelled from rural white areas. Police forcibly moved blacks to the homelands; partly as a result of this forced migration, the population of the homelands grew from 4.5 million to 11 million between 1960 and 1980.[19] But the land area of the homelands did not increase.

In addition to this in-migration, the homelands experienced high natural population growth rates. The total fertility rate for blacks from 1985 to 1990 was estimated at 5.12 children per woman.[20] In 1990, Alan Durning observed, "Black couples . . . have larger families because apartheid denies them access to education, health care, family planning, and secure sources of livelihood— the things that make small families possible and advantageous."[21] Gender discrimination contributed to these high fertility rates. Priya Deshingkar, a researcher for the Land and Agriculture Policy Centre in Johannesburg, describes the responsibilities of women in informal settlements and rural regions:

> As opposed to men, the lives of a majority of women in rural and peri-urban areas of South Africa are linked intimately with their natural environment in the course of their daily activities. Women are responsible for providing food, water and fuel (survival tasks); preparing food and caring for children (household tasks) and income generating activities such as trading of forest products. At the same time they are poor and face many legal and cultural obstacles which deny them the rights to own and control natural resources.[22]

Research conducted by Cambridge economist Partha Dasgupta shows that women who lack paid employment have less decision-making authority in their families. Weak authority, combined with the usefulness of children for labor in subsistence conditions—for collecting fuelwood and water and for herding animals—leads to high fertility rates.[23] In South African rural areas, black women's responsibilities are largely unpaid, and high fertility rates are to be expected. High infant and child mortality rates also raise fertility rates, as families have no guarantee that their children will survive to adolescence. The infant-mortality rate among black children was estimated at 74 per 1,000 from 1985 to 1990.[24]

Population size, growth rate, and geographical distribution in KwaZulu-Natal are shown in tables 4.4 and 4.5. These tables demonstrate that all areas in KwaZulu-Natal are experiencing population growth, with the most dramatic increases in informal settlements. In 1992, the population of informal settlements made up 26 percent of the total KwaZulu-Natal population—and the percentage was steadily increasing.

Supply-induced Scarcity

The apartheid regime situated the homelands in fragile environments with thin topsoil not suitable for supporting the level of agricultural production

TABLE 4.4
Population Size and Growth Rate, KwaZulu-Natal

Year	Size (Thousands) and Growth Rate (Percentage)			
	Rural	Urban	Informal Settlements	Total
1985	4,281	2,592	1,143	8,019
1990	4,518 (1.1%)	2,936 (2.5%)	1,419 (4.4%)	8,874 (2.0%)
1995	4,747 (1.0%)	3,400 (3.0%)	1,733 (4.1%)	9,882 (2.2%)

Source: Doug Hindson and Jeff McCarthy, "Defining and Gauging the Problem," in *Here to Stay: Informal Settlements in KwaZulu-Natal,* ed. Doug Hindson and Jeff McCarthy (Dalbridge: Indicator Press, 1994), 2. Reprinted with Permission.

TABLE 4.5
Population Location, KwaZulu-Natal, 1992

	Population	
	Thousands	Percentage of Total
Metropolitan	2,290	24.7
Towns	350	3.8
Total Urban Formal Settlement	2,640	28.5
Informal Metro	1,550	16.7
Informal Towns	470	5.1
Transitional (Rural/Urban)	400	4.3
Total Urban Informal	2,420	26.1
Total Urban	5,060	54.6
Total Rural	4,210	45.4
Grand Total	9,270	100.0

Source: Doug Hindson and Jeff McCarthy, "Defining and Gauging the Problem," in *Here to Stay: Informal Settlements in KwaZulu-Natal,* ed. Doug Hindson and Jeff McCarthy (Dalbridge: Indicator Press, 1994), 3. Reprinted with Permission.

required by their populations.[25] The result has been severe erosion: "Dongas [erosion gullies] have become small valleys which split the hillsides; soil has given way to a crumbling grey shale, stone-built huts squat in a scene which is almost lunar in its desolation."[26] Per capita food production in the former homelands has fallen; these areas have become net importers of food, partly a result of land degradation and high population growth rates.[27] South Africa's overall rate of topsoil loss is 20 times higher than the world's average.[28] Experts estimate that South Africa has lost 25 percent of its topsoil since 1900 and that 55 percent of South Africa is threatened by desertification.[29] One study puts the daily cost to the national economy of lost production due to reduced soil fertility at about $250,000. Yet maintaining agricultural productivity is crucial, because South Africa's food needs are predicted to double by 2020.[30]

Deforestation is an important form of supply-induced environmental scarcity. By destabilizing soils and changing local hydrological cycles, it disrupts key ecosystem links.[31] Unfortunately, fuelwood remains the most accessible and inexpensive energy source for many rural blacks, which encourages deforestation. Inadequate energy services force about 40 percent of the South African population to depend on fuelwood for cooking and heating. Estimates place the annual volume of fuelwood consumed at 11 million metric tons.[32] In the past 50 years, 200 of KwaZulu's 250 forests have disappeared.[33] A comparison of forest consumption rates with noncommercial forest growth rates shows that all ten former homelands are in a fuelwood deficit, with supplies expected to be almost gone by the year 2020.[34] Wood for fuel is perceived as free, and collection costs are seen in terms of women's time, which is generally undervalued. Moreover, "frequent fires, the high opportunity cost of land, the long time periods for tree growth, and the use of both arable and uncultivated land for grazing all discourage tree planting. Trees can be seen as a threat to crops if they compete for space, water, and labor, and if they are seen to harbor pests."[35]

The scarcity and degradation of water resources is also a problem. South Africa is a water-scarce country: twelve to sixteen million people lack potable water supplies, and twenty-one million people—half the country's population—lack adequate sanitation.[36] Seventy percent of urban blacks do not have access to running water and are forced to rely on severely contaminated river systems for their daily water needs.[37] The water used by residents in informal settlements tends to have the highest concentrations of suspended solids and the highest level of fecal bacterial contamination.[38] The wider health of South African society is at risk as the probability rises in these settlements of epidemics of cholera, gastroenteritis, dysentery, parasitic infections, typhoid, and bilharzia. Pollution from industrial sources and seepage from coal, gold, and other mines threatens the quality of both river and ground water. The level of industrial pollution is particularly severe in the former homelands, where environmental controls were nonexistent.

Summary of Environmental Scarcity in the Former Homelands

Figure 4.1 summarizes the causes and effects of environmental scarcity in the former homelands. Apartheid created homelands in areas with few natural resources. Resources were also inequitably distributed within the homelands themselves, as elites controlled access to productive agriculture and grazing land. Populations sustained themselves through subsistence agriculture with added remittances from family members working in industry and mines outside the homelands. Homeland agricultural producers suffered from a chronic lack of investment capital, were denied access to markets, and lacked knowledge of appropriate land-use management techniques—a product of discriminatory education and agricultural extension services. Opportunities to move into urban areas were restricted by influx control; these restrictions combined with high fertility rates to increase population densities. Soils were fragile and susceptible to erosion. Inadequate supplies of electricity and fossil fuels forced people to use fuelwood, which became more scarce. Rural poverty escalated as agricultural and grazing productivity declined from land degradation, and daily water and energy needs became ever more difficult to satisfy.

This rising scarcity of vital environmental resources boosted incentives for powerful groups within the homelands to secure access to remaining

FIGURE 4.1
Environmental Scarcity Within South African Homelands

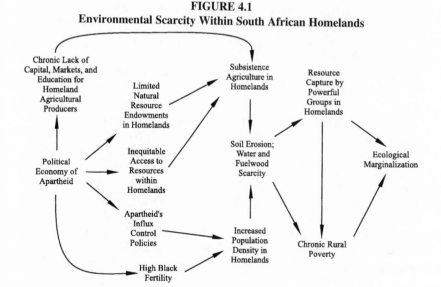

stocks—a process we call resource capture. Land rights were traded for political favors in the homelands' highly corrupt system of political rule. The combination of overpopulation, depleted resources, and unequal resource access resulted in ecological marginalization: To survive, people migrated first to marginal lands within the homelands—hillsides, river valleys, and easily eroded sweet veld. Then, as the apartheid system began to show signs of limited reform in the early 1980s, people started moving to ecologically and infrastructurally marginal urban areas.

Environmental Scarcity in Urban Areas

Even before the collapse of apartheid, an estimated ten million people lived in informal housing in urban areas—corrugated shacks, outbuildings, and garages.[39] Although the system of apartheid was initially successful in curtailing the movement of the black population to urban areas, influx control broke down in the early 1980s. In 1993, the *New York Times* described the implications of rapid growth in the city of Durban:

> Albert and Nellie Brown need no newspaper to tell them South Africa's old order is collapsing. They can step out on their porch in a white university neighborhood and look across the street. There, on an overgrown slope where they once expected to see a new hospital or terraces of comfortable homes like their own, is a burgeoning squatter village of mud huts, recycled plywood, plastic tents and sheet metal. The Browns can hear the whack of machetes chopping the neighborhood trees for firewood. They can smell the stink of pit toilets, and watch the daily procession of new black settlers walking up Cato Manor Road, some pushing grocery carts full of building scrap, to join an estimated 15,000 people encamped near the heart of South Africa's second largest city.[40]

South Africa's recent economic decline combined with its infrastructural shortcomings to produce a dire marginal existence for most blacks within urban areas. Urban growth has placed natural vegetation under constant attack, as the poor struggle to satisfy their basic needs. A growing population, concentrated in a limited area, coupled with the structural inequalities that deny them access to basic services, such as electricity, running water, refuse collection, and adequate sewage disposal facilities, results in environmental degradation. An estimated 25 percent of the population of informal settlements have no access to piped water, 46.5 percent have no access to electricity, and 48 percent lack adequate sanitation facilities.[41] Trees are cut down for fuel, grasses are used for feeding livestock and thatching, and residents often burn the veld to promote rapid regrowth, which depletes the soil of its humus content. These processes increase soil erosion, which is particularly high during intense rainstorms.[42] Devegetation leads to floods, mud slides, and sinkholes, because informal settlements are frequently in water catchment areas.[43]

Table 4.6 provides statistics on water and electricity services in informal settlements in KwaZulu-Natal and shows the degree to which the population must rely on the local environment to provide its daily needs.

Social Effects of Environmental Scarcity

We have shown that environmental scarcity has reached alarming levels in many of the former homelands and informal urban settlements in South Africa. Rural areas are unable to support their growing populations: soil is degraded, water resources are inadequate and decreasing in quality, and fuelwood is scarce. Urban areas cannot adequately provide for the needs of the people living and moving within their boundaries. Below we examine the four main social effects that arise from rural and urban environmental scarcity: decreased agricultural production, economic decline, population movement, and weakened institutions.[44]

TABLE 4.6
Basic Services in Informal Settlements, KwaZulu-Natal, 1994

Service	Population	
	Number	Percentage of Total
Water		
Only Springs and Streams	229,878	76.2
Taps in Homes	300	0.0
Standpipes	45,434	15.0
Reservoirs	4,800	1.6
None	21,205	7.1
Electricity		
Some Domestic Supply	108,816	36.2
No Supply	191,501	63.8

Source: Adapted from Doug Hindson and Jeff McCarthy, "Defining and Gauging the Problem," in *Here to Stay: Informal Settlements in KwaZulu-Natal,* ed. Doug Hindson and Jeff McCarthy (Dalbridge: Indicator Press, 1994), 20.

Falling Agricultural and Economic Productivity

Agricultural potential decreased in the homelands due to growing population densities, water scarcity, and soil erosion. In Bophuthatswana in the 1940s, farmers harvested 110 kilograms (kg) of maize and sorghum for each person. By the late 1950s, this decreased to 80 kg per person, and by the late 1970s, to 50 kg.[45] The rural black South African population is increasingly unable to sustain itself. David Cooper of the Land and Agriculture Policy Centre describes the situation:

> Family incomes in South African "homelands" are among the lowest in Africa; migrant remittances, state pensions and local employment account for 90 percent of village income. Agriculture, however, accounts for only 10 percent. Malnutrition-related diseases, including kwashiorkor and pellagra in children and tuberculosis in adults, are widespread. Not only are impoverished families unable to invest in tree-planting or soil conservation schemes, but they are forced to strip the land of its resources. Families burn dung as fuel, instead of using it as manure; they strip trees for firewood, leaving hillsides bare.[46]

As agricultural and forest resources are depleted, people switch to low-paying jobs in villages and towns. A study of a rural community in Bophuthatswana found that such wage labor was the major source of income for more than 90 percent of households; less than 5 percent could make a living from agriculture. Approximately 55 percent of the households studied had no agricultural land at all, and 37.5 percent had too little land to make a living.[47]

Finding wage labor is more and more difficult because South Africa has such a serious unemployment problem: formal jobs are available for only 50 percent of the country's population, whites and blacks included.[48] Poverty is therefore endemic and deep within the rural black community. In 1980, 81 percent of the rural population earned less than the minimum subsistence wage.[49] In urban areas the situation is little different:

> It is estimated . . . that some 40 percent of the metropolitan African population, outside the "homelands," earns incomes below the poverty datum line of R700 per month and that 25–40 percent of the potential economically active African population is formally unemployed. As a result, vast numbers of people are engaged in a desperate daily struggle to meet basic needs.[50]

Marginal rural and urban blacks are trapped between worsening environmental scarcities and inadequate investment in the physical and human capital that might eventually generate alternative employment opportunities. The result is chronic poverty. In 1993 in KwaZulu, 80 percent of all rural households and 40 percent of urban households were living below the poverty line. The average rural monthly household income was 43 percent below urban income. Moreover, the average rural worker supported 4 people, while the average urban worker supported 2.5 people. It was estimated that only 25 percent of the urban population in KwaZulu—and a dismal 16 percent of the rural population—had formal jobs.[51]

Migration

Migrations from rural areas to urban and peri-urban areas have increased sharply in recent years.[52] "Push" factors are difficult to distinguish from "pull" factors. The former clearly include environmental degradation, unequal access to land, and high population densities within the homelands. Three major pull factors are "the repeal of the pass laws in 1986, the rapid construction of backyard shacks in formal townships, especially in the Pretoria-Witwatersrand-Vereeniging area, and the increasing designation of land outside the 'homelands' as suitable for African residential development."[53] Although the number of blacks moving into cities is estimated to be 750,000 a year,[54] rural-urban migration rates are disputed, and determining the precise rate will require more research.

Researchers, however, have identified some basic trends. The Durban Functional Region (DFR), an administrative region that includes Durban and surrounding areas, provides an example of the way the process generally proceeds:

> [Rural migrants scout] to find their first urban base, often within a formal township. This transforms, however, into indirect migration within the DFR as the recently arrived rural migrants tend to move around within the DFR, from formal to informal settlements, and then from one informal settlement to another. Once a rural migrant family is established within an informal area, it becomes possible for some direct migration from rural source areas to take place.[55]

Although most migrants to urban regions are of rural origin, the percentage is falling. Families moving into informal settlements increasingly move from closely adjacent communities. Urban-urban migration is driven by the housing shortage (currently estimated at over a million units), migrant laborers bringing families to urban areas, and the unemployed attempting to avoid exploitive rents for backyard shacks in the townships.[56] Violence also plays a role in determining migration: people often leave their homes after violence erupts, but their places are quickly taken by migrants desperate for housing.[57]

We can make three generalizations regarding migration in South Africa. First, the majority of those moving into most urban settlements are still rural migrants. Second, the same processes of resource capture and ecological marginalization that occur in the homelands are occurring in urban informal settlements. The concentration of many people on a limited resource base, in the context of weak local government authority, leads to resource capture: "violence [becomes] entrenched with formation of competing local power structures whose leaders seek to gain and secure power through the control of basic residential resources such as land, home allocations, services, business rights etc."[58] And third, the combination of this resource capture and environmental problems forces greater urban-urban migration.

KwaZulu-Natal experiences particularly high levels of migration to urban areas. Catherine Cross and her colleagues at the University of Natal identify the sources for the DFR:

> The most important areas of origin for the DFR informal population are the rural districts of former Natal, which contribute some 46 percent of the informal population. At some 5 percent the peri-urban districts are relatively less significant sources of inflow, as is the Transkei at 8 percent. The contribution from other former homelands and countries outside South Africa represents a negligible 2 percent, but these may be under reported. The informal population is thus predominantly from KwaZulu-Natal or Transkei, and is mostly of rural origin, although there is a substantial urban origin component.[59]

Although the population of both rural and urban areas within KwaZulu-Natal is growing, the population growth rate of urban areas is about three times greater than that of rural areas. Moreover, the growth of informal settlements, which now represent more than a third of the total urban population and more than half of the total black urban population, exceeds growth within formal urban boundaries.[60] Migration from rural regions is largely responsible for these differentials. Nick Wilkins and Julian Hofmeyer note that "by the mid-1980s it was clear that rural poverty was undermining the system of oscillating migration, and that people were migrating permanently into urban areas. Migrants appear to follow several routes into urban areas, and once there may move several times from area to area."[61]

Declining Institutional Capacity

Civil violence is a reflection of troubled relations between state and society. Peaceful state-society relations rest on the ability of the state to respond to the needs of society—to provide, in other words, key components of the survival strategies of the society's members—and on the ability of the state to maintain its dominance over groups and institutions in society.[62] Civil society—groups separate from but engaged in dialogue and interaction with the state—presents the demands of its constituents.[63] Grievances against the state will remain low if groups within society believe the state is responsive to these demands. Opportunities for violence against the state will rise when the state's ability to organize, regulate, and enforce behavior is weakened in relation to potential challenger groups. Changes in state character and declining state resources increase the chances of success of violent collective action by challenger groups, especially when these groups mobilize resources sufficient to shift the social balance of power in their favor.[64]

Severe environmental scarcity causes groups to focus on narrow survival strategies, which reduces the interactions of civil society with the state. Society segments into groups, social interactions among groups decrease, and each group turns inwards to focus on its own concerns.[65] Civil society retreats, and, as a result, society is less able to articulate effectively its demands on the state. This segmentation also reduces the density of "social capital"—the trust, norms, and networks generated by vigorous, crosscutting exchange among groups.[66] Both of these changes provide greater opportunity for powerful groups to grab control of the state and use it for their own gain. The legitimacy of the state declines, as it is no longer representative of or responsive to society.

Opportunities for violent collective action can decrease, even under conditions of environmental scarcity, when the power of potential challenger groups is diffused by vigorous horizontal interaction within society and vertical interaction between civil society and the state. However, if poor socioeconomic conditions persist, grievances will remain. These grievances will probably be expressed through an increase in deviant activity, such as crime. Unless the grievances are addressed, the legitimacy of the government will decrease, society will once again become segmented, and opportunities for violent collective action will correspondingly increase.

These phenomena were all visible in South Africa during the transition period. When he received the 1993 Nobel Peace Prize with Mandela, President de Klerk stated that it was not international sanctions or armed struggle that forced apartheid to change, but instead the movement of millions of people into the cities that created social upheaval and strained community and state institutions.[67] The township of Khutsong in the province of Gauteng (formerly the Pretoria-Witwatersrand-Vereeniging administrative region) is one of many examples of urban migration initially straining and finally overwhelming the capacity of institutions:

> The official township of Khutsong was set up in 1958 to house labor for the mines near the "white's-only" town of Carletonville. Khutsong's population has grown so fast that today more people live in shacks than in formal houses. State surveys, although dated, suggest that there are more than 29,400 informal squatter dwellings in and about Khutsong and only about 17,757 formal houses. The township no longer even meets the needs of people residing within its official boundaries. For the growing population of squatters the authorities take almost no responsibility—apart from a few taps there are no other services.[68]

Strong community institutions are crucial for managing the social conflicts that inevitably arise from large numbers of migrants. Institutional strength is a function of an institution's financial resources, the adequacy and relevance to community needs of its expertise, and its flexibility in novel circumstances; these factors, in turn, are influenced by the depth of the community's social capital. Uncontrolled influxes of people and the degradation of resources that often ensues can, as we have noted, cause social segmentation as subgroups within the community withdraw into themselves to protect their own interests. Segmentation breaks down social networks, weakens community norms, and erodes trust. This loss of social capital, in turn, undermines the ability of institutions to function. In South Africa, segmentation often takes the form of divisions among ethnic groups, among family-based clans, and among the residents of townships, informal settlements, and work hostels.

Marginal urban communities of blacks are often trapped in a downward spiral. Because community institutions are debilitated by the processes just described, they are unable to provide infrastructure—including sewers, electricity, and running water—to keep residents from wrecking local environmental resources. As people become more dependent on these resources for basic services, and as the resources are thus further degraded, community segmentation increases. This segmentation again weakens essential community institutions, allows powerful "warlords" to capture critical resources, and sets the stage for outbreaks of violence among competing groups.

KwaZulu-Natal has seen huge influxes of people into its cities. Approximately half the population in the Durban-Pietermaritzburg region now lives in informal settlements, lacking infrastructure and basic services.[69] According to the Urban Foundation, the region has the largest concentration of informal settlements in the country.[70] These settlements are often run by warlords— local leaders who control their own paramilitary forces and owe "only nominal allegiance to any higher authority."[71] Warlords establish patron-client relations with settlement residents: the residents support the warlord in return for essential resources and services, including policing and dispute settlement. Paramilitary forces allow warlords to exercise strict control over the right to conduct business and over environmental resources, such as land and water. Resource control multiplies warlord power and wealth, permitting extraction of surpluses in the form of taxes, rents, and levies.[72]

Warlords, in fact, have limited ability to provide their communities with infrastructure or services. They have no real control over electricity, refuse removal, roads, and other services, since these services—to the extent that they are available—are provided by the local municipality.[73] They control only their paramilitary forces, the residents in their territories, and the local land and water (including taps into municipal pipelines) that residents depend on. Resource control therefore becomes a main source of legitimacy within the warlords' communities.

As resources are degraded within their territories, warlords often try to maintain power by pointing to resources in neighboring townships and informal settlements and mobilizing their communities to seize them. This mobilization can set in motion a cycle of appalling violence among African communities. "Squatters are mobilized to fight for access to resources in neighboring townships, and township youth organize military style units to defend their areas and counter-attack squatter areas."[74]

Figure 4.2 summarizes the variables and causal relations identified in this section. As described above, chronic poverty, ecological marginalization, and high fertility rates in the former homelands cause rural-urban migration. These migrations, along with high urban fertility rates, boost urban population densities. High urban densities, in turn, combine with the impoverishment produced by apartheid to force people to rely on the urban environment to provide for their daily needs. Where too many people rely on a limited resource base, there is urban environmental scarcity.

The huge movement of people to and within an urban area increases demands on local institutions. Rising environmental scarcity, meanwhile, causes ever more social segmentation. These two processes together produce a sharp weakening of the institutions needed to meet the needs of the local population. Warlords are able to seize control of key environmental resources, which further weakens local institutions. A cycle begins: institutions cannot provide for the population, which forces people to rely on, and subsequently degrade, the

FIGURE 4.2
Environmental Scarcity and Urbanization in South Africa

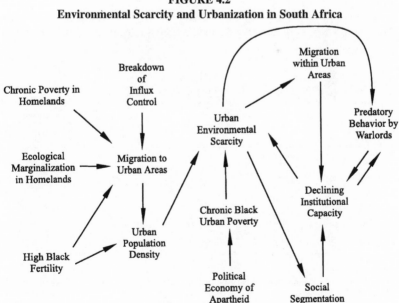

local environment; weak institutions provide warlords with increased opportunities for predatory behavior.

Violent Conflict

Between September 1984 and the end of 1989, an estimated 3,500 people died in political violence throughout South Africa. After Mandela's release in February 1990, violence became pervasive. From that date until December 1993, political violence killed an estimated 12,000 people—an annual rate more than four times that prior to 1990.[75] In 1992 alone, criminal and political violence together produced more than 20,000 deaths.[76]

In July 1990, the so-called Reef Township War began in the regions around Johannesburg. Clashes broke out between migrant workers residing in hostels and residents of townships and informal settlements.[77] In 1992, the annual incidence of violence escalated 133 percent in the Central Rand, the area immediately surrounding Johannesburg. The area south of Johannesburg saw a jump of 200 percent, whereas the region east of Johannesburg witnessed an increase of 84 percent.[78]

Table 4.7 contains totals for deaths and injuries for the former provinces of Transvaal (primarily the area around Johannesburg) and Natal. The table does not include deaths from criminal violence, but the distinction between political and criminal motivations is somewhat arbitrary in a politically charged atmosphere, such as that of the pre-1994 election period.[79]

Environmental scarcity is not the sole cause of this violence, yet analysts should not ignore how scarcity has undermined South Africa's social stability.

TABLE 4.7
Unrest-related Deaths and Injuries, Natal and Transvaal, 1989–93

Year	Deaths		Total Casualties	
	Natal	Transvaal	Deaths	Injuries
1989	(est.) 800	NA[*]	1,403	1,425
1990	1,685	924	2,609	4,309
1991	1,057	1,197	2,254	3,166
1992	1,430	1,822	3,252	4,815
1993	2,009	2,001	4,010	4,790

*Not available.

Source: Anthony Minnaar, *An Overview of Political Violence and Conflict Trends in South Africa with Specific Reference to the Period January–June 1994* (Pretoria: Center for Socio-Political Analysis, Human Sciences Research Council, July 1994), 1.

Below, we examine the effect of scarcity on grievances, group segmentation, and opportunities for violent collective action. Most theorists of civil conflict assume that these factors are causally independent. However, in this chapter we argue, first, that grievances powerfully influence the meaning of group membership and the formation of groups and, second, that grievances can shift these groups' perceptions of opportunities for violence. The potential for group formation increases as people identify with one another due to their shared perception of grievance, and the meaning of group membership is influenced by the degree and character of the grievance. In addition, more salient group identity influences the perception of opportunity for group action: it ensures that the costs of violent challenges to authority are distributed across many individuals, and it increases the probability that these challenges will succeed.

Escalating Grievances

Environmental scarcity reduced rural incomes and helped push many black South Africans into urban areas. The segmentation of urban black communities weakened local institutions, which often could not deliver basic services to their people and as a consequence lost legitimacy. The apartheid state depended upon its ties to co-opted local institutions, such as municipal and tribal councils, to maintain order within black communities. With the debilitation of these institutions, the apartheid state lost its tenuous link to black society and was forced to relinquish control over communities, which made it impossible for the state to address local grievances.

Research conducted on black South Africans' happiness and perception of personal well-being shows that, although levels of happiness have historically been low, grievances escalated during the late 1980s. "Being black in South Africa was a strong predictor of negative life satisfaction and [un]happiness, even when other background factors were controlled."[80] From 1983 to 1988, the percentage of blacks satisfied with life declined from 48 to 32, and the percentage stating they were happy declined from 53 to 38 (see table 4.8).[81]

Group Divisions

Group divisions, reinforced and in some instances created by the institution of apartheid, became the basis of politics in South Africa. Identification with one's ethnic group was necessary for survival and advancement within apartheid's ethnically divided political system. These divisions were reinforced by the territorial boundaries of the homelands. When people moved to the cities, therefore, they tended to carry their ethnic identities with them. A survey taken just prior to the 1994 election shows the salience of ethnic identity: when asked to name their nationality, 16 percent of blacks replied South Afri-

TABLE 4.8
Quality of Life Trends in South Africa

	Blacks	Coloreds	Indians	Whites
		Percentage Satisfied or Very Satisfied		
Life Satisfaction				
1983	48	81	89	89
1988	32	77	77	82
Happiness				
1983	53	80	88	93
1988	36	83	83	92

Source: Adapted from Valerie Moller, "Post-Election Euphoria," *Indicator SA* 12, no. 1 (summer 1994): 28.

can or black South African, while 63 percent gave the name of their tribe.[82] Much of the recent violence in South Africa has been between supporters of the ANC and those of the Inkatha movement. The Inkatha-based Freedom Party is primarily a Zulu organization, and the ANC's leadership is dominated by members of the Xhosa ethnic group. Thus ethnic divisions reinforce the political differences between the two groups.

Ethnic groups are not only divided among themselves; they are also divided internally. Environmental scarcity increases the salience of group boundaries, which causes the segmentation of communities. Competition within and among groups grows under conditions of economic hardship and influxes of migrants.[83] Powerful individuals manipulate group identities within their communities to capture resources, and they distribute resources according to group affiliation to maintain their support. Mary de Haas and Paulus Zulu describe this process in KwaZulu-Natal:

> As with any ethnic identity, the emotional appeal of Zuluness does not, of course, operate in a vacuum. There seems little doubt that Inkatha's success in appealing to the ethnic sentiment of many of its supporters is enhanced by its ability to disperse patronage, both through its administrative structures—jobs, housing, franchises for shops and bottle stores, etc.—and sanctioning and facilitating the operations of warlords who preside over what amount to be private fiefdoms.[84]

While international attention has often focused on the interethnic conflict between Zulu and Xhosa, the Zulu population itself is cleaved into factions. These cleavages have political overtones and often manifest themselves as conflicts between the ANC and Inkatha. Group divisions are constructed and manipulated by political leaders and warlords on each side. ANC members tend to support political and social change, while Inkatha members support more traditional tribal institutions. The ANC is strong in the townships, while Inkatha draws its strength from informal settlements, often through connections to warlords.

Opportunities for Violence

The strife in South Africa and its links to changing opportunities for violence can be better understood by examining the phases of conflict in the country. Before 1983, almost all black political violence aimed to dismantle apartheid; it was sporadic and of relatively low intensity. In 1983, the UDF was formed to oppose the new constitution. An organized wave of protests against both the white regime and black local authorities, seen as puppets, caused President Botha to declare a state of emergency in June 1986. From 1983 to 1990, the violence against symbols of apartheid steadily increased in intensity. Although instances of violence within the black community rose, they remained relatively isolated, confined mostly to outbreaks at migrant workers' hostels and to protests against puppet local governments.

Before 1983, the apartheid state was strong enough to control violent protest. With reform in 1983, however, power relations began to change; the new constitution ceded some power to nonwhite groups. The small political space provided by reform was astutely exploited by opposition groups, such as the UDF, and their power relative to the state increased rapidly. Boycotts of schools, white businesses, and township rents further weakened the state at the local level. The regime's inability to control protest in subsequent years clearly showed that the balance of power had shifted in favor of the opposition.

After Mandela's release in February 1990, the nature of protest and violence changed, since it became clear that apartheid was about to collapse. The climate of reform made it easier to express grievances publicly. Both the ANC and the Inkatha Freedom Party, led by Mangosuthu Buthelezi, were transformed into political parties. The townships went to war with each other as the ANC and Inkatha struggled for political dominance.

In just one month, between August and September 1990, the death count around Johannesburg stood at more than 700, dwarfing the final death toll after four months of the Soweto uprisings of 1976. In the first three months of 1991, more than 400 people died in political violence, 260 of them after the long-awaited and much-applauded Mandela-Buthelezi peace summit. Watching the death count on television and reading about the carnage in newspapers gave the impression that nearly every major South African city, large town, and even outback farming districts was experiencing turmoil more fierce than the 1984–6 upheavals. More than 7,000 lives were lost in the 14 months that followed the unbanning of the ANC, and other liberation movements, from February 1990 to April 1991.[85]

The events of 1990 radically changed the opportunities for political violence in South Africa. As the ANC and Inkatha became fully fledged political organizations battling for control of the institutions of power, they mobilized huge numbers of people and substantial financial resources for their political ends. At the same time, the capacity of the state to do anything about the violence between the ANC and Inkatha was debilitated by the reform process. The apartheid state seemed to retreat into the white areas of the country, leaving the ANC and Inkatha to fight it out between themselves.

The South African state was unable to control violence at the local level because communities were segmented and institutions were weak. The withdrawal of the state from these communities made it possible for the ANC and Inkatha to mobilize large numbers of alienated and underemployed young men for their political battle. The battle took place within a deeply aggrieved society, brutalized for generations, and well rehearsed in fighting the system of apartheid. It resulted in the worst outbreak of violence in the country's history.

Figure 4.3 diagrams the surge of violence after 1990 in South Africa. The reform process raised expectations for better socioeconomic conditions, while declining capacity limited the ability of institutions to meet these expectations. Unmet expectations, further frustrated by the poverty endemic to the black South African community, increased grievances within black society and promoted group cleavages and competition for resources. Opportunities for collective action changed with the transformation of South African politics. Predatory warlords and opportunistic members of the ANC and Inkatha took advantage of a weakened state, debilitated local institutions, and an aggrieved population to mobilize group identities and instigate group rivalries. These factors dramatically increased the incidence of violence.

KwaZulu-Natal Conflict

The conflict in KwaZulu-Natal began much earlier than in the rest of South Africa. Before 1985, it took the form of opposition to the state, particularly in UDF-dominated townships resisting incorporation into Inkatha-dominated KwaZulu. The 1985 murder of civil rights lawyer Victoria Mxenge sparked intensified fighting between the UDF and Inkatha. In battles between these groups from 1985 to 1990, the UDF gained control of most townships. Since the informal settlements were not under the clear rule of either faction, violence shifted into these areas, with the UDF and Inkatha vying for political dominance.

Political leaders and warlords on both sides manipulated the conflicts among communities over access to resources, such as land, housing, water, and services.[86] The large numbers of people moving into and within the KwaZulu-Natal region made the situation worse: migrants contributed to turmoil

FIGURE 4.3
Outbreak of Violence in South Africa

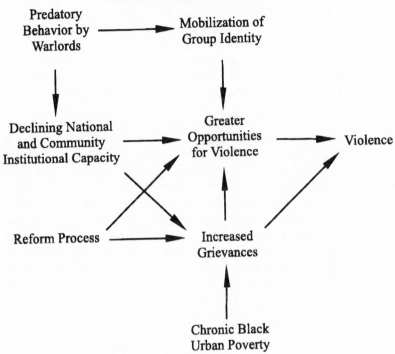

by increasing demands on resources and straining relations among groups. Disputes over scarce resources within informal settlements were transformed into political battles between the UDF—later the ANC—and Inkatha.[87]

Inkatha came to dominate the informal settlements by striking political deals with warlords and manipulating the conservative group identities of many residents who had only recently arrived from rural areas.[88] Warlords, in turn, used the charged political climate to gain protection and favors from Inkatha. The ANC promoted a revolt against tradition among Zulu youth, who expressed their opposition to traditional tribal structures through participation in ANC recruitment drives.[89] Divisions between the ANC and Inkatha polarized social relations within townships and informal settlements, mobilizing and politicizing their residents.[90] The region seemed locked into a spiral of violence, as conflict created migrants that, in turn, strained social relations in receiving communities:

The number of refugees and displacees from violence over the years runs into thousands. Conflict has arisen when these people either move into new communities or try to return to their homes. This, along with migration of people for economic reasons, puts extra pressure on scarce resources creating the potential for violent conflict.[91]

Table 4.9 shows how political violence soared during this period in the DFR. Although violence increased everywhere, the informal settlements became the main zones of conflict. The table also shows that in Durban—as elsewhere in the country—Mandela's release in 1990 substantially boosted violence.

After 1990, the use of lethal weapons rose and attacks targeted specific persons, not property or police.[92] Deaths in KwaZulu-Natal doubled again in 1992–93. Between 1992 and the 1994 election, more than one hundred violent events occurred per month, making the conflict in KwaZulu-Natal, and in the DFR in particular, the most sustained in the country.[93]

After the election, violence subsided in both KwaZulu-Natal and the region around Johannesburg. Although conflict levels have remained relatively low around Johannesburg, they have risen in Kwazulu-Natal. Buthelezi has called on his supporters to rise up and resist the control of the central government. In response, Mandela has threatened to cut the flow of federal funds to Kwa-Zulu-Natal. The lives of people in the province continue to be disrupted by violence that shows little sign of ending.

Conclusions

It is impossible to prove that the upsurge of violence in the early 1990s would not have occurred in the absence of severe environmental scarcity. The data available are simply not adequate for such proof. Moreover, environmental scarcity is always enmeshed in a web of social, political, and economic factors, and its contribution to violence is exceedingly difficult to disentangle from contributions by these other factors. Yet we show in the South African case that scarcity pushed up grievances and changed opportunities for violent collective action, thus contributing to social instability.

We argue that analysts must understand the relationship between state and society if they are to understand the complex links between environmental scarcity and violent conflict. During the 1980s and early 1990s, South African society's demands on the state increased as thousands of people migrated to urban areas, while the ability of both national and local institutions to meet these demands decreased. With the decline of local governments, the apartheid regime lost its already tenuous links to society. Society segmented, and powerful groups seized control of resources. These groups married their local conflicts over resource access to the struggle for political control between the ANC and Inkatha.

TABLE 4.9

Total Deaths Resulting From Political Violence in the Durban Functional Region, 1986-1992

Area	Deaths						
	1986	1987	1988	1989	1990	1991	1992
Formal	100	88	186	227	289	151	246
Proportion of Total	70%	63%	50%	44%	36%	34%	30%
Informal	43	51	188	288	515	290	566
Proportion of Total	30%	37%	50%	56%	64%	66%	70%
Grand Total	143	139	374	515	804	441	812

Source: Doug Hindson, Mark Byerley, and Mike Morris, "From Violence to Reconstruction: The Making, Disintegration and Remaking of an Apartheid City," *Antipode* 26, no. 4 (October 1994): 339. Reprinted by permission.

The election of Mandela has changed the relationship between state and society. State legitimacy has jumped upward. The RDP recognizes the needs of society, and interactions between state and society are now more constructive and vigorous. The government has established forums around the country to discuss local implementation of the RDP—forums that boost civic engagement and generate social capital. Levels of grievance have fallen: the proportion of black South Africans expressing satisfaction with their lives rose from 32 percent in 1988 to 80 percent in 1994, while the proportion expressing happiness went from 38 percent in 1988 to 86 percent in 1994.[94] A sharp rise in expectations of change has accompanied this decline in grievances. Table 4.10 identifies blacks' expectations of their new government. When asked what their reaction would be if their expectations were not met, 20 percent cited violent action, while only 5 percent cited peaceful mass protest.[95]

The election of Mandela may have boosted expectations for change, but for most blacks objective living conditions remain dismal. Blacks are not happier because their living conditions have changed; rather, they are happier because they think these conditions are going to change. If change is not quickly forthcoming, therefore, the regime will lose legitimacy, and linkages between state

TABLE 4.10
What Blacks Expect from Their New Government

Item	Percentage Who Expect Item
Enforced Minimum Wages	58
Subsidies to Lower Transport and Food Prices	56
Ready-built Houses Provided by Government	58
Government to Provide Work to All Unemployed	71
Free Schooling for All Children	70
White Schools to Accept All Black Applicants	71
White Farmers to Give Up Part of Their Land to Black Farmworkers	54
Heavier Taxation on Whites to Provide Welfare for the Poor	50
White Companies to Appoint More Blacks	41
Whites in Civil Service to Make Way for Blacks	46

Source: Adapted from *Indicator SA* 12, no. 1 (summer 1994): 73.

and society will once again weaken. Unfortunately, already severe environmental scarcity makes the process of positive change much harder. Social demands on local institutions continue to expand, and the potential for violence between the ANC and Inkatha remains high.

Violence between these groups continues to be serious in areas where political control is contested, especially in KwaZulu-Natal. The *Economist* recently reported rising conflict in that province.

Since the general election 13 months ago, political violence across the country has subsided. At first it fell back also in KwaZulu-Natal. But at the start of this year political murders there began to multiply again, against the national trend. In April, Gauteng, the province around Johannesburg, had 11; KwaZulu-Natal had 83.[96]

Local elections, scheduled for May 1996, may produce widespread violence as Inkatha and the ANC fight to dominate local governments. Crime rates remain at alarming levels, indicating that underlying grievances and social alienation in the black community are still high. Many analysts predicted a decrease in crime after the 1994 election.[97] However, overall levels of crime—in both KwaZulu-Natal and the region surrounding Johannesburg—appear to have increased, although the precise degree awaits complete statistical analysis.[98]

In conclusion, it is still too early to establish whether South Africa will make the transition to a stable and prosperous democracy. If a successful transition is to occur, national and local institutions must understand and break the links between environmental scarcity and conflict: they must redress the chronic and brutal structural scarcities impoverishing the black community; they must promote rapid, but sustainable, economic growth to absorb huge numbers of unemployed blacks in a still growing population; and they must preserve political channels for the peaceful expression of grievances. The state needs to provide agricultural extension services to black farmers, to target informal settlements for new infrastructure, and to increase opportunities for civic engagement. Women must be provided with investment capital, employment opportunities, and family-planning services to increase their authority within families and communities. Gender equality and increased female participation in society not only reduce fertility rates but also enhance economic growth.

South Africa's transition to majority rule was a miracle few anticipated. Nelson Mandela's victory gave many hope that the ills of apartheid and the violence of recent years would give way to peace and prosperity. Nothing can detract from the accomplishments so far. But without careful attention to the environmental factors contributing to violence, South Africa may once again be locked into a deadly spiral of conflict.

Notes

This essay was first published as Valerie Percival and Thomas Homer-Dixon, "Environmental Scarcity and Violent Conflict: The Case of South Africa," *Journal of Peace Research* 35, no. 3 (May 1998). Reprinted with permission of Sage Publications Ltd. For their valuable help, the authors thank Chris Albertyn, Marc Van Ameringen, Peter Ewang, Saliem Fakir, George Grant, Craig Johnson, Tim Hart, Doug Hindson, Antoinette Louw, Jennifer Mander, Karen MacGregor, Anthony Minaar, Mike Morris, Jim Mullin, Johan Olivier, Garth Stead, and Daniel Weiner.

1. Especially in the townships, many people earn their livelihood by buying and selling outside the formal economy of South Africa.

2. In this study, "informal settlement" denotes a legal or an illegal settlement with little infrastructure. Housing is constructed from unconventional building materials. Normally, illegal settlements are described as squatter communities, yet this distinction will not be made here. Derik Gelderblom and Pieter Kok, *Urbanization: South Africa's Challenge* (Pretoria: Human Sciences Research Council, 1994), 255.

3. Quoted in Rich Mkhondo, *Reporting South Africa* (London: Heinemann, 1993), 19.

4. Sebastian Mallaby, *After Apartheid: The Future of South Africa* (New York: Times Books, 1992), 43.

5. African National Congress, *The Reconstruction and Development Programme: A Policy Framework* (Johannesburg: Umanyano Publications, 1994), 1.

6. Bill Keller, "Mandela's Rising Star in Corporate Circles," *New York Times*, 22 April 1995, 17, 31.

7. Under the new constitution, the formerly white-dominated province of Natal has been integrated with the neighboring Zulu-dominated homeland of KwaZulu to form the province of KwaZulu-Natal.

8. Henk Coetzee and David Cooper, "Wasting Water," in *Going Green: People, Politics, and the Environment in South Africa*, ed. Jacklyn Cock and Eddie Koch (Cape Town: Oxford University Press, 1991), 130.

9. Craig MacKenzie, *Degradation of Arable Land Resources: Policy Options and Considerations Within the Context of Rural Restructuring in South Africa*, Agriculture Policy Centre Working Paper 8 (Johannesburg: Land and Agricultural Policy Center, December 1994), 2.

10. Bruce Liggitt, *An Investigation into Soil Erosion in the Mflozi Catchment: Final Report to the KwaZulu Bureau of Natural Resources*, Institute of Natural Resources, University of Natal, Investigational Report I/R 28 (Pieter-Maritzburg: Institute of Natural Resources, University of Natal, February 1988), 2.

11. MacKenzie, *Degradation of Arable Land*, 1.

12. According to its Gini coefficient, South Africa was the most inequitable nation in the world. In 1976, the Gini coefficient based on household income was estimated at 0.68, and in 1991 it was 0.67. The coefficient for the United States is 0.34, and that for Canada, 0.29. Mike McGrath and Andrew Whiteford, "Disparate Circumstances," *Indicator SA* 11, no. 3 (winter 1994): 49.

13. David Cooper, "From Soil Erosion to Sustainability," in *Going Green: People, Politics, and the Environment in South Africa*, ed. Jacklyn Cock and Eddie Koch (Cape Town: Oxford University Press, 1991), 176.

14. Alan Durning, *Apartheid's Environmental Toll*, World Watch Paper 95 (Washington, D.C.: World Watch Institute, 1990), 14.

15. Cooper, "From Soil Erosion to Sustainability," 179.

16. Lesley Lawson, "The Ghetto and the Greenbelt," in *Going Green: People, Politics, and the Environment in South Africa*, ed. Jacklyn Cock and Eddie Koch (Cape Town: Oxford University Press, 1991), 61.

17. David Barnard, "Housing: The Reconstruction Challenge," *Prodder Newsletter: Program for Development Research* 6, no. 4 (November 1994): 1.

18. Mkhondo, *Reporting South Africa*, ix. Mkhondo gets these figures from the South African Development Bank.

19. Francis Wilson, "A Land Out of Balance," in *Restoring the Land*, ed. Mamphela Ramphele (London: Panos Institute, 1991), 32.

20. Charles Simkins, "Population Pressures," in *Restoring the Land*, ed. Mamphela Ramphele (London: Panos Institute, 1991), 22.

21. Durning, *Apartheid's Environmental Toll*, 13.

22. Priya Deshingkar, *Integrating Gender Concerns into Natural Resource Management Policies in South Africa* (Johannesburg: Land and Agriculture Policy Centre, April 1994), 1.

23. Partha Dasgupta, "Population, Poverty and the Local Environment," *Scientific American* 272, no. 2 (February 1995): 40–42.

24. Simkins, "Population Pressures," 23. The white infant mortality rate for the period 1985–1990 is 9.0 per thousand (see "Republic of South Africa," *South Africa Statistics 1992* [Pretoria: Central Statistical Service, 1992], 3.8).

25. Land use management practices, not just natural vulnerabilities, must be analyzed when soil erosion is discussed: "Factors such as climate, soil erodibility and topography determine the potential erosion hazard in an area. Nevertheless, the difference in erosion caused by differing management of the same soil is very much greater than the difference in erosion from different soils under the same form of management. Thus cropping and management practices provide the key to controlling soil loss." Liggitt, *An Investigation into Soil Erosion*, 27.

26. Wilson, "A Land Out of Balance," 34.

27. Durning, *Apartheid's Environmental Toll*, 12–13.

28. John Collings, "The Vanishing Land," *Leadership* (1993): 24.

29. Dan Archer, *Twenty-Twenty, A Working Report*, Working Paper 111 (Pietermaritzburg: University of Natal, Institute of Natural Resources, August 1994), 5.

30. Ibid.

31. Mark Gandar, "The Imbalance of Power," in *Going Green: People, Politics, and the Environment in South Africa*, ed. Jacklyn Cock and Eddie Koch (Cape Town: Oxford University Press, 1991), 98.

32. David Cooper and Saliem Fakir, *Commercial Farming and Wood Resources in South Africa: Potential Sources for Poor Communities*, Land and Agriculture Policy Centre Working Paper 11 (Johannesburg, South Africa: Land and Agriculture Policy Centre, 1994), 1.

33. Francis Wilson and Mamphela Ramphele, *Uprooting Poverty: The South African Challenge* (New York: W. W. Norton and Co., 1989), 44.

34. Gandar, "Imbalance of Power," 98–99.

35. Morag Peden, *Tree Utilization in KwaZulu and the Future Provision of Tree Products*, Working Paper 88 (Pietermaritzburg: University of Natal, Institute of Natural Resources, March 1993), 7.

36. David Brooks, *Field Study Report: South Africa, Mozambique and East Africa* (Ottawa: International Development Research Centre, Environment and Natural Resources Division, 31 May 1995), 17.

37. David Dewar, "Cities Under Stress," in *Restoring the Land*, ed. Mamphela Ramphele (London: Panos Institute, 1991), 92.

38. Dean Simpson, "The Drowning Pool," in *Rotating the Cube: Environmental Strategies for the 1990s*, Indicator South Africa Issue Focus (University of Natal, Durban: Centre for Social and Development Studies, 1993), 28.

39. Barnard, "Housing," 1.

40. Bill Keller, "Squatters Testing Limits as Apartheid Crumbles," *New York Times*, 14 November 1993, p. A3.

41. Barnard, "Housing," 1.

42. H. R. Beckedahl and D. G. Slade, "Minimise Soil Loss in Urban Areas," *Muniviro* 9, no. 3: 12.

43. Lawson, "The Ghetto and the Green Belt," 54.

44. Thomas Homer-Dixon, "On the Threshold: Environmental Changes as Causes of Acute Conflict," *International Security* 16, no. 2 (fall 1991): 91.

45. Durning, *Apartheid's Environmental Toll*, 13.

46. Cooper, "From Soil Erosion to Sustainability," 179. Kwashiorkor results from a lack of protein in the diet and causes skin problems and muscle wasting. Pellagra is a riboflavin deficiency that results in joint deformities and gastrointestinal ailments and affects the nervous system.

47. N. Boersema, "Making the Right Move: Migration Decision Making in a Rural Community," in *Making a Move: Perspectives on Black Migration Decision Making and Its Context*, ed. H. P. Steyn and N. Boersema (Pretoria: Human Sciences Research Council, 1988), 113–14.

48. Barnard, "Housing," 2.

49. H. P. Steyn and N. Boersema, "Introduction," in *Making a Move: Perspectives on Black Migration Decision Making and Its Context*, ed. H. P. Steyn and N. Boersema (Pretoria: Human Sciences Research Council, 1988), 3.

50. Dewar, "Cities Under Stress," 91–92.

51. South African Institute of Race Relations, *Race Relations Survey, 1993–94* (Johannesburg: South African Institute of Race Relations, 1994), 493.

52. In addition, South Africa has an estimated seven to eight million homeless people drifting from countryside to cities and also among cities. Barnard, "Housing," 1.

53. Simkins, "Population Pressures," 23–24. See also H. P. Steyn and N. Boersema, "Conclusion," in *Making a Move: Perspectives on Black Migration Decision Making and Its Context*, ed. H. P. Steyn and N. Boersema (Pretoria: Human Sciences Research Council, 1988). In this publication, written before the repeal of the pass laws, Steyn and Boersema state: "The rural-urban migration of blacks in South Africa centers around the inability of the rural areas to provide for the material needs of the local people. Structural determinants such as land shortage and the inaccessibility of available land, overpopulation, and the general underdevelopment of rural areas on the

one hand, and the attractions of cities and city life such as job opportunities, general infrastructure and facilities on the other hand are relevant in this regard" (134).

54. This estimate was produced by the Urban Foundation. Lawson, "The Ghetto and the Green Belt," 47.

55. Catherine Cross, Simon Bekker, and Craig Clark, "People on the Move: Migration Streams in the DFR," *Indicator SA* 9, no. 3 (winter 1992): 42.

56. Inga Moltzin, "Do-It-Yourself Urban Living," *New Ground*, no. 3 (March 1991): 15–16.

57. Cross, Bekker, and Clark, "People on the Move," 43.

58. Doug Hindson and Mike Morris, "Violence in Natal/KwaZulu: Dynamics, Causes, Trends," unpublished paper, March 1994, 1.

59. Catherine Cross, Simon Bekker, and Craig Clark, "Migration into DFR Informal Settlements: An Overview of Trends," in *Here To Stay: Informal Settlements in KwaZulu-Natal*, ed. Doug Hindson and Jeff McCarthy (Dalbridge, South Africa: University of Natal, Indicator Press, 1994), 88–89.

60. Doug Hindson and Jeff McCarthy, "Defining and Gauging the Problem," in *Here to Stay: Informal Settlements in KwaZulu-Natal*, ed. Doug Hindson and Jeff McCarthy (Dalbridge, South Africa: University of Natal, Indicator Press, 1994), 2.

61. Nick Wilkins and Julian Hofmeyer, "Socio-Economic Aspects of Informal Settlements," in *Here to Stay: Informal Settlements in KwaZulu-Natal*, ed. Doug Hindson and Jeff McCarthy (Dalbridge, South Africa: University of Natal, Indicator Press, 1994), 109. Oscillating migration is the movement of people, predominantly for employment purposes, back and forth between urban and rural areas.

62. Joel Migdal, "The State in Society," in *State Power and Social Forces*, ed. Joel Migdal, Atul Kohli, and Vivienne Shue (Cambridge: Cambridge University Press, 1994), 27.

63. Both Robert Putnam and Naomi Chazan emphasize the importance of interactions between civil society and the state for effective state policy. See Robert Putnam, *Making Democracy Work: Civil Traditions in Modern Italy* (Princeton, N.J.: Princeton University Press, 1993); Naomi Chazan, "Engaging the State: Associational Life in Sub-Saharan Africa," in *State Power and Social Forces*, ed. Joel Migdal, Atul Kohli, and Vivienne Shue (Cambridge: Cambridge University Press, 1994), 255–92.

64. Ted Gurr, *Minorities at Risk: A Global View of Ethnopolitical Conflicts* (Washington, D.C.: U.S. Institute of Peace, 1993), 130.

65. Chazan, "Engaging the State," 269. Chazan argues that under conditions of economic strain, both state and society become more insular.

66. Putnam, *Making Democracy Work*, 167.

67. John Darnton, "Note of Unity Pervades Peace Prize Ceremony," *New York Times*, 11 December 1993, 7.

68. Moltzin, "Do-It-Yourself Urban Living," 14.

69. Antoinette Louw, "Conflicting Views," *Indicator SA* 11, no. 1 (summer 1992): 17–18.

70. Philip Harrison, "The Policies and Politics of Informal Settlement in South Africa: A Historical Perspective," *Africa Insight* 22, no. 1 (1992): 14.

71. Anthony Minnaar, "Undisputed Kings: Warlordism in Natal," in *Patterns of Violence: Case Studies of Conflict in Natal*, ed. Anthony Minnaar (Pretoria: Human Sciences Research Council, 1992), 63.

72. Hindson and Morris, "Violence in Natal/KwaZulu," 6–7.

73. Ibid., 8.

74. Doug Hindson, Mark Byerley, and Mike Morris, "From Violence to Reconstruction: The Making, Disintegration and Remaking of an Apartheid City," *Antipode* 26, no. 4 (October 1994): 341.

75. Anthony Minnaar, *An Overview of Political Violence and Conflict Trends in South Africa with Specific Reference to the Period January-June 1994* (Pretoria: Centre for Socio-Political Analysis, Human Sciences Research Council, July 1994), 1.

76. South African Institute of Race Relations, *Race Relations Survey, 1993–94*, 296.

77. Minnaar, *An Overview of Political Violence and Conflict Trends*, 17.

78. The percentage increases are based on the following numbers:

Central Rand—203 incidents to 473

East Rand—145 incidents to 266

South of Johannesburg—53 incidents to 160

From Matha Ki and Anthony Minnaar, "Figuring Out the Problem: Overview of PWV Conflict from 1990–1993," *Indicator SA* 11, no. 2 (autumn 1994): 26.

79. Antoinette Louw, "Post-Election Conflict in KwaZulu-Natal," *Indicator SA* 11, no. 4 (Conflict Supplement, spring 1994): 16.

80. Valerie Moller, "Post-Election Euphoria," *Indicator SA* 12, no. 1 (summer 1994): 27.

81. Ibid., 28.

82. John Battersby, "Blacks Prepare to Cast Their Ballots," *Christian Science Monitor*, 28 February 1994, 11.

83. Susan Olzak and Johan Olivier, "The Dynamics of Ethnic Collective Action in South Africa and the United States: A Comparative Study," unpublished paper, June 1994, 2–7.

84. Mary de Haas and Paulus Zulu, "Ethnic Mobilization: KwaZulu's Politics of Secession," *Indicator SA* 10, no. 3 (winter 1993): 49.

85. Mkhondo, *Reporting South Africa*, 48.

86. Mike Morris and Doug Hindson, "The Disintegration of Apartheid: From Violence to Reconstruction," in *South African Review*, ed. Glen Moss and Ingrid Obery (Braamfontein, South Africa: Raven Press, 1992), 158.

87. Mike Morris and Doug Hindson, "Power Relations in Informal Settlements," in *Here to Stay: Informal Settlements in KwaZulu-Natal*, ed. Doug Hindson and Jeff McCarthy (Dalbridge, South Africa: University of Natal, Indicator Press, 1994), 160.

88. Hindson, Byerley, and Morris, "From Violence to Reconstruction," 340.

89. Louw, "Conflicting Views," 21.

90. Antoinette Louw, "Political Conflict 1989–92," *Indicator SA* 9, no. 3 (winter 1992): 57.

91. Louw, "Conflicting Views," 21.

92. Antoinette Louw, "Wars of Weapons, Wars of Words," *Indicator SA* 11, no. 1 (autumn 1994): 65–70.

93. Antoinette Louw, "Conflict of Interest," *Indicator SA* 11, no. 2 (autumn 1994): 17.

94. Moller, "Post-Election Euphoria," 28.

95. *Indicator SA* 12, no. 1 (summer 1994): 73.

96. "A Zulu Irritant," *The Economist* 335, no. 7916 (27 May 1995): 39.

97. Mark Shaw, an analyst with the Centre for Policy Studies, wrote: "The number of murders increased dramatically from 1980 to 1990 after which levels surged. Some of these statistics reflect political violence, but the line between political and criminal violence is fine. This implies that the murder rate should decline from 1994 when political violence decreased." Mark Shaw, "Exploring a Decade of Crime," *Crime and Conflict*, no. 1 (autumn 1995): 13.

98. See Lorraine Glanz, "Patterns of Crime," *Crime and Conflict*, no. 1 (autumn 1995): 9–10. Glanz compares crime levels from 1988 to 1993 and to the first ten months of 1994. The following table is adapted from this article and is based on crime statistics compiled by the commissioner of the South African Police. Rates are calculated per hundred thousand of the population of South Africa, including the former self-governing territories. The "big six" crimes are rape, murder, aggravated assault, aggravated robbery, burglary (business and residential), and theft of motor vehicles.

TABLE 4.11
Crime Levels in South Africa, 1988–1994

Type of Offense	1988		1992		1993	
	No.	Rate	No.	Rate	No.	Rate
Big Six	422,116	1,440	557,426	1,764	587,030	1,821
Total	1,423,763	4,857	1,781,861	5,639	1,852,223	5,747

Type of Offense	Jan.–Oct. 1994		Percentage Change in Rate	
	No.	Rate	1988–93	1992–93
Big Six	545,158	2,522	+26.5	+3.2
Total	NA	NA	+18.3	+3.2

5

The Case of Pakistan

Peter Gizewski and Thomas Homer-Dixon

Overview

Rapid population growth and degradation of a nation's environmental resources may impair its economy, disrupt its social relations, and destabilize its political system. These stresses can cause civil or even international strife.[1] Today, such conflicts appear likely in certain parts of the developing world where growing populations with rising expectations struggle to sustain themselves on a dwindling resource base.

Some commentators view the Islamic Republic of Pakistan as increasingly vulnerable to environmentally induced conflict. They argue that with a population growth rate that ranks among the highest in the world, a declining resource base, and growing evidence of societal strife, environmental and demographic stresses are already destabilizing Pakistan.[2]

However, there has been no adequate investigation of whether and how population growth and scarcities of renewable resources, such as cropland, forests, and fresh water (which we refer to here as "environmental scarcities"[3]), contribute to the intensity and extent of violence within Pakistan. In general, commentators assert rather than demonstrate causation; they ignore other variables—some long associated with the onset or perpetuation of conflict in the country—and they do not specify the precise causal processes by which scarcity produces violence.[4]

Identifying these linkages is a daunting task in part because of severe data limitations. Nevertheless, a systematic investigation of the nature and sources of environmental scarcity and of its societal effects in Pakistan yields important insights.

This chapter first examines the character of the Pakistani state, its political and economic development, and the tensions that have historically marked Pakistani society. It then turns to the issue of environmental scarcity, examining its nature, its social impacts, and the degree to which linkages between scarcity and conflict exist in Pakistan.

We conclude that environmental scarcity rarely if ever acts as the sole cause of conflict. Other variables—most notably the character of the state, its development, its policies, and its relationship to the society at large—not only have increased environmental degradation but also have interacted with environmental scarcity to generate social instability and conflict. We show that, together, these forces are triggering resource capture, marginalization of poor groups, rising economic hardship, and a weakening of the state. This interaction is heightening ethnic, communal, and class-based rivalries that have long plagued Pakistani society. This conjunction of pressures increases group-identity and deprivation conflict as groups turn to violence as a means of addressing their mounting grievances.

These conflicts are increasingly urban in character. Environmental scarcity is now a major contributor to the rapid expansion and fractionation of the urban population and to the growing inability of the state to meet this population's demands. Within the Pakistani urban context, opportunities for competition among rival groups rise, struggles over scarce urban resources mount, and grievances proliferate. Yet as the relative capacity of the state erodes, means of addressing grievances and nonviolent channels for expressing them are less and less available. The result in Pakistan is a persistent escalation of urban violence.

Lasting solutions to this turmoil will require fundamental reforms in the Pakistani state and its policies. In their absence, strife will increase and could eventually contribute to regional instability.

Background

The Land and its People

Pakistan, which means "land of the pure,"[5] is a predominantly Muslim state located in the northwest of the Indian subcontinent. Extending from the northern Himalayan mountain ranges one thousand miles down to the Arabian Sea, it is bounded on the northwest by the mountain ranges of Koh Sulaiman and by Afghanistan and on the southwest by the Iranian section of Baluchistan. In the east, Pakistan is separated from India along the Sutlej River, the deserts of Rajasthan, and the Rann of Kutch; and a cease-fire line dividing the Kashmir Valley separates the two countries in the north.[6]

The country has a total land area of approximately 310,322 square miles, much of which consists of desert and mountainous regions. Yet the river system of the Indus and its tributaries has provided Pakistan with some of the most fertile and best-irrigated land in the Indian subcontinent, and a majority of the population lives along its banks. Frequent, occasionally severe earthquakes occur in the northern and western regions, while flooding plagues the Indus valley after heavy rainfall.

Agriculture is the nation's principal occupation, employing half of the country's population and accounting for 25 percent of its GNP. Wheat, cotton, rice, barley, sugarcane, maize, and fodder are the main crops. In addition, the western province of Baluchistan supplies a rich crop of fruits and dates. The industrial sector is growing and employs over 20 percent of the formal workforce. Key industries include textiles, construction materials, sugar, paper products, and rubber. Mineral resources are modest. In addition to oil and gas reserves, Pakistan has deposits of uranium, coal, sulfur, chromate, limestone, and antimony.

The state has four constituent political units: the North West Frontier Province (NWFP), and the provinces of Punjab, Sind, and Baluchistan; a number of tribal areas are also administered by the federal government. Of the provinces, Punjab is the most populated and agriculturally rich, followed by Sind. Baluchistan, which is primarily desert, is sparsely populated, while much of the NWFP is also barren and predominantly tribal in character.

The physical diversity of Pakistan's provinces is more than matched by the complex ethnic and cultural composition of the general population. The chief ethnolinguistic groups are Punjabis, Sindhis, Pathans, Baluchis, and a significant population of Muhajirs—Urdu-speaking refugees and their descendants who migrated to the country en masse following the partition of the subcontinent and the country's independence in August 1947. The dominant language is Punjabi (the first language of 65 percent of the population), followed by Sindhi (11 percent), Pushto (8 percent), and Urdu (9 percent). Gujarati, Sahraike, and Baluchi are among the languages of other ethnic minorities. English is generally spoken in business circles and in government.[7] Islam, the state religion, is practiced by the vast majority of the populace. Muslims make up 97 percent of the population (77 percent Sunni and 20 percent Shia), while Hindus, Buddhists, and Christians constitute the remaining 3 percent.

State and Society

In theory, Pakistan is a federal polity, committed to Islamic religious principles and parliamentary rule. The executive consists of a prime minister, who heads the government, with a president acting as chief of state. The legislative branch is bicameral and consists of a popularly elected National Assembly and a largely advisory Senate, elected indirectly by members of the provincial assemblies.[8]

Yet the "practice" of truly democratic and representative politics has proven elusive. Nonelected institutions hold sway over their elected counterparts, and the state has long been dominated by a military and bureaucratic elite dedicated to advancing its own interests largely to the exclusion of those of society at large.

The contours of Pakistan's "bureaucratic-authoritarian" state emerged soon after independence in 1947, as the challenges of nation building threatened to overwhelm the modest resources of the newly created country. Almost overnight, enormous social dislocations arising from partition, pressing defense requirements, and the need to assert authority over newly acquired and disparate territories confronted the state machinery with demands it could not meet.

Partition had yielded Pakistan 18 percent of the population, 17.5 percent of the financial assets, less than 10 percent of the industrial base, and slightly over 7 percent of the employment facilities of an undivided India.[9] Organizational machinery was inadequate—particularly in the regions the regime acquired—and the largely migrant political leadership had little direct contact or rapport with the indigenous population of the lands it inherited.[10]

The pressing need to consolidate territory and defend the nation prompted a rapid expansion of administrative machinery and wholesale adoption of the colonial British "vice regal" system of administration and resource management. This system had been long geared to maintaining law, order, and the collection of revenues on behalf of the British Empire. It included a professional civil service with a deep knowledge of local conditions as well as great access to and influence over provincial populations.[11] It was an effective tool—and one readily available to the new Pakistani regime—for augmenting state revenues and financing burgeoning defense budgets.

Military influence within the society expanded apace. The outbreak of war with India over the northern princely state of Kashmir only months after independence, lingering doubts over provincial loyalties to the newly formed state, and the internal dislocations and communal conflicts that attended independence all gave the military a critical role in the creation and maintenance of the state. Defense spending became a top priority and—along with the cost of civil administration—accounted for more than three-quarters of the federal government's budget during the first decade after independence.[12] This spending was soon supplemented by Western aid, as Pakistan adopted the role of junior guardian of the Persian Gulf in the Cold War.[13]

Yet there was little corresponding effort to ensure the supremacy of elected institutions within Pakistani society. Administrative-bureaucratic influence over the state rapidly increased, and democratic institutions decayed. By the late 1950s, the civil-military bureaucracy had consolidated its hold on the government,[14] and the country settled into a mode of state rule that remained largely unchanged for the next three decades. A succession of military and civilian regimes followed, and while each professed some commitment to greater political participation, all ultimately fell short of popular expectations. Elites often opted for a controlled form of democracy; they saw politics less as a participatory affair than as something to be steered from above.[15]

Recently, however, this pattern appears to have changed. After more than seven years of civilian-led government, some analysts now speak of a trend toward greater democratization of Pakistani politics.[16] There has been a routin-ization of some key elements of a democratic system, including more frequent general elections, somewhat more robust political parties, and a freer press. Nevertheless, nonelected institutions continue to have great power. The first prime ministerial tenure of Benazir Bhutto and that of her successor, Nawaz Sharif, were both, in effect, terminated following clashes with members of the permanent government.[17] In short, while the grip of bureaucratic authoritarian-ism may have loosened, its final demise is a distant prospect at best.[18]

Character of the Pakistani Regime

Burdened by an overdeveloped civil-military bureaucracy and exceedingly weak elected institutions, the Pakistani government has long been marked by a lack of accountability. Power and expertise are highly concentrated and largely reside in nonelected institutions and their supporters. Politicians often serve as junior partners in state rule, sometimes providing a cloak of legiti-macy for the actions of the permanent government, and at other times acting as lightning rods to deflect popular criticism as bureaucrats run the nation from behind the scenes. Not surprisingly, rule by executive ordinance has dominated legislative action, and coercion has frequently eclipsed negotiation in federal-provincial deliberations.[19]

Meanwhile, institutional avenues for broad-based popular expression have remained weak. Although general elections have occurred more regularly in recent years, they were infrequent for much of Pakistani history. The first general election based on a broad franchise took place in 1970, a full 23 years after independence. Political parties are still poorly evolved; they resemble movements and factions that do not generally articulate national goals and concerns.[20] Banned by government at various points in the nation's history, their precarious existence encourages them to adopt narrow political plat-forms, often appealing to the aspirations of particular ethnic and religious groups.[21]

Economic development has generally reflected the attitude that prevailed during the colonial period, stressing efficient resource exploitation, rapid eco-nomic growth, and state profit over conservation and human welfare. Over the past five decades, the country has witnessed the emergence of a profusion of low-cost, high-polluting industries governed by few environmental guide-lines.[22] Similarly, during the 1960s agriculture began to stress techniques intended to boost short-term production, often at the expense of long-term sustainability.

Despite relatively impressive GNP growth rates (in 1996 about 6 percent a year), economic returns have been largely directed toward meeting defense, debt-servicing, and administrative costs while neglecting human development. Improvements in the social well-being of the population have been marginal. Long ranked among the lowest in the world in terms of human development, the country lags in such areas as infant mortality, education (particularly for females), and the alleviation of poverty.[23] Social services are poor and often funded through foreign aid. Today, approximately 31 percent of the population lives in absolute poverty, infant morality stands at 95 per thousand live births, and 65 percent of the adult population aged 15 and over is illiterate.[24]

Meanwhile, strong traditions of environmental consciousness have been absent, both within government and in society at large. Environmental legislation has been weak or nonexistent. While adoption of the Environmental Protection Ordinance in 1983 marked the country's first explicit attempt to deal with the environment, governmental practice often does not reflect the spirit of the legislation, and efforts to improve the environment continue to confront old mind-sets, political gridlock, and institutional weakness.

Underlying the system's lack of political accountability and its developmental approach is a state structure deeply penetrated by powerful vested interests. In the years following independence, alliances among the state bureaucracy, large landowners, and a nascent industrial bourgeoisie were secured through patronage and bribes. Thereafter, the interests of the state and its supporters largely took precedence over all else. Dominated by a mainly Punjabi elite, the political and economic system concentrated power and investment in the western half of the country, to the great disadvantage of East Pakistan (now Bangladesh).

Ownership of land and industry remains highly concentrated, and it lies mainly in the hands of the bureaucracy and its supporters.[25] Meanwhile, land grants, lucrative defense contracts, permits, loans, licenses, and jobs are awarded on the basis of personal contacts and the ability to perform political favors rather than on the basis of merit. Over time, such practices have become accepted as necessary and inevitable ways of conducting business, both within and outside government. Today, a culture of greed and an absence of civic-mindedness pervade Pakistani society.

The political and economic system has resulted in some extension of privilege. However, more often than not, this extension is a result of elites' use of state resources to co-opt rivals and dissipate the potential challenges they pose. In the face of provincial discontent and threats of secession, the regime offers development money to provincial elites in exchange for political stability.[26] Similarly, favors are conferred upon industrialists and commercial entrepreneurs to shore up loyalties. Combined with the narrow sectional politics encouraged by weak representative institutions, these elite tactics cause greater segmentation of society along lines of class and ethnicity, as well as a debilitation of organized opposition to elite interests.

Consequences of Regime Character

Such political practices exacerbate regional, ethnic, and class divisions within Pakistani society. As the state supplies patronage to certain regions and ethnic groups, it creates classes that tend to reflect regional and ethnic divides.[27] Moreover, efforts to harness provincial resources to fill federal coffers breed regional alienation and resentment among provincial elites. Punjabi dominance of the civil-military bureaucracy, along with a high concentration of wealth and investment in Punjab Province, fuel accusations of unfair treatment and exploitation from other provinces and ethnic groups.

Before 1971, neglect of East Pakistan was particularly glaring. Dominance of the political system by West Pakistani elites resulted in marked economic disparities favoring West over East and wholly inadequate representation of the East's Bengali majority in government services. Bengali resentments mounted, and support for provincial autonomy increased. By late 1970, West Pakistan's gestures of electoral reform[28] and, by extension, more equitable representation proved illusory: general election results that did not favor West Pakistan's elite were disallowed. Consequently, in 1971 civil war and secession led to the creation of Bangladesh. Further fragmentation has been avoided, yet secessionist pressures persist, with Baluchistan, in particular, rebelling during the 1970s.

Today, provinces continue to quarrel over distribution of resources and power relative to one another and to the central government. Disputes over the waters of the Indus River are especially frequent: major canal and dam diversions in Punjab prompt accusations by Sind of unfair distribution of water. The constant contention among provinces results in costly delays in infrastructure projects.[29]

State practices have also fueled tensions within the provinces, particularly in Sind, Pakistan's most multiethnic province. Neglect of the long-standing demands of a burgeoning Muhajir population in Sind's urban centers and the general absence of broad-based representative institutions have brought ethnic and class tensions to the political breaking point.

Problems followed the division of the subcontinent in 1947, as waves of Urdu-speaking Muhajirs migrating from northern India marginalized the province's local Sind population both ethnically and linguistically. Primarily settling in Sind's urban centers (Karachi and Hyderabad), the new arrivals promptly filled the void created by the departure of Sind's Hindu population to form the bulk of the middle class. They also took over a substantial portion of property left by Hindus fleeing to India. The Muhajirs came to dominate various forms of commercial and industrial activity in the province, and Urdu replaced Sindhi as the province's official language. They also retained considerable strength in the bureaucracy, despite growing Punjabi dominance.

However, over the years waves of non-Muhajir migrants (for example, Punjabis and Pathans) in search of employment, along with the implementation of a system of placement quotas for government jobs and college entrance, curtailed Muhajir opportunities.[30] Combined with efforts by Prime Minister Zulfikar Ali Bhutto to redress Sindhi grievances during the 1970s, Muhajir alienation and resentment grew. Increasingly underrepresented within the corridors of political power and influence, yet constituting a dynamic economic and commercial force in Sind's urban centers, Muhajirs gradually identified themselves as a people without a state.

Rural Sindhi were equally dissatisfied. Deep resentment of Muhajirs was accompanied by similar animosities toward Punjabis, who dominated a civil and military bureaucracy stationed in the interior of Sind and owned vast tracts of land within the province. Sindhi underrepresentation within commerce and industry magnified these resentments.[31]

By the early 1980s, the long absence of nationally based political parties had reinforced organization of loyalties along narrow ethnic lines. In rural areas, rising Sindhi nationalism led to clashes between Sindhi guerrilla bands and Punjabi troops. Rural-urban migration continued unabated, taxing the absorptive capacities of cities and heightening competition among diverse groups for limited urban resources. War in Afghanistan added a heavy influx of refugees, narcotics, and arms to the urban mix, creating a huge black market economy and strengthening the power and influence of organized crime in the process. Not surprisingly, violence became commonplace in Sind's urban centers, with the Muhajir Qaumi Movement (MQM) championing the Muhajir cause.

As turmoil has escalated in the 1980s and 1990s, the Muhajirs have demanded recognition as the fifth nationality of Pakistan, a fairer allocation of provincial resources, and greater representation in elected bodies, federal and provincial services, and the police force.[32] Yet official efforts to address these problems have been inadequate, because of chronic institutional weakness at both the provincial and the national levels and a lack of support for the Muhajir cause within political elites.[33] The conflict has bred suspicions of collusion between India and MQM "terrorists." In addition, efforts to meet Muhajir demands would compromise powerful vested interests, especially in rural Sind.[34]

The highly inegalitarian character of the state also influences economic policy, often to the detriment of stability. Although successive regimes have achieved relatively impressive aggregate economic growth, they have not, for the most part, concerned themselves with the equitable distribution of the results of that growth. As a result, the ranks of the dispossessed have grown and their grievances have intensified. Meanwhile, the political strength of the military, the need to maintain internal order, and the rivalry with India have kept military spending high. As a result, Pakistan has relied heavily on foreign borrowing and development assistance and has accumulated considerable foreign debt. Today, along with annual defense spending averaging 6.8 percent of GDP—the highest in South Asia—debt servicing represents a major constraint on government spending. By the early 1990s, defense spending and debt servicing accounted for more than 80 percent of total government expenditures.[35]

For a time, remittances from nationals working abroad tended to mask the severe resource constraints facing the government. They accounted for almost 40 percent of exchange earnings and nearly 8 percent of GNP at their height in the early 1980s.[36] Yet by middecade, their decline combined with a low domestic savings rate and tightening conditions on international loans to dampen growth.

By 1987–88, loans from the International Monetary Fund (IMF) and the World Bank were tied to a structural adjustment package requiring deficit reduction, controls on inflation, and a series of other measures intended to cut spending and boost revenues. Policies aimed at meeting IMF guidelines included a withdrawal of food subsidies, bans on government recruitment, increased privatization, and higher taxation of the business community. Unemployment increased and incomes of labor and the poor declined throughout the late 1980s and early 1990s.[37]

Recent improvements in aggregate economic performance and some signs of renewed investor confidence in the country suggest a better economic picture. Yet problems remain. Domestic savings and investment are still low. Revenues from direct taxation are especially troubling, with only about 1 percent of the population paying direct income tax.[38] The existing system of tax collection is plagued by corruption and inefficiency, and vested interests oppose major reform; Punjab's politically powerful feudal landlords are especially intransigent.

Also troubling is the low employment intensity of recent growth. This phenomenon is partly attributable to a shift from labor-intensive to more capital-intensive industries and to continuing state subsidies that favor capital over labor. Since 1977, the number of jobs generated per unit of investment in industry has declined at a rate of 11 percent per year.[39] Current estimates suggest that each 1 percent gain in GDP translates to a mere 0.4 percent growth in employment.[40] Meanwhile, efforts to develop human resources remain weak, and civil strife in the nation's urban centers drains revenues and deters the creation of a truly stable climate for investment and job creation. These trends threaten long-term prospects for a healthy economy.

Environmental Scarcity and the Pakistani State

Pakistan's physical environment has deteriorated markedly since independence. State policies and the character of the state itself have created critical environmental scarcities throughout the country. Such scarcities and the patterns of behavior they generate owe much to the state's lack of accountability, its vice regal approach to economic development, and its penetration by special interests.

Lack of Accountability and Rising Scarcity

Over the years, the widespread lack of accountability of state officials and their supporters, along with Pakistan's vice regal approach to development, has produced excessive exploitation of the country's resource base. The result has been a progressively increasing nationwide scarcity of renewable resources (figure 5.1).

Fashioned to meet the needs of a colonial ruler, the vice regal system was founded on the principle of efficient resource exploitation of the "hinterland" to generate maximum profit for the British Empire. With rapid economic growth as this system's chief aim and Britain as its sole focus, issues of resource sustainability and of the host population's welfare were, at best, secondary. Early on, therefore, the perception of the appropriate relationship between natural resources and human need was distorted.[41]

With independence, Pakistan's elite adopted this colonial model wholesale. The system and its organizational culture remained intact, only the identities of its chief beneficiaries changed. Exploitation of the nation's resource base continued apace, although now in the service of the new state's elites and their supporters instead of a foreign colonizer. The masses remained the last to be considered.

Models of national development stressed growth in commodity production and consumption as the benchmarks of success,[42] and industrial and agricultural strategies emphasized cheap and rapid production at the expense of conservation. Industries using low-cost, highly polluting technologies proliferated. Mega-projects, such as reservoirs and dams, were conceived with an eye

FIGURE 5.1
Some Causes of Increased Environmental Scarcity

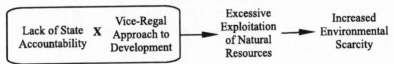

more to boosting national development than to their impact on local communities.[43] And agriculture relied on techniques aimed at increasing short-term production. Although heavy use of fertilizers and pesticides raised yields, the potential long-term impacts were generally ignored.

The pervasive lack of accountability inherent in the political system reinforced these features of the Pakistani development process. Strong and institutionalized means for popular expression and input were not available to constrain social exploitation and environmental degradation. The state did not legislate rigorous environmental guidelines; elites unburdened by concerns of responsibility to the broader public ignored those guidelines that did exist.

It was also impossible to change significantly the distribution of wealth yielded by development. Since elites could not be held responsible for their actions, the fruits of development went mainly to the government and its supporters. There was minimal articulation of popular demands for greater investment in human development, and there was little pressure on elites to respond to such demands.

Over time, the effects of vice regal development and low accountability became increasingly apparent. Unhampered exploitation of resources in the name of economic growth encouraged the rise of supply-induced scarcity as development practices degraded and depleted renewable resources, such as agricultural land, water, and forests. At the same time, lack of investment in human development and social welfare fueled scarcity from the demand side, as a highly impoverished, poorly educated, and politically disenfranchised Islamic population grew rapidly. Meanwhile, the weakness of institutional constraints on elite practices ensured that a seriously inequitable form of development proceeded largely unchecked, which perpetuated elite privilege and, consequently, structural scarcity.

Scarcity and the Penetrated State

Environmental scarcity and resource degradation have been accompanied by a gradual increase in resource capture by elites and a consequent ecological marginalization of large numbers of poor and disadvantaged. Here, environmental scarcity has interacted with the highly penetrated nature of the Pakistani state to encourage both processes (figure 5.2).

As noted above, unhampered exploitation of resources along with high population growth have progressively eroded the country's natural resource base. As scarcities of critical renewable resources—such as forests, land, and water—worsen, their prices increase, which in turn increases the incentive for powerful groups to acquire them and extract quasimonopolistic economic rents. The deeply penetrated structure of the Pakistani state encourages this

FIGURE 5.2
Resource Capture and Ecological Marginalization

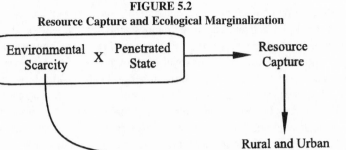

appropriation or "capture" of scarce natural resources: elites often already have preferential access to and control over resources; moreover, resources are a key means by which power and privilege are retained and expanded in the country's corrupt political system.

To reward, co-opt, or bribe potential challengers, the Pakistani regime often distributes concessions allowing powerful individuals and groups to exploit natural resources. This political behavior breeds chronic corruption and inefficiency: bribes and buy-offs are commonplace at the highest levels of the state, and these practices are replicated at lower levels and in private transactions. Most importantly, it allows favored individuals and well-connected entrepreneurs to appropriate valuable state lands, forests, and other resources at relatively low cost.

Such activity yields great profit for those involved, since they can sell, rent, or speculate on the resources in question. It also leads to misery for the local communities that depend on these resources for their livelihoods. The result is often the ecological marginalization of those affected. As resources are appropriated and exploited for profit, they become less available to local populations, increasing pressure on remaining stocks. These stocks are quickly depleted and degraded, and growing impoverishment eventually leads people to migrate, often to Pakistan's urban centers.

The rural-urban migrants generally settle in low-income areas, characterized by high population densities and rudimentary living conditions. Because of high urban land prices, they are often forced to build their settlements on the least desirable lands—areas that frequently flood, that lack basic services, or that lie beside transportation infrastructure, such as highways and railways. Despite their low quality, these lands are also often subject to resource capture by powerful urban entrepreneurs, and the terms of settlement for incoming migrants can be highly exploitive.

Environmental Scarcity

Pakistan is exhibiting increasingly severe demand, supply, and structural scarcities of key natural resources, as well as the resource capture and ecological marginalization associated with these scarcities.

Demand-induced Scarcity

Today, Pakistan is the tenth most populous nation in the world with more than 128 million inhabitants. Its current population growth rate of 3.1 percent implies a population doubling time of 22 years. Given present trends and the absence of an effective population policy, the population will likely exceed 200 million by 2010.[44]

There is considerable variation in population distribution. Some arid areas of Baluchistan average as few as 2 persons per square kilometer, while irrigated districts of the Punjab average 400 persons. Water and soil availability are the chief reasons for such variation. Thus, areas of low density have little spare absorption capacity.[45]

The high growth rate (table 5.1) is largely due to sustained high fertility

TABLE 5.1
Pakistan's Demographic Profile, 1970–1985

	1970	1975	1980	1985
Crude Birth Rate (per 1000 population)	36.5[a]	40.5[b]	41.5[c]	43.3[c]
Crude Death Rate (per 1000 population)	10.5[a]	10.5[d]	10.7[c]	11.5[c]
Total Fertility Rate (per woman)	6.25[a]	6.28[b]	6.48[e]	6.9[c]
Infant Mortality Rate (per 1000 live births)	139[b]	125[e]	121[c]	115[c]
Average Household Size	6.6	6.0[df]	6.7[f]	6.4[c]
Male Life Expectancy	53.6[a]	54.5[d]	56.6[g]	57.1[c]
Female Life Expectancy	47.6[a]	55.5[d]	57.8[g]	58.6[c]
Percentage Urban	23.4[f]	26.0[f]	28.0[f]	30.0[f]

Sources:
a. *Pakistan Growth Survey Series I,* 1968–1971
b. *Pakistan Fertility Survey,* 1970–75
c. *Pakistan Demographic Survey,* 1984–86
d. *Pakistan Growth Survey Series II,* 1976–79
e. *Population Labor Force, Migration Survey,* 1975–1979
f. Census 1972–81, Interpolation
g. *Pakistan Growth Survey Series II* and *Pakistan Demographic Survey,* Extrapolation

coupled with rapid declines in mortality brought on by the introduction of modern health care methods and improved nutrition. Over the past 24 years, Pakistan's fertility rate has not dropped below 6.25 and currently stands at 6.6.[46] Interestingly, reductions in infant morality have not been as dramatic as those for the general population as a whole. Many children continue to perish due to diseases contracted through unsanitary habits, bad water, and contaminated food. High infant mortality, along with a lack of education among poorer groups (particularly women), has discouraged family planning and kept birth rates high.

Efforts at family planning have met with limited success, particularly in rural areas. Pakistan now has a population pyramid with an extremely wide base. About 45 percent of the population is under 15, while 55 percent is under 20 years of age.[47] This demographic structure results in steadily rising demands for social services, especially schools, housing, and jobs.

The impacts of rapid population growth are pervasive. They include the subdivision of rural agricultural holdings, which decreases the amount of cultivated land per rural inhabitant; the denudation of well-forested hillsides; the migration of villages en masse from high mountain pastures to valleys; and the migration of large numbers of young people to cities.[48]

Supply-induced Scarcity

Land

Pakistan comprises 88.2 million hectares of land, of which 61.8 million has been surveyed. Approximately 20 million hectares are used for agriculture, while some 31 million hectares are forest, rangeland, unutilized, or unutilizable (map 5.1).[49]

Since independence, the area of land under cultivation has increased by approximately 40 percent.[50] Yet today the country is approaching its physical limits. Of the total surveyed land area, less than 20 percent retains the potential for intensive agricultural use, while 62 percent is classified as having low potential for crop, livestock, and forestry production. Overall, land categorized as cultivable represents less than one-quarter of the country's total area. Today, nearly all of this land is already under cultivation. Very little additional land is available for the expansion of agriculture.[51]

Shortages of arable land do not, of course, preclude an increase in agricultural production. Practices such as double-cropping, increases in labor productivity, and better technical inputs (such as new grains) can boost agricultural output. But a number of forces have combined to prevent the realization of the country's full agricultural potential. These include poor water management practices (which restrict double-cropping), a system of absentee landlords, the fragmentation of landholdings, the reduction in farm size from generation to

MAP 5.1
Pakistan's Agroecological Regions

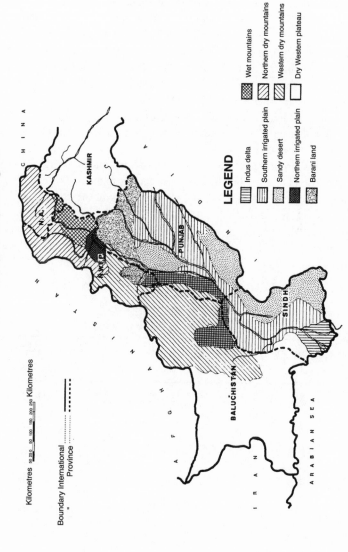

LEGEND

Indus delta	Wet mountains
Southern irrigated plain	Northern dry mountains
Sandy desert	Western dry mountains
Northern irrigated plain	Dry Western plateau
Barani land	

Kilometres

50 25 0   50 100   150 200 250   Kilometres

Boundary International
"   Province

Source: Arif Hasan and Amenah Azam Ali, *Environmental Repercussions of Development in Pakistan* (Karachi: OPP-RTI, 1993), 9.

generation as farming populations rise, poor access to agricultural capital, poor technology transfer to farmers, and a lack of information concerning the use of agricultural inputs, such as fertilizers and pesticides.[52] The heavy use of fertilizers (table 5.2), particularly during the 1960s and 1970s, has also left soils deficient in a number of nutrients essential to plant growth.[53]

Soil maps of the central-western region (an area representing approximately 40 percent of the country) reveal land affected by light water and wind erosion, a loss of topsoil, and some terrain deformation. In the southwest and along the southern coastal fringe west of Karachi, wind-eroded and salinized soils predominate. Desert soils, highly salinized soil, and some severely eroded areas are found along the Indo-Pakistani border, and soil in the lowlands of the Indus River valley also suffers from salinization. Meanwhile, lands in and around the northeastern tip of the country are classified as "stable" under normal conditions.[54]

The most important causes for reduced land productivity are water and wind erosion, salinity and sodicity,[55] waterlogging, flooding, and loss of organic matter (tables 5.3, 5.4, and 5.5). According to the government's Report on the Pakistan National Conservation Strategy, 17 percent of surveyed soils (which include most of the soils usable for agriculture, forestry, or ranching) are affected by water erosion, 7.6 percent by wind erosion, 8.6 percent by salinity and sodicity, and 8.6 percent by flooding and ponding; fully 96 per-

TABLE 5.2
Fertilizer Use in Pakistan, 1960–87

Period	Fertilizer Offtake (1,000 Nutrient Tons)	Growth Rate (Annual Percentage)
1960–65	3 – 71	17.7
1965–70	71 – 283	31.2
1960–70	31 – 283	24.6
1970–75	283 – 584	14.3
1975–80	548 – 1079	14.5
1970–80	283 – 1079	14.2
1980–87	1079 – 1784	8.8

Source: Arif Hasan and Amenah Azam Ali, *Environmental Repercussions of Development in Pakistan* (Karachi: OPP-RTI, March 1993), 36.

TABLE 5.3
Area Affected by Water Erosion

Degree of Erosion	Province					Pakistan
	Punjab	Sind	NWFP+FATA	Baluchistan	N.A.*	
	(1,000 Hectares)					
Slight (sheet & rill erosion)	61.2	-	156.3	-	180.5	398.0
Moderate (sheet & rill erosion)	896.8	-	853.8	1,805.0	25.8	3,581.4
Severe (rill, gully, and/or streambank erosion)	588.1	58.9	1,765.1	829.6	504.2	3,745.9
Very Severe (gully, pipe, and pinnacle erosion)	357.9	-	1,517.0	-	1,571.6	3,446.5
Total	1,904.0	58.9	4,292.2	2,634.6	2,282.1	11,171.8

* Northern Areas
Source: Alim Mian and Yasin Javed Mirza, *Pakistan's Soil Resources:: Pakistan National Conservation Strategy Sector Paper* (Karachi: IUCN-World Conservation Union, 1993), 13.

TABLE 5.4
Area Affected by Wind Erosion

Degree of Erosion	Province					Pakistan
	Punjab	Sind	NWFP+FATA	Baluchistan	N.A.*	
			(1,000 Hectares)			
Slight	2,251.4	295.0	13.1	36.0	-	2,595.5
Moderate	279.1	70.2	3.8	143.6	-	496.7
Severe to Very Severe	1,274.0	273.8	19.6	100.9	-	1,668.3
Total	3,804.5	639.0	36.5	280.5	-	4,760.5

* Northern Areas
Source: Alim Mian and Yasin Javed Mirza, *Pakistan's Soil Resources: Pakistan National Conservation Strategy Sector Paper* (Karachi: IUCN-World Conservation Union, 1993), 14.

TABLE 5.5
Area Affected by Salt

		Punjab	Sind	NWFP	Total Indus Plains
			(1,000 Hectares)		
Total Command Canal Area (CCA):		7,891	5,351	320	13,562
Within CCA:	Salt Affected Area	1,614	1,532	14	3,160
	Percentage	20.4	28.6	4.3	23.3
Outside CCA:	Salt Affected Area	1,129	1,019	502	2,650
Total		2,743	2,551	516	5,810

Source: Ministry of Food and Agriculture, Government of Pakistan, *Report of the National Commission on Agriculture* (Islamabad: Government of Pakistan, March 1988), 295.

cent suffer from less-than-adequate organic matter. These problems often occur simultaneously and produce synergistic impacts on agricultural productivity. Soils can suffer from both water and wind erosion, and poor organic-matter content is universal, reducing the potential productivity of the best as well as the worst of soils.[56]

Water

An arid and semi-arid country, Pakistan's water sources have always been limited. The country has regularly experienced critical water shortages, which lead to power blackouts and also to inadequate supplies of irrigation water for the main crop-growing season. To compensate, a finely balanced system of water management for irrigation, electricity, and industry has been developed. The system is shaped in part by the Indus Waters Treaty. Signed in 1960 by India and Pakistan following long-standing water disputes,[57] the treaty gives Pakistan control over the Indus and its western tributaries the Jhelum and Chenab, while India controls the Ravi, Beas, and Sutlej branches in the east. The treaty also allowed Pakistan to construct two large storage and hydroelectric dams: the Tarbela on the Indus and the Mangala on the Jhelum, as well as a system of smaller dams, inter-river canals, and irrigation canals. This irrigation network now services about 16 percent of the country and is one of the largest such systems in the world. As much as 65 percent of agricultural land is irrigated, accounting for about 90 percent of the country's food and fiber production.

Approximately 175 billion cubic meters of water enters the Indus Basin annually. Of this, 128 billion cubic meters is diverted for irrigation purposes to the canal heads, while remaining water flows to the sea. Although this flow to the sea is needed to maintain a viable river ecosystem, especially in the Indus estuary, experts agree that much of it could be stored for irrigation.[58] Yet, Pakistan currently lacks the necessary storage capacity, in part because of heavy silting of reservoirs. The absence of this water is one of the factors preventing the nation from attaining food self-sufficiency.[59]

The existing irrigation system is also highly inefficient. Of the 128 billion cubic meters diverted for irrigation, about 52 billion cubic meters are lost to seepage and evaporation from canals and watercourses. This loss is a major cause of waterlogging and salinity of soils in the Indus Basin. Vertical pumping systems used for drainage are proving unsustainable: the recycled water contains chemicals that produce sodicity[60] and reduce the life of pumping machines.

No serious effort has been made to develop a drainage system to parallel the irrigation system. In Punjab alone there are about 280,000 tube wells pumping 51 billion cubic meters of water and using about 2,400 megawatts of subsidized power. One hundred million metric tons of salts have been pumped up in the process.[61] The salts have decreased crop productivity in 1.2 million hectares of prime land in the Canal Command Area, which is about 5 percent of the total agricultural land in Pakistan. Another 2.1 million hectares of salt-affected lands exist in Punjab's non-sweet water areas. The result is lower crop productivity.[62]

Beyond the Indus Basin, sharp drops in the water tables of underground aquifers—of 15 centimeters (cm) to over 60 centimeters per year—are occurring in a number of areas. The water table in the Northern Basin of the Quetta Valley is falling at the extraordinary rate of 200 cm per annum, while the Southern Basin has registered a yearly decline of 60 cm.[63] The groundwater table in Lahore is falling at a rate of 30 cm per year in the central part of the city due to excessive withdrawals by a growing urban population.[64]

An inadequate sewage treatment infrastructure adds to problems. Many of Pakistan's rivers are now badly polluted with domestic sewage and industrial waste. A recent study of the Kabul River (near Peshawar) reveals that parts of the river and some of its tributaries have become open sewers.[65] Much of this polluted river water is used for drinking and irrigation. In fact, inadequate drinking water represents a long-standing and serious problem in several parts of the country.[66] It is increasingly common to see people in many parts of the country walking for kilometers to fill a container with water.[67]

Forests

As legally defined by the government, areas designated as "forests" include both natural and plantation forests, as well as areas with closed forest cover and open cover; the definition even includes some territory with little tree cover.[68] Clearer are the designations of "production" and "protected" areas offered in the Forest Act of 1927. Production forests are used mainly for the direct material products of their growth. They have a high tree density and, in most instances, a closed tree canopy. They represent the chief source of timber and currently make up 27.6 percent of total forest area.[69] Protected areas are largely intended to guard against soil erosion and today account for a full 72.4 percent of total forest area.[70]

Such distinctions have nonetheless done little to prevent the decline of forest areas generally. Over the past 75 years, forests have decreased from 14.2 percent to 5.2 percent (4.57 million hectares) of Pakistan's total land area, with less than 3 percent currently under tree cover. Closed cover forests account for under 1 million hectares.[71]

Efforts at afforestation and watershed management have not kept pace with increased demand for timber and excessive cutting and overgrazing. Between 1974 and 1985, timber supplies from state forests declined by 45 percent, in part because of reduced forest area. The total loss of forest occurred at a rate of 0.4 percent from 1981 through 1984 and has now decreased to 0.2 percent per annum.[72] This figure translates into the destruction of 7,000 to 9,000 hectares of forested land every year.[73] Today, Pakistan imports about 30 percent of the timber it uses.[74]

The heavy deforestation stems from a number of factors. During both the colonial and the post independence periods, entrepreneurs took over and commercially exploited large forest tracts to satisfy the demands of a growing rural and urban population. With the development of canals, hundreds of thousands of hectares of riverine, scrub, and forest land in the Indus plains were cleared for agriculture. Energy demand also has increased pressure on the forests. Wood currently meets approximately one-half of national energy requirements. Annual consumption now stands at an estimated 19.70 million cubic meters and is expected to rise to 30.66 million cubic meters by the year 2000. According to the 1980 housing census, approximately 70 percent of all households in Pakistan relied upon wood for cooking and heating, with dependence reaching 80 percent in rural areas.[75] Given continuing high population growth, reports of a further rise in timber demand for cooking and heating are hardly surprising.[76]

The negative consequences of uncontrolled forest exploitation are ever more obvious. They include serious soil erosion and sedimentation, desertification of once-productive upland areas, the silting up of waterways in the plains (making them more prone to flooding), and marked scarcities of fuelwood and building timber (creating an economic burden on low-income communities).[77] The decline in tree cover has already resulted in a large reduction in watershed and reservoir efficiency. Except for a small headpond with daily storage capacity, Pakistan's important Warsak Reservoir—built in 1960—is now completely silted up. The water's silt burden has caused serious wear on all rotating parts of the reservoir's hydroelectric generating station, and the main powerhouse structure is suffering from alkali-aggregate reaction.[78] Efforts at watershed management should lengthen the life of more recent projects, such as the Mangela and Tarbella Reservoirs; yet reports indicate that, even in these cases, sedimentation is occurring at a rate that could render them inoperative in as little as forty years.[79]

These processes have major implications for the availability of water for irrigation and power generation. Indeed, some experts predict large deficits of water and electricity in the future, with considerable impact on agriculture and the economy. According to the World Bank, while less than 10 percent of Pakistan's hydroelectric potential has actually been exploited, further development is heavily constrained by silting.[80] Nevertheless, projected stagnation in growth of supplies of natural gas—Pakistan's chief energy source—is likely to heighten demand for electricity.[81] Energy supplies have been growing at 7.2 percent per year, while demand is increasing at 8.3 percent annually[82] and the country has already experienced serious loadshedding due to electricity shortfalls.[83]

The effects of flooding are even more salient. Floods have not only pro-duced loss of life and property, but also serious damage to irrigation networks, crops, and transportation and communication systems and utilities. Between 1973 and 1978, a succession of floods in Punjab and Sind affected over 12 million people and over 8 million hectares of land and destroyed an estimated 70 percent of the total standing crop.[84] More recently, in 1992, landslides, accelerated soil erosion, and large quantities of felled, unclaimed timber mov-ing down the Kunhar, Siran, Daur, and Jhelum Rivers in Hazara resulted in widespread destruction of lives and infrastructure. According to a report re-leased by the Sungi Development Foundation, the felled timber:

> destroyed approximately 30 to 35 water mills on the banks of the Kunhar River in the Kaghan Valley, demolished bridges used as links between remote villages and commercial centers, damaged much needed sources of irrigation, and wiped out precious agricultural land.[85]

Overall, Pakistan's Economic Survey reported devastating floods as a chief cause of a 3.9 percent drop in agricultural output for fiscal 1992–93. Direct losses from flooding were estimated at PRs. 40 million (approximately US$1.5 million) for that year.[86]

Structural Scarcity

Regional resource disparities have always existed. Of Pakistan's four prov-inces, both Punjab and Sind contain the majority of the nation's population, industrial capacity, irrigation networks, and prime agricultural land. In con-trast, the NWFP and Baluchistan are less endowed. Long-standing distribu-tional inequities also exist among groups, including between landlords and peasants in rural areas, among classes in the urban context, and among ethnic communities throughout the country.

As discussed above, the state has often exacerbated these inequalities rather than ameliorated them. Pakistan's overdeveloped military-bureaucratic oligar-chy is marked by corruption and patronage and an almost total lack of ac-countability. Truly independent and representative political institutions have never developed at any level of governance.

This situation has virtually guaranteed that economic and social policy has been unbalanced or excessively influenced by parochial interests. The elite and middle class represent narrow strata of society but control an exceedingly large share of resources and industry. Even in Pakistan's most troubled cities, they ensure themselves a comfortable lifestyle and access to services through political pressure and bribes, while those in less fortunate areas are ignored.[87] High- and middle-income groups in fact absorb the vast majority of urban resources, with the wealthiest 25 percent of the urban population receiving almost two-thirds of housing and services.[88]

The military is especially privileged. Over the years, military personnel have become deeply entrenched in the economic life of the country, heading up numerous corporations in the public sector and strongly represented on the boards of many private companies. According to Ayesha Jalal, each of the three defense services have trusts and foundations with extensive investments in the national economy. For instance, the Fauji Foundation—run by the army—owns eight manufacturing units that produce sugar, fertilizer, cereals, liquid gas, and metals; in addition, it has a gas field, transportation companies, schools, hospitals, and investments in defense production industries. All are exempt from taxation and legislation covering the manufacturing sector and are not required to disclose their assets or make shares available for public subscription.[89]

Meanwhile, in rural areas, large landowners dominate life and derive the majority of benefits from agriculture. State policy often strengthens their position. For instance, while policies implemented during Pakistan's "green revolution" significantly boosted overall agricultural productivity through the use of high-yield crops, fertilizer, and irrigation, these technologies favored large landholders (those with over 40 hectares). Large, well-connected landholders thrived, while many smaller farmers were eventually left landless.[90]

Land reforms have failed to alter fundamentally the highly skewed distribution of rural wealth. Both in 1959 and in 1972, reform legislation imposed ceilings on individual rather than family ownership, which ensured that the vast bulk of land under cultivation remained in the hands of a privileged minority.[91] According to one source, a mere 1 percent of landless tenants and small peasant holders directly benefited from the reforms.[92] Still another notes that between 1972 and 1980, the share of total agricultural land held by the poorest 40 percent of agricultural households declined from 11 percent to 10 percent, while the share of the top 20 percent jumped from 55 percent to 57 percent. Rural income distribution moved in the same direction.[93]

Recent evaluation of the relationship between resources and society in Pakistan suggests little change in the patterns of inequality producing such scarcities or in the mentality underlying them. According to a recent report on the environment by the Pakistan Administrative Staff College, Pakistan is "a predatory and factional country. Economic policy and management . . . are often designed to serve the interests of the elite, who are engaged in obtaining advantages for themselves."[94]

Resource Capture and Ecological Marginalization

Accompanying widespread supply-induced, demand-induced, and structural scarcities is growing evidence of resource capture and ecological marginalization in the agricultural and timber industries and in urban areas.

Resource Capture

The Green Revolution

The introduction of green revolution technologies in Pakistan contributed to resource capture. Launched in the early 1960s, the revolution was an attempt to increase agricultural production to meet the rising food demands of a growing population. In short, it was launched as part of an effort to address real and impending resource scarcities within the nation.

Application of these new technologies—which combined high-yield hybrid grains with greater use of fertilizers and irrigation—improved agricultural performance and increased grain output. However, the economically efficient use of these technologies demanded particularly large tracts of agricultural land. Consequently, the green revolution favored large, well-connected landowners. Not only could they exploit the new technologies to maximum effect, but the revenues generated from their use enabled large landowners to take over additional land for cultivation. Farmers with smaller land holdings were eventually bought out, and many became landless. Those with medium-sized holdings (3 to 10 hectares) were hit especially hard.

Indeed, census data for 1960 to 1972 in Punjab Province (where green revolution technologies were most widely adopted) reveal that the new technologies resulted in a polarization of farm-size distribution: the percentage land area of large and small farms increased, while that of medium-sized farms declined (table 5.6).

Motivated by the potential profits of green revolution technologies, large

TABLE 5.6
Percentage of Farms and Farm Area by Size of Farm, 1960 and 1972, in Punjab

Size of Farm (Hectares)	Farm Area	
	1960 (Adjusted)	1972
Less than 3	9.9	11.8
3 to 10	51.2	46.4
10 and above	38.9	41.8
Total	100.0	100.0

Source: Adapted from Akmal Hussain, *Strategic Issues in Pakistan's Economic Policy* (Lahore: Progressive Publishers, 1988), 188.

landowners resumed self-cultivation of land previously rented out to both small- and medium-sized farmers. The latter suffered disproportionately because a higher percentage of them were tenant farmers. The result was a shift of farmers from the lower-medium- to the small-farm category over the intercensual period. Polarization in farm size also contributed to landlessness among the poor peasantry. According to Akmal Hussain, census data reveal that 794,000 peasants—43 percent of all agricultural laborers in Pakistan in 1973—entered the category of wage laborers from 1961 to 1973.[95] Many of these peasants were evicted from their land during the process of change ushered in by the green revolution.

In short, concern over resource scarcities, the structure of Pakistan's agrarian economy, and new agricultural technologies combined to increase the incentives and opportunities for rural elites to appropriate, or capture, cropland, in the process increasing the number of small holder and landless peasants. Many were forced to move to other areas in search of employment, with small towns and cities receiving the largest share of the migration.

The Timber Mafia

The exploitation of Pakistan's forests exhibited a similar process. While deforestation has a long history, rates have been particularly high over the past decade, in large part because of rising demand for fuelwood. Land management and property rights legislation have failed to ensure adequate regulation of the forest industry.

In many cases, strong urban and rural groups have appropriated both community and government lands for themselves. According to a recent report published by the Pakistan Administrative Staff College in Lahore, a "timber mafia"—a term coined to describe persons and groups having a commercial interest in rapid forest exploitation—is now ravaging Pakistan's dwindling forests.[96]

Those involved in the timber business have acquired leading roles in forest institutions and are deeply entrenched in the state's administrative machinery. These individuals, who are traditional tribal leaders and Sayyeds (direct descendants of Muhammad), have been able both to manipulate legislation to serve their interests and to block changes in the law that would make forest management more participatory and sustainable.[97]

During the late 1970s and early 1980s, such individuals used large transfers of state development funds to open up forest areas for exploitation. Road and electrification programs facilitated commercial cutting while reinforcing the political and social control of tribal leaders over indigenous populations.[98] Thereafter, the collusion of forest officials, large forestland owners, and contractors allowed timber extraction to proceed with little significant regulation.

The Chitral District in the NWFP is an example of such activity and its effects. The felling and smuggling of timber has been a constant source of irritation for the Kalush ethnic minority who reside there. Yet efforts to stop these practices have often been weak and unorganized and have at times prompted retaliation from timber interests. In one case, a Kalush leader survived an attempted murder, while his brother was killed after filing a court case about timber, grazing, and land rights in Rumbur Valley. Meanwhile, overharvesting of timber by colluding special interests continues in the Kalush valleys, causing migrations of villagers from high mountain pastures to valleys and of young people to cities in search of work.[99] The districts of Malakand and Hazara have experienced similar problems.[100]

Land Barons and the Tanker Mafia

Meanwhile, in large urban centers, such as Karachi, dramatically rising population and expanding commercial and industrial activity have resulted in a steady increase in the value of land. Technically, about four-fifths of all lands in Karachi are publicly owned.[101] However, deep-seated government corruption, along with bribery, has allowed entrepreneurs to appropriate these lands for profit.

This resource capture has not only led to widespread land speculation, but also to a thriving business founded on illegal squatter settlements. Settlement land is subdivided into plots and sold to low-income groups, usually for a moderate initial outlay. Yet interest rates for money borrowed for the initial purchase and for services are high.

Moreover, given that such dwellings are illegal, constant bribes are required to prevent demolition by local authorities, and tenants face a similar threat for delinquency in payment to the landlord.[102]

Corrupt civic agencies have allowed similar practices to govern the distribution of essential services. In Karachi, high demand for water along with rampant corruption and mismanagement in the Karachi Water Supply Board have created a "tanker mafia." Tankers obtain water from illegal hydrants or from poorer districts in the city and then sell it for profit.[103] The customers are often the inhabitants of the very districts from which the water was taken, and exorbitant prices force many to purchase the water on credit.[104] The results of such practices are increasing profit for entrepreneurs and local authorities and growing impoverishment of low-income urban dwellers.[105]

Ecological Marginalization

Resource capture often prompts a flight of dispossessed inhabitants from affected areas in search of a better life. Receiving areas—whether rural or urban—are frequently ecologically vulnerable and are further degraded as incoming migrants place additional stress on existing resources.

According to the 1981 census, of the 5.92 million persons who had migrated within the country, 87.6 percent moved from rural to urban areas, while only 12.4 percent moved in the opposite direction. Over half permanently settled in cities.[106] The chief forces driving such migration have been identified as:

> slow progress in the agricultural sector, a decline in per capita cropped area, low crop yields due to inefficient water management practices, failure to absorb skilled labor by modern technological systems, lack of alternate employment opportunities and environmental degradation due to deforestation and desertification.[107]

The large rural influx has, in turn, contributed to the overburdening of urban infrastructure and urban services. There has not only been a rapid decline in the quality and availability of basic urban resources and amenities such as housing, potable water, transportation, electricity, gas, drainage and sewerage, but also a mushrooming of katchi abadis (squatter settlements), often located on the most marginal land (table 5.7).

Today, squatter settlements account for about 25 to 30 percent of Pakistan's overall urban population. In Karachi, they comprise an estimated 41 percent and are growing by approximately 200,000 persons per year, twice as fast as the city's population.[108] In short, rural migration has contributed significantly to urban growth and to the marginalization of those within the urban environment.

The impact of migratory movements among rural areas is somewhat less clear. Available data do not permit definitive judgments about the degree to which rural ecological marginalization has occurred. Still, in the case of tenants left land-poor or landless as a result of the green revolution, data do support the conclusion that they have suffered a decline in real income and in the quality of their diets.[109] It is also clear that in addition to their migration into cities and towns, some supplemented their incomes by undertaking wage labor on neighboring farms.[110] In short, data support the conclusion that resource capture prompted some decline in the living standards of affected rural groups.

Social Effects of Environmental Scarcity

The effects of environmental scarcity, resource capture, and ecological marginalization have been wide-ranging. Most notably, they have: constrained agricultural productivity; exacerbated rural poverty and helped cause large waves of migration; contributed to widespread urban decay; and hindered economic growth and disrupted legitimized and authoritative institutions and social relations in the society.

TABLE 5.7
Population Trends for Katchi Abadis (Squatter Areas) in Karachi

	1970s (1978)	1980s (1985)	Most Recent (1988)	2000 (Projection)
SQT Population	2,000,000	2,600,000	3,400,000	7,070,000
SQT Households	227,000	356,000	465,000	960,000

Source: Arif Hasan, *Seven Reports on Housing: Government Policies and Informal Sector and Community Response* (Karachi: OPP-RTL, 1992), 152.

Agricultural Production

Notwithstanding marked industrial growth over the past two decades, agriculture remains an important sector of Pakistan's economy, contributing 23 percent to GDP, employing roughly 51 percent of the labor force, and generally supporting about 70 percent of the country's total population (either directly or indirectly).[111] Total agricultural output has been rising at an average of 4 percent per annum since the beginning of the green revolution in the 1960s—a rate that exceeds average population growth.[112]

Still, as noted above, there has been a general decline in the country's agricultural resource base. Uncertain and variable water supplies affect agriculture. The majority of irrigated lands suffer from some degree of waterlogging and salinization, which causes the loss of about 40,000 hectares of irrigated lands each year; a total of 5.7 million hectares (well over one-quarter of all agricultural lands in the country) are salt-affected.[113]

Food production has increased 50 percent over the past 20 years, yet the area under cultivation has risen 8 percent. This differential indicates a marked increase in the intensity of Pakistani agriculture: higher productivity has come from irrigation, fertilizer, pesticides, the introduction of new crop varieties, and changes in cropping practices. Although there is still significant potential for further improvement in yields (table 5.8), the country's food supply remains highly dependent on good harvests rather than on any institutionalized process of technical change, and it is therefore vulnerable to sharp downturns.[114] Furthermore, many of the improvements in agriculture are not distributed equally throughout the country (for example, extension services in the mountains are weak).

Meanwhile, fragmentation of landholdings due to rapid population growth and prevailing laws of inheritance is continuously reducing the efficiency of small farms. Indeed, while total cropland increased from 14.6 million to 20.6 million hectares between 1947 and 1987, per capita cropland declined from 0.44 to 0.2 hectares during the same period. At present rates, cultivable land per person could drop as low as 0.08 hectares within 40 years.[115] By 1988, largely as a result of these problems, Pakistan's National Commission on Agriculture was reporting a steady decline in farm yields and a rising tendency among the rural population to farm marginal land.[116]

More recently, the final report of the Pakistan National Conservation Strategy claims that per capita agricultural growth is currently stagnating.[117] While increases in agricultural inputs can compensate somewhat, sharply diminishing returns to land are ultimately unavoidable.[118] As population increases, greater demands will be placed on the finite resource base. In the absence of major change, the report argues, economic growth is bound to suffer and food deficits are likely to threaten a number of regions—most notably, sandy deserts, the western dry mountains, and barani (rainfed) areas.[119]

TABLE 5.8

Yield Gap of Various Crops in Pakistan: Average versus Potential Yield

Commodity	Potential Yield	Average Yield	Yield Gap	Unachieved Potential (Percentage)
		(Kilograms per Hectare)		
Wheat	6,425	1,695	4,730	74
Paddy	9,489	1,703	7,786	82
Maize	6,944	1,272	5,672	82
Sugar Cane	256,000	35,672	220,328	86
Rape & Mustard	2,743	641	2,102	77
Potato	38,128	10,403	27,725	73

Source: G. R. Sandhu, *Sustainable Agriculture: A Pakistan National Conservation Strategy Sector Paper* (Karachi: IUCN-World Conservation Union, 1993), 3.

Rural Poverty and Migration

Constraints on agricultural productivity contribute to rural poverty and unemployment. Despite the fact that over 70 percent of all rural households are classified as agricultural, many do not earn enough income to meet their basic needs. In 1981, a study of agriculture in Punjab found that one-quarter of all small farmers (who make up the majority of all farmers in the province) were forced to supplement their agricultural earnings by other means.[120] Other sources have reported that rural underemployment approaches 60 percent nationwide.[121]

Accompanying such problems is a marked lack of basic infrastructure and human services. Less than one-third of the country's 45,000 villages have access to wholesale trading centers through a network of all-weather roads.[122] Access to education is lower in rural than in urban areas, fertility rates are slightly higher, and cases of undernutrition among children are more widespread.[123] Only 17 percent of the rural population has access to potable water, a full 95 percent obtains some portion of its water supply from groundwater, and only 4 percent of the population has access to sewerage and drainage facilities.[124] Although these deficiencies promote disease, hospitals and other health centers are sorely lacking: there are only 455 health centers to service the approximately 70 percent of the total population (about 89.5 million people) who live in rural areas.[125] Not surprisingly, the rural mortality rates are higher than urban rates.

The poor quality of rural life encourages a heavy movement of migrants from rural to more prosperous urban areas. Much of the migration has been from the north; particularly from the NWFP to Karachi, but the large industrial cities of Punjab also draw workers: migrants from economically stressed areas such as Peshawar, Malakand, Rawalpindi, and Sargodha are especially prevalent (table 5.9).[126]

These migrants are usually young adult males in search of improved economic opportunities for themselves and their families. Their absence often serves to deepen rural poverty. The loss of healthy, able-bodied youth reduces agricultural productivity by placing increased demands on those who remain (women, children, and the aged). Gains in rural household income due to remittances from migrants tend to be directed toward increased consumption rather than investment in capital. The result is often greater awareness of a more affluent urban lifestyle, yet lingering rural impoverishment.

Urban Decay

Urban growth has been staggering, averaging from 4 percent to almost 5 percent per year in most major cities (table 5.10); such rates imply a doubling time for urban population of between 14 and 18 years. Over the past decade,

TABLE 5.9

Rural-Urban Migration by Province of Origin and Province of Destination
(percentage of rural-urban migratory movement), 1972–79

Province of Origin	Province of Destination				Total
	Punjab	Sind	NWFP	Baluchistan	
Punjab	52.0	13.8	5.1	1.8	72.6
Sind	-	3.1	-	-	3.1
NWFP	4.7	10.4	7.0	0.3	22.4
Baluchistan	-	0.6	-	1.3	1.9
Total	56.7	27.8	12.1	3.4	100.0

Source: S. Akbar Zaidi, "The Economic Bases of the National Question in Pakistan: An Indication," in *Regional Imbalances and the National Question in Pakistan,* ed. S. A. Zaidi (Lahore: Vanguard Books, 1992), 111.

TABLE 5.10

Rural and Urban Population Size and Rates of Growth, 1951–1991

Year	Total Population (1,000)	Average Growth Rate Per Annum (Percent)	Urban Population (1,000)	Intercensal Urban Growth Rate Per Annum (Percent)	Rural Population (1,000)	Intercensal Rural Growth Rate Per Annum (Percent)
1951	33,370	1.8	3,109	4.1	27,487	1.4
1961	42,880	2.4	9,655	4.8	33,324	1.8
1972	63,309	3.6 (3.0[a])	16,594	4.8	48,727	2.6
1981	84,254	3.1	23,841	4.4	60,412	2.5
1991 (Est[a])	108,909	2.9[b]				
1991 (Est[b])	114,333	3.1[c]				

[a] The intercensal rate of growth of 3.6 percent assumes no undercount in the 1961 census. The rate of 3.0 percent assumes an undercount of 7.5 percent.

[b] NIPS estimate.

[c] Population Census Organization/NEMIS projection.

Source: Lee L. Bean, "Growth Without Change: The Demography of Pakistan," in *Contemporary Problems of Pakistan*, ed. J. Henry Korson (Boulder, Colo.: Westview Press, 1993), 21.

some of the influx has been produced by the entry of about 3 to 3.5 million Afghan refugees into the country (as a result of the Afghan War) and the return of over 1 million Pakistani workers from the Middle East. Still, the majority of migration emanates from rural areas within the country, accounting for a full 22 percent of total urban growth.[127]

Along with already high natural growth, such migration has placed enormous demands on urban infrastructure, facilities, and services. Invariably, however, municipal institutions cannot accommodate these needs. In particular, there has been insufficient investment capital to meet the absorption costs of the rapidly growing population. According to Syed Ayub Qutub, the investment resource pool generated by Pakistan's recent annual 6 to 7 percent GNP growth covers only 28 to 32 percent of urban investment requirements. With capital investment per capita likely to remain low, and with trends indicating that over three-fifths of future Pakistani population growth will occur in urban areas, an increase—absolute and proportionate—in unserviced urban populations is inevitable.[128]

Evidence of Pakistan's inability to cope with the "urban explosion" is abundant. In Karachi, while the population rises at 6 percent per annum, far above the current national rate of 3.1 percent, urban services expand by only 1.2 percent.[129] Housing for low-income groups has become a major problem, with the government able to meet only about one-eighth of demand. Meanwhile, an informal system of illegal occupation and subdivision of state land for sale to low-income families has developed. The uncontrolled growth often encroaches on valuable agricultural land and the plant and animal life inhabiting it. While Lahore and Faisalabad had several tracts of good agricultural land 25 years ago, there is now no arable land within their city limits.[130] Similarly, the city of Peshawar has lost over 2,700 hectares of agricultural land to urban users over the last 20 years.[131]

Acute shortages of electricity and water are pervasive in Karachi, and sanitation services are often nonexistent. In 1983, per capita water consumption stood at approximately 80 liters per day—a level well below international standards.[132] Only 40 percent of all households received piped water, usually for only a few hours a day. Others were served either by standpipes (about one pipe per 270 persons) or purchased water from tankers.[133] And one-fifth of all households had sewerage connections.[134]

The Karachi Electric Supply Corporation generates over 1,700 megawatts against a peak demand of approximately 1,450 megawatts, yet the city faces constant electricity shortages due to a decaying distribution system and inadequate maintenance.[135] Theft rates have been reported to be as high as 20 percent.[136] And in the absence of additional generation capacity, the corporation anticipates a net shortfall of over 1,200 megawatts by the year 2000.[137]

Karachi and Islamabad are the only two cities in Pakistan possessing sewage treatment plants and these facilities are overtaxed. In Karachi, only 15 to

20 percent of sewage is treated, while the rest flows directly into the sea. Similarly, only 33 percent of the city's solid waste is transported to dump sites; the remaining refuse is picked over by scavengers in the streets.[138] Water-borne illnesses due to poor sanitation account for 25 to 30 percent of total cases in public hospitals and dispensaries nationwide and for an estimated 40 percent of deaths.[139]

Industrial pollution of water and air from chemical plants, cement factories, and the like poses additional hazards. In Karachi, industrial activities result in high concentrations of metals, metal salts, bacteria, acids, and oils in bodies of water and their surrounding lands. Tests also show industrial contamination of seawater.[140] Studies indicate that in Punjab, large segments of the population are suffering from respiratory ailments and eye problems due to air pollution, and plant and crop damage is evident as well.[141] A growing number of automobiles, along with widespread burning of solid wastes for heating, lighting, and disposal, compounds this pollution problem (solid waste is one of the nation's chief fuels). According to the final report on the Pakistan National Conservation Strategy, "the average Pakistani vehicle emits 20 times as much hydrocarbons, 25 times as much carbon monoxide, and 3.6 times as much nitrous oxide in grams per kilometer as the average vehicle in the United States."[142]

Quantitative studies of the economic impact of this pollution are rare, yet, based on evidence from other developing countries, there are strong grounds to assume that the costs are large, in terms of both labor productivity and income. In India, for instance, waterborne diseases alone are responsible for the loss of some 73 million workdays annually; the cost in medical treatment and lost production is estimated at US$600 million per year. A comparative study of health and economic output across 22 African, Asian, and Latin American nations has found that the influence of health on economic output is quite high relative to other factors, including agricultural production.[143] Pollution also has indirect costs; in particular, it boosts the expenditure of time and energy required to secure clean services. The search for adequate water supplies and sanitation facilities reduces the resources and labor available for activities that increase economic output and earnings.[144]

Economic Decline and State Weakness

Reduction of crop yields due to water, soil, and air pollution; loss of agricultural land resulting from salinization, waterlogging, erosion, and urban expansion; nutrient loss stemming from erosion and deforestation; loss of hydroelectric power owing to the siltation of reservoirs; and loss of timber due to poor harvesting practices all inevitably reduce an economy's capacity to produce wealth.[145] These economic effects weigh disproportionately on already marginal regions and groups.

Financial and political demands on government increase. Resource scarcities raise the demand for compensating industry and infrastructure and for aid to affected marginal groups, especially rural-urban migrants. At the same time, scarcity-induced reductions in economic productivity can restrict state revenues. A widening gap between demands upon the state and its capacity to meet these demands can, in turn, progressively weaken the state.[146]

Scarcity and Economic Vulnerability

In general, aggregate growth of Pakistan's economy appears strong: annual GDP has climbed by more than 6 percent in real terms for most of the 1980s and early 1990s.[147] A marked expansion in industrial activity has been key to this growth. Industry today accounts for 27 percent of total GDP and has registered annual growth rates of 9 percent over the past decade.[148] Meanwhile, agriculture and services have registered average growth rates of 4 and 7 percent respectively; the former now accounts for 23 percent of GDP.[149]

Nevertheless, these aggregate statistics mask serious structural weaknesses in the economy—weaknesses that are aggravated by environmental scarcities and that have disproportionate effects on poorer segments of Pakistan's population. Ownership of land and industrial wealth is highly concentrated and relatively free of direct taxation. Industry tends to be capital- rather than labor-intensive; in fact, manufacturing has registered a net decline in its contribution to employment over the past 25 years.[150] Meanwhile, agriculture continues to employ over half the workforce, it contributes a substantial part of manufacturing value added (for example, textile industries often draw their raw material from the agricultural sector),[151] and it accounts for 70 percent of exports.[152] In sum, a significant portion of Pakistan's population and economy remains strongly tied to the country's resource base.

The average annual rate of increase in agricultural production has been only slightly greater than annual population growth. According to the report on the Pakistan National Conservation Strategy, the inadequate performance of Pakistan's agricultural sector has already forced the import of food grains worth millions of rupees annually, severely straining the national treasury.[153] Similarly, Pakistan's 1991 report to the United Nations Conference on Environment and Development notes that because large increases in irrigation cropland are now unlikely, "it will be difficult for crop production to keep pace with population growth in future." Consequently, serious food shortages over the next two decades "cannot be ruled out."[154]

Problems with the country's power sector have caused substantial economic losses. As of late 1994, the country's total installed electrical capacity was 10,586 megawatts, with chronic shortages of about 2,000 megawatts. These shortages have resulted in loadshedding during the summer dry season, costing the economy an estimated $950 million annually.[155] Transmission losses and theft are currently estimated at over 12 percent of power capacity nationally and over 20 percent in some cities—a level twice that regarded as acceptable by international agencies.[156]

Perhaps most troubling is the growing problem of unemployment and underemployment throughout the country.[157] At one time, the export of labor to the Middle East and the West, and generous aid packages from a number of foreign donors (the United States in particular), helped compensate for Pakistan's surplus labor problem. But such opportunities are less available in the post–Gulf War environment. Many people working in the Middle East returned as demand for their services contracted. Such migrants had long provided a source of valuable remittances, yet they are now a growing proportion of the unemployed.

Demands for government spending continue to grow, yet investment in development is constrained by high defense costs and Pakistan's heavy debt load. Moreover, state revenues have not grown as rapidly as needed. In recent years, development projects for which some foreign financing has been provided have been canceled because the state could not secure matching funds. In its search for credit, the government has crowded the private sector out of the capital market. Pakistan's annual international debt-servicing costs amount to almost 3 percent of GNP or 23.6 percent of export receipts. Tighter conditions on loans from international lending agencies are restricting foreign borrowing.

In short, despite apparently robust aggregate economic growth, the current pattern of Pakistani economic development reinforces impoverishment for the majority of the population and an increasing polarization of society into rich and poor. The benefits of Pakistan's development are not widely shared—a situation unlikely to change in the near future—and most Pakistanis remain highly dependent on a limited, and ever more fragile, resource base.

State Weakness

Alongside signs of growing economic trouble and societal polarization are signs of increasing weakness of the Pakistani state. Nowhere is this weakness more obvious than in the nation's cities. In Karachi, government has literally lost control over the management of housing allocations, land taxes, and policing. The urban land market in the city is unique. Approximately 80 percent of Karachi's land is owned by the government. These lands are often under long-term lease and managed by various governmental agencies. Yet despite large-scale public ownership, many serviced sites developed by the Karachi Development Authority have been sold to investors at well below market value.[158] Moreover, while restrictions govern the number of plots that can be individually owned, these rules are circumvented with relative ease. The result is widespread speculation and rent seeking, much to the benefit of the rich.[159] An estimated 5 square kilometers of serviced land in the center of the city lie vacant due to speculation, while surrounding areas are packed with slums. Only middle- and high-income groups can afford good housing, while those of lower income encroach on public land.

The city's tax base is very narrow. In 1987–88, property taxes accounted for only 10 percent of government receipts. More than half of all properties were not taxed;[160] assessments on those that were taxed were invariably badly outdated. Public services, however, are heavily subsidized and underpriced, which increases rural-urban migration and causes demand for these services to rise.

Nor have urban governments proved themselves capable of coping with the violence that plagues Pakistani cities. Police lack the equipment and expertise to conduct effective investigative work. According to Jamiel Youssef, head of a civilian committee that liaises with the Karachi authorities, "the Karachi police have no fingerprinting facility, no computerized national data system for criminal records, and . . . [outmoded] ballistic and forensic equipment."[161]

Some experts insist that the main problem is corruption. In certain areas of Karachi, police connections to organized crime are so tight that residents feel they cannot report criminal acts or injustices they witness. The police often use the people they detain to extort money from anxious relatives; the "cash value" of a suspect is determined by such factors as ethnicity, family wealth, and possible family connections to the administration and pro-government politicians.[162]

Increasingly, in fact, state power has been eclipsed by a "parallel government" composed of heavily armed, organized criminal elements, capable of holding legitimate authorities at bay with force and bribes. In urban areas, local crime syndicates have often proved more adept than local authorities at managing some neighborhoods, offering individuals access to shelter, security, and employment that the state cannot match. During the mid-1980s, in Orangi Township, Karachi, crime bosses even threatened to orchestrate ethnic riots if local authorities attempted to launch raids against their drug operations.[163]

Rural areas have fared little better. Rather than place their trust in local authorities, large landowners have long employed security staffs to guard their holdings against encroachment by covetous neighbors. Such staffs are often tempted to exploit their power for additional profit—frequently at the expense of other landholders. Recent years have witnessed a marked rise of lawlessness in Sind, the NWFP, and Baluchistan.

The Tando Allahyar region of Sind provides a vivid example of the government's inability to ensure law and order. Located some 150 kilometers northeast of Karachi, this region is one of the most fertile areas of the country. During the late 1980s and early 1990s, organized gangs of armed bandits literally held it for ransom. Largely composed of migrants from the barren and resource-scarce northern regions of Sind, the gangs formed a federation that acted to gather and disseminate information concerning planned raids by law enforcement agencies and to divide the region's spoils among themselves.

Each time a new crop was harvested, the gangs descended on farmers for protection money. Those who refused to pay were subject to abduction or the destruction of their crops and electricity transformers. Enforcement agencies were unable to protect the rural population. At times, victims failed to register complaints with authorities because they did not trust the police. Only direct involvement by the army restored order.[164] Still, many of the gangs have not been eradicated, and recent incidents of violence in rural Sind indicate a resurgence of their activity.[165]

Such intimidation not only shakes government legitimacy but also produces a climate unfavorable to investment and the generation of economic growth and tax revenues. The financial resources upon which the state can draw to address the demands of its growing population are further constrained. Many landlords have moved to cities, forcing down agricultural harvests, and large numbers of entrepreneurs have deserted Sind Province entirely.

Urban violence has had similar effects. Noteworthy are the severe economic consequences of turmoil in Karachi, which is Pakistan's largest city, premier industrial port, and home to more than 65 percent of its industry and 80 percent of its finance. In 1987, political violence closed the port and industrial areas for days. Businesses closed down, industrialists fled to the north, and unemployment soared.[166] According to John Adams, the violence, curfews, and plant closings cost the economy an estimated $175 million in the early part of the year alone.[167] In December 1994, the army's withdrawal from Karachi caused a 207-point drop in the Karachi Stock Exchange Index (about 15 percent of the total value of the exchange), and U.S. and Japanese companies pulled their executives and their families out of the city. More recently, industry sources claimed that armed violence along with a three-day general strike resulted in the loss of $260 million in revenue and left potential investors reluctant to even visit the city.[168]

The economic impact of Karachi's civil strife extends far beyond the city itself. Businesses have suffered nationwide. Fan manufacturers in Gujrat anticipate a 25 percent drop in sales largely due to the market shutdowns caused by turmoil in Karachi in 1995.[169] Textile manufacturers in Multan and Faisalabad have reported rising difficulties in recovering payments from Karachi traders due to falling sales in the city, and businessmen in the NWFP expect problems from a large influx of unemployed youth returning to the region in the wake of layoffs from Karachi factories.[170]

Violent Conflict

Environmental scarcities and the processes accompanying them are encouraging the violent expression of long-standing ethnic, communal, and class-based rivalries in Pakistani society. As resource scarcities mount, grievances rise, especially across existing social cleavages within society; at the same time, the capacity of the state to address these grievances and to prevent violent challenges to its authority is diminished.

Scarcity and Rural Conflict

Developments in the country's rural areas suggest that growing deprivation among particular groups has caused an increase in violence over the last decade. Environmental pressures have played a significant role in generating the grievances behind this conflict.

The bandits (or "dacoits") of rural Sind are a case in point. Although banditry has a long history in Pakistan, the 1980s witnessed a sharp increase in the frequency and scope of this activity.[171] It was no longer the vocation of a few isolated individuals but rather involved organized gangs that were increasingly capable of eluding punishment by local authorities. The bandits are mostly migrants from the barren northern regions of Sind; many were once sharecroppers, but they lost their livelihoods because of multiple economic problems.

According to Christina Lamb, members of one group of bandits—operating in and around the forest of Dadu—describe their actions as driven by "a combination of the feudal system, unemployment and the difficulty of eking a living from the unforgiving land through which salinity is creeping like a white plague, rendering thousands more acres uncultivable each year."[172]

The bandits place their criminal activities in a context of revolt against a landed elite whose control over resources has combined with severe resource scarcity to threaten the livelihood of rural laborers. In other words, supply, demand, and structural scarcities conjoin to increase grievances and violence in rural areas.

Less obvious is the violence among tribal groups in the forest regions of the NWFP. The actions of the timber mafia have not only marginalized indigenous groups, but also produced conflict between haves and have-nots in forest areas. Growing protests from those threatened by the unchecked exploitation of the forests have led to reprisals by profiteers. Although widespread conflict has been avoided, incidents occur regularly.

Scarcity and Urban Violence

Urban violence represents the predominant form of civil strife in Pakistan today. There are many causes of this violence, and they are rooted in the particular configuration of geographical, economic, ethnic, and political forces shaping each city. Nevertheless, the rural-urban migration partly induced by rural environmental scarcities has worsened grievances among rival groups and classes in the cities. In combination with weakening state institutions, these rising grievances have raised the likelihood of violence.

High natural population growth and a rapid influx of migrants have pushed diverse and contending societal groups into close contact. Inequalities among economic classes and ethnic groups are therefore more obvious than would be the case in rural areas, and these inequalities are exacerbated by competition for exceedingly limited urban resources. The result is greater group affiliation and cohesion and violence along predominantly ethnic and class-based lines.[173]

Karachi exhibits these processes. While the Muhajirs continue to run much of the city's business and industry, they face increasing competition from other groups—for example, Punjabis. Pathans make up the majority of the working class and have gained a virtual monopoly over Karachi's transport sector. Retaining deeply rooted tribal traditions and support systems, they are in effect a separate state within the city. Meanwhile, the Sindhi minority has kept its dominance of provincial government and educational institutions through a system of quotas.

Rivalries among these groups are long-standing and flow largely from the relative position each group occupies and each group's efforts to maintain, if not improve, its status. The city's high urban growth rate—about three to four hundred thousand persons per year—has accentuated these conflicts. Local government is characterized by murky lines of authority, few taxing powers, rampant corruption, and little accountability.[174] It lacks the capacity and basic institutions needed to accommodate the demands of an expanding, diverse, and quarreling Karachi population. With institutionalized and peaceful channels of action on grievances unavailable, government legitimacy has plummeted. Popular loyalties and allegiances remain local, and efforts to redress grievances often take the form of ethnic and class-based violence. Such violence has been on the rise (table 5.11).

At times, an isolated, seemingly chance incident—for example, a traffic accident or a breakdown in services—serves to ignite turmoil. The cause of the mishap is attributed to a particular community and quickly escalates into a spiral of retaliation among contending ethnic groups. For instance, minibus accidents have sparked ethnic riots, owing to Pathan dominance of Karachi's transport sector. Fights between residents and an underfunded police force are also common; the fact that the police are heavily drawn from the northern provinces heightens ethnic tension. In one incident, the death of a Muhajir student triggered a succession of clashes between Muhajirs, police, and transporters that lasted over a month. By the time the situation was brought under control, over 40 had died and hundreds had been wounded in clashes.[175]

Frustration stemming from the lack of urban services in poorer areas of the city also prompts violence. Attacks on the offices of the Karachi Electric Supply Corporation and the Karachi Water and Sewage Board are common. In

TABLE 5.11
Trends in Violent Crimes in Karachi, Number of Incidents, 1990–94

Nature of Crime	Year				
	1990	1991	1992	1993	1994
Murder	584	466	387	365	1,113
Attempted Murder	1,035	814	672	646	1,069
Serious Injury	501	372	414	465	502
Kidnapping	572	352	373	345	276
Armed Robberies	2,557	2,483	2,211	2,191	1,464
Vehicle Snatching at Gunpoint	676	524	965	1,060	1,177

Source: Methab Karim, "Deaths Due to Violence in Karachi, Pakistan: Patterns, Differentials and Their Impact on the Community" (paper presented at the 22nd Annual Conference of the National Council for International Health, "Violence as a Global Health Issue," Washington, D.C., June 25–28, 1995), 3.

summer 1994, the city's overloaded electricity distribution system broke down—leaving entire areas of Karachi in darkness. But fear of violence deterred repairmen from providing help. Demonstrations against power shortages were organized. And in July 1994, violence erupted as police opened fire on angry crowds demanding better service.[176] The scarcities and inefficiencies of a decaying urban environment may thus act as a trigger by providing a specific incident—and a ready-made pretext—for the unleashing of ethnic or class-based hatreds.

Current Trends, Future Dangers

The general climate of insecurity pervading Karachi persists. Horizontal polarization of ethnic and religious groups is unabated, as is vertical polarization by economic stratum. The city's educational system is now crippled: some colleges have been forced to close, and others serve as armed strongholds for warring factions. Education is increasingly privatized and segregated along class lines.

Outbreaks of violence are increasingly common in Hyderabad, Islamabad, and Rawalpindi.[177] Some of this violence appears to involve similar scarcities of resources. In spring 1994, water shortages in Islamabad produced widespread protest, the hijacking of water trucks by residents in harder-hit poorer districts, and violent confrontations with police.[178] Moreover, in the NWFP, high natural population growth along with large influxes of Afghan refugees into such cities as Peshawar and Mingora is causing depletion of natural resources in surrounding areas and growing concern over the ability of urban infrastructure to handle the rising population. A recent report observes that in Mingora, a "shortage of basic services, narrow economic base, and bad governance have [had] visible impacts on the social fabric and [are] resulting in a steady decay of the urban environment and a growing sense of deprivation among the people."[179] This decay has bred a "highly volatile situation in and around Mingora."[180] Although widespread violence has been avoided, sporadic incidents have caused general worries about sharply deteriorating law and order.[181]

More broadly, there are mounting concerns over the potential for conflict arising from major development projects that promote national economic growth at the expense of local communities. A good example is the Ghazi-Barotha hydropower project. Consisting of a barrage, a power channel, and a 1,425-megawatt generating complex, the project aims to use the drop of the Indus River between the tailrace of the Tarbela Dam and the confluence of the Indus and Haro Rivers to produce electricity.[182] It promises to provide a much-needed renewable and emission-free source of energy to the country.

Yet the project will also cut off almost the entire downstream flow of water for seven months of the year, reducing the quantity to less than 12 percent of the current flow in the river during the dry season.[183] Environmental groups point out that planners have paid insufficient attention to the environmental, economic, and social consequences of the enterprise,[184] neglecting important questions concerning the project's impact on groundwater, on local water quality, and on a downstream population highly dependent on the river for economic and social activity.[185] The project could precipitate acts of violence against authorities by people in the affected communities.[186]

Such events may never come to pass, and evidence of environmental scarcity contributing to conflict in urban areas other than Karachi does not necessarily imply that such conflict will reach the scale or intensity of the violence witnessed in Karachi. The particular social, economic, and political context of each case crucially determines the likelihood and severity of conflict, and environmental scarcity never represents a sole cause of conflict. In recent years a number of grassroots initiatives have emerged to provide services to communities in need. Exemplary is the Orangi Pilot Project, which has created a series of community-based organizations to improve urban services and infrastructure in Orangi Township (Karachi's largest squatter settlement).[187] Since its creation in 1980, the project has evolved into a model of effective grass-roots development, with the community actively involved in the creation, financing, operation, and maintenance of an expanding sanitation system as well as housing, health, and welfare programs.[188] The project has attracted a number of national and international donors and has led to similar efforts in other areas, including Lahore and Faisalabad.[189]

Nevertheless, success stories remain few and far between, and they are in part noteworthy precisely because of their absence elsewhere. At the same time, promising official initiatives, such as the Pakistan National Conservation Strategy, confront problems of implementation due to political intransigence and lack of funds. Indeed, such realities, along with trends indicating a continuation of rapid population growth, declining resources, and rising shortfalls in services, suggest that scarcity-induced conflict—both rural and urban—will persist, if not increase, in years to come.

Conclusions

Much of the ethnic, communal, and class-based rivalry in Pakistan is intimately linked to the state—the manner in which it has evolved and its character, policies, and practices. Following independence, the country's leadership quickly adopted a state apparatus heavily weighted in favor of nonelected institutions and particular ethnic groups. This institutional structure, along with a pervasive lack of accountability and rampant corruption and patronage within government, progressively exacerbated regional, ethnic, class, and linguistic differences in the nation's population.

The imperatives of authoritarian central government overrode provincial rights and regional autonomy, Punjabi interests generally eclipsed those of other ethnic groups, and government elites and their supporters continually reaped the spoils of development with little regard for the needs of a rapidly growing population. Not surprisingly, political tension—in the form of regional, ethnic, and class conflicts—has long been a feature of the nation's landscape.

At the same time, certain characteristics of the Pakistani state worsened environmental scarcity, while others interacted with the resulting scarcities to produce resource capture, economic hardship, huge migrations of the poor from ecologically stressed rural areas into cities, and a weakening of the state's ability to respond to these rising challenges. The result has been an increase in group-identity and deprivation conflicts.

Ethnic and group rivalries have been increasingly urbanized, and grievances and opportunities for violence have correspondingly risen. Rival groups are increasingly pushed together in an urban context, heightening chances for interaction and intensifying competition for ever-more-scarce resources. All the while, legitimate channels for the resolution and prevention of conflict have grown weaker and weaker.

A lasting solution to this tangle of problems requires fundamental reforms to the state and its policies. In their absence, environmental scarcity will worsen and civil strife will probably increase. Scarcity could eventually become so severe that the conflict and institutional breakdown it generates become self-sustaining. In that event, the regime may try to divert attention from internal crisis by exacerbating tensions with its neighbors. Long-standing regional disputes (for instance, in Kashmir) would provide a ready pretext for such behavior. The potential dangers of such a course—for regional as well as global security—would be considerable.

Notes

An earlier version of this chapter was published as Peter Gizewski and Thomas Homer-Dixon, *Environmental Scarcity and Violent Conflict: The Case of Pakistan*, Occasional Paper of the Project on Environment, Population, and Security (Washington, D.C.: American Association for the Advancement of Science and the University of Toronto, 1996). The authors thank the Aga Khan University, Karachi, Pakistan, and the Sustainable Development Policy Institute (SDPI), Islamabad, Pakistan, for their support during the preparation of this study. Mohammad Tahir of SDPI provided particularly valuable comments and research assistance. We also thank David Runnalls, Tariq Banuri, Methab Karim, Francois Bregha, Roger Schwaas, Arthur Rubinoff, Iqbal Noor, John Dirks, Stephan Fuller, and Aban Marker Kabraji for additional suggestions and comments on earlier drafts.

1. Thomas Homer-Dixon, "Environmental Scarcities and Violent Conflict: Evidence from Cases," *International Security* 19, no. 1 (summer 1994): 5–40; Jack Goldstone, *Revolution and Rebellion in the Early Modern World* (Berkeley, Calif.: University of California Press, 1991).

2. See, for instance, Norman Myers, "Environmental Security: The Case of South Asia," *International Environmental Affairs* 1, no. 2 (spring 1989): 138–54.

3. For further elaboration, see Homer-Dixon, "Environmental Scarcities and Violent Conflict," 8–9.

4. See, for example, ibid.

5. Manzooruddin Ahmed, "Introduction," in *Contemporary Pakistan: Politics, Economy, and Society* (Durham, North Carolina: Carolina Academic Press, 1980), 3.

6. Ibid.

7. Arthur S. Banks, ed., *Political Handbook of the World: 1994–95* (New York: CSA Publications, 1994), 661.

8. Ibid., 664.

9. Ayesha Jalal, *Democracy and Authoritarianism in South Asia: A Comparative and Historical Perspective* (Lahore: Sang-E-Meel Publications, 1995), 23.

10. Ibid., 49.

11. Ibid., 49–50.

12. Ibid., 141.

13. Ibid., 37–38.

14. Ibid., 54.

15. Rasaul Bakhsh Rais, "Pakistan: Hope Amidst Turmoil," *Journal of Democracy* 5, no. 2 (April 1994): 134.

16. See for instance, ibid., 132–43. Similar optimism is expressed in Leo E. Rose, "Pakistan: Experiments with Democracy," in *Democracy in Developing Countries*, ed. Larry Diamond, Juan Linz, and Seymour Martin Lipset (London: Adamantine Press, 1989), 2: 105–41, and Robert LaPorte Jr., "Another Try at Democracy," in *Contemporary Problems in Pakistan*, ed. J. Henry Korson (Boulder, Colo.: Westview Press, 1993), 171–92.

17. Indeed, both ran afoul of President Ghulam Ishaq Khan, who, along with the army chief of staff, formed the "linchpin" of Pakistan's military-bureaucratic state structure. See Jalal, *Democracy and Authoritarianism*, 110–14.

18. In this regard, Ayesha Jalal notes that political processes remain hostage to a highly inequitable state structure. Continuing imbalances within the state and between the state and civil society "foreclose the possibility of a significant reapportioning of political power and economic resources in the very near future." See Jalal, *Democracy and Authoritarianism*, 121. Similar pessimism is expressed in S. John Tsagronis, *Pakistan: Prospects for Democracy* (Washington, D.C.: Hudson Institute, December 1992).

19. Jalal, *Democracy and Authoritarianism*, 49.

20. William Richter, "Pakistan," in *World Encyclopedia of Political Systems*, ed. George E. Debury (New York: Facts on File Ltd., 1987), 2: 839.

21. The major political parties are the Pakistan Muslim League (PML); the Pakistan People's Party (PPP), currently headed by Prime Minister Benazir Bhutto; and the Jamaat-e-Islami-Pakistan (JIP). Inter-party rivalries and splits have often led to the formation of broader coalitions. Examples include the Movement for the Restoration of Democracy (a loose coalition of forces opposing the PPP and the regime of General Mohammed Zia ul-Haq during the 1980s) and the more recently formed Islamic Democratic Alliance, led by PML majority-faction leader and former Prime Minister Nawaz Sharif.

22. Parvez Hassan, "The Growth of Environmental Consciousness in Pakistan," in *Beyond Shifting Sands: The Environment in India and Pakistan*, ed. The World Conservation Union (New Delhi: Centre for Science and the Environment and IUCN, May 1994), 7.

23. Shahid Javed Burki, "Pakistan's Economic Performance," in *Contemporary Problems in Pakistan*, ed. J. Henry Korson (Boulder, Colo.: Westview Press, 1993), 9.

24. See World Bank, *Trends in Developing Economies* (Washington, D.C.: The World Bank, 1994), 384.

25. Jalal, *Democracy and Authoritarianism*, 142–45.

26. Ibid., 192.

27. See for instance, ibid., 156.

28. These reforms included the abolition of the "one-unit" through which Punjab, Sindi, the NWFP, and Baluchistan had been merged into West Pakistan, the establishment of a one-person–one-vote system, and recognition of East Pakistan's larger population through allotment of more seats to that province in the National Assembly. See LaPorte, "Another Try at Democracy," 176.

29. The Kalabaugh Dam is a case in point. Conceived in 1953, it was supposed to be constructed on the border between Punjab and the NWFP. However, the project quickly bogged down in endless interprovincial haggling. Punjabi support for the dam was opposed by the NWFP on grounds that it would flood villages around Nowshera

and Attock. Sind and Baluchistan warned that the dam would lower water levels and cause drought further down the Indus. The dispute continues to this day. While countless rupees have been wasted on surveys of even less suitable sites, the country's power deficit worsens. See Christina Lamb, *Waiting for Allah: Pakistan's Struggle for Democracy* (New Delhi: Penguin Books, 1991), 182.

30. Ibid., 148–49.

31. For a good general discussion, see Feroz Ahmed, "Pakistan's Problems of National Integration: The Case of Sind," in *Regional Imbalances and the National Question in Pakistan*, ed. S. Akbar Zaidi (Lahore: Vanguard Books, 1992), 163–65.

32. Aziz Siddiqui, "Sparring with the Enemy," *Newsline*, July 1995, 29.

33. Pakistan has failed to conduct a census since 1981, in part because of the implications new census numbers could have for the relative power of ethnic groups in various political, economic, and social institutions.

34. Siddiqui, "Sparring with the Enemy," 30.

35. As reported in Robert E. Looney and David Winterford, *Economic Causes and Consequences of Defense Expenditures in the Middle East and South Asia* (Boulder, Colo.: Westview Press, 1994), 193.

36. Omar Noman, "The Impact of Migration on Pakistan's Economy and Society," in *Economy and Culture in Pakistan: Migrants and Cities in Muslim Society*, ed. Hastings Doonan and Prina Werbner (London: Macmillan, 1991), 79. See also Jonathan S. Addleton, *Undermining the Centre: The Gulf Migration and Pakistan* (Karachi: Oxford University Press, 1992), 113–35.

37. Shabruki Rufi Khan and Safiya Aftab, *Structural Adjustment and the Poor in Pakistan*, Sustainable Development Policy Institute Research Report 8 (Islamabad: Sustainable Development Policy Institute, January 1995), 4.

38. See Ahmed Rashid, "Begging to Differ," *The Herald* (Karachi), July 1995, 80.

39. As reported in Akmal Hussain, *Strategic Issues in Pakistan's Economic Policy* (Lahore: Progressive Publishers, 1988), 8.

40. See Aftab Ahmad Khan, "Unemployment Rising Unabatedly Needs Effective Emergent Measures for Containment," *The News* (Karachi), 1 April 1995, 9.

41. Khawar Mumtaz and Mehjabeen Abidi-Habib, *Pakistan's Environment: A Historical Perspective and Selected Bibliography with Annotations* (Karachi: Joint Research Council–International Union for the Conservation of Nature Pakistan, 1989), 9–10.

42. Ibid., 10.

43. Part of the problem lies in the huge capital requirements of such megaprojects—a feature that automatically calls for high-level, centralized decision making in government as well as considerable foreign backing and input. These characteristics tend not only to shrink opportunities for local community involvement but also to encourage corruption by increasing the number of governmental and financial agencies likely to demand kickbacks for the project's completion. See Sungi Development Foundation, *Ghazi-Barotha Hydro Power Project: A Report on the Key Issues* (Islamabad: Sungi Development Foundation, 1995), 6–7.

44. Government of Pakistan, *The Pakistan National Conservation Strategy* (Karachi: Government of Pakistan/Joint Research Council–International Union for the Conservation of Nature Pakistan, 1992), 68.

45. Ibid., 70.

46. Ibid., 69.

47. Ibid., 70.

48. Ibid., 68.

49. Ibid., 21.

50. As reported in G. R. Sandhu, *Sustainable Agriculture: A Pakistan National Conservation Strategy Sector Paper* (Karachi: IUCN-The World Conservation Union, 1992), 35.

51. Government of Pakistan, *The Pakistan National Conservation Strategy* (Karachi: GOP/JRC-IUCN Pakistan, 1992), 21–22.

52. Ibid., 26.

53. See Arif Hasan and Amenah Azam Ali, *Environmental Repercussions of Development in Pakistan* (Karachi: OPP-RTI, March 1993), 35.

54. Global Assessment of Soil Degradation, *World Map on the Status of Human-Induced Soil Degradation*, Sheet 2, Europe, Africa and West Central Asia (Nairobi, Kenya/Wageningen, The Netherlands: United Nations Environment Programme/ International Soil Reference Center, 1990).

55. "Salinity" is the accumulation of salts in a given amount of water or soil, primarily due to overirrigation and a lack of adequate drainage. See Peter Collin, *Dictionary of Ecology and the Environment* (London: P. Collin Publishers, 1988), 158, and Andy Crump, *Dictionary of Environment and Development* (London: Earthscan, 1991), 219–20. "Sodicity" refers to the impact of high concentrations of sodium on soil. While saline soils generally have normal properties, sodic soils undergo physicochemical reactions that cause the slaking of aggregates and the swelling and dispersion of clay materials, leading to reduced permeability and poor tilth. The loss of permeability may so restrict water infiltration into the root zone that plants become stressed from lack of water. Crusting can also impede seedling emergence and reduce crop stand. For an extended discussion, see Kenneth K. Tanji, ed., *Agricultural Salinity Assessment and Management* (New York: American Society of Civil Engineers, 1990), 18–28.

56. Government of Pakistan, *The Pakistan National Conservation Strategy*, 26.

57. For an in-depth discussion of these disputes and the eight years of negotiations that led to their successful resolution, see Niranjan D. Gulhati, *The Indus Waters Treaty: An Exercise in International Mediation* (New York: Allied Publishers, 1973).

58. Pakistan Administrative Staff College, *Environmental Issues and Problems in Pakistan*, National Management Paper (Lahore: Pakistan Administrative Staff College, July 1994), 46.

59. Ibid., 47.

60. Ibid.

61. Ibid.

62. Ibid.

63. Government of Pakistan, *The Pakistan National Conservation Strategy*, 39.

64. Ibid.

65. Pakistan Administrative Staff College, *Environmental Issues and Problems*, 48. See also Government of Pakistan, *The Pakistan National Conservation Strategy*, 80.

66. Pakistan Administrative Staff College, *Environmental Issues and Problems*, 48.

67. Zafar Samdani, "Bigger Power Crisis in the Offing," *The Globe* (Karachi), July 1994, 26.

68. Government of Pakistan, *The Pakistan National Conservation Strategy*, 33.

69. Ibid.

70. Ibid.

71. Ibid., xvi. According to agricultural specialists, the level of forested area should be between 20 and 25 percent of a nation's total land area. See Tom Rogers, "Population Growth and Movement in Pakistan: A Case Study," *Asian Survey* 30, no. 5 (May 1990): 457.

72. "Deforestation Enigma—Afforestation Drives," *The Muslim* (Peshawar), 21 July 1995, 1.

73. As reported in ibid.

74. Arif Hasan and Amenah Azam Ali, "Environmental Problems in Pakistan: Their Origins, Development and the Threats They Pose to Sustainable Development," *Environment and Urbanization* 4, no. 1 (April 1992): 13.

75. Sandhu, *Sustainable Agriculture*, 26.

76. Hasan and Ali, "Environmental Problems," 13.

77. Ibid.

78. Water and Development Authority, *National Power Plan Pakistan* (Islamabad: Government of Pakistan and the Canadian International Development Agency, April 1994), 2–2.

79. Hasan and Ali, *Environmental Repercussions*, 31.

80. Mudassar Imran and Philip Barnes, *Energy Demand in the Developing Countries: Prospects for the Future*, World Bank Staff Commodity Working Paper 23 (Washington, D.C.: The World Bank, 1990), 41.

81. Ibid., 32.

82. Sungi Development Foundation, *Ghazi-Barotha Hydro Power Project*, 2.

83. Loadshedding occurs when managers of an electricity grid deliberately reduce the flow of electricity to some parts of the grid because total electricity demand across the grid exceeds total supply.

84. As reported in Sandhu, *Sustainable Agriculture*, 34–35.

85. Sungi Development Foundation, *Forests, Wealth and Politics: A Focus on Hazara* (Islamabad: Sungi Development Foundation, April 1995), 1.

86. Finance Division, Government of Pakistan, *Economic Survey 1992–93* (Islamabad: Government of Pakistan, June 1993), 2.

87. Arif Hasan, "Karachi and the Global Nature of Urban Violence," *The Urban Age* 1, no. 4 (summer 1993): 4.

88. Syed Ayub Qutub, "Rapid Population Growth and Urban Problems in Pakistan," *Ambio* 21, no. 1 (February 1992): 47.

89. As reported in Jalal, *Democracy and Authoritarianism*, 143.

90. Hasan and Ali, "Environmental Problems," 11.

91. Prior attempts at land reform failed entirely. In 1952–53, for instance, Punjab's bigger landlords subverted an attempt by the progressive wing of the Muslim League to initiate redistributive reforms by refusing to bring their produce to market and by precipitating a "man-made" famine in the province. See Jalal, *Democracy and Authoritarianism*, 145.

92. Ibid., 147.

93. As reported in John Adams, "Population and Urbanization," in *Foundations of*

Pakistan's Political Economy: Towards an Agenda for the 1990s, ed. William E. James and Subroto Roy (New Delhi: Sage Publications, 1992), 245.

94. Pakistan Administrative Staff College, *Environmental Issues and Problems*, 43.

95. Hussain, *Strategic Issues*, 186–87.

96. Pakistan Administrative Staff College, *Environmental Issues and Problems*, 43.

97. Sungi Development Foundation, *Forests, Wealth and Politics*, 1–3.

98. Ibid., 4.

99. Ibid., 44.

100. Pakistan Administrative Staff College, *Environmental Issues and Problems*, 52. See also, Sungi Development Foundation, *Forests, Wealth and Politics*.

101. United Nations Department of International, Economic and Social Affairs, *Population Growth and Policies in Mega-Cities: Karachi*, Population Policy Paper 13 (New York: United Nations, 1988), 18.

102. See, for instance, Lamb, *Waiting for Allah*, 151–52. Nor are businesses and merchants excluded from such exploitation. According to Arif Hasan, a recent study of the Saddar area of Karachi reveals that the police and local administration collect over PRs 110 million a month (US$3.4 million) as bhatta (tribute) from hawkers and encroachers (including beggars). See Arif Hasan, "What Is Karachi Really Fighting For?" *The Herald* (Karachi), September 1995, 62.

103. See Nafisa Shah, "Karachi Breakdown," *Newsline*, July 1994, 35, 37.

104. As reported in Ahmed Rashid, "Mean Streets: Chaos and Violence Rule in Karachi," *Far Eastern Economic Review* 157, no. 43 (27 October 1994): 19.

105. Ibid., 152.

106. See Sandhu, *Sustainable Agriculture*, 36.

107. Ibid., 36–37.

108. Kenneth Fernandes, "Katchi Adabis: Living on the Edge," *Environment and Urbanization* 6, no. 1 (April 1994): 51; Environment and Urban Affairs Division, Government of Pakistan, *Pakistan National Report to the United Nations Conference on Environment and Development: August, 1991* (Karachi: Government of Pakistan–Joint Research Council, 1991), 11.

109. According to field surveys, 33 percent of poorer farmers (those with less than three hectares of land) reported a decline in the quantity of their diet, and a full 67 percent indicated a drop in its quality. See Hussain, *Strategic Issues*, 286.

110. Ibid.

111. Sandhu, *Sustainable Agriculture*, 1.

112. Ibid.

113. Ibid.

114. For example, while seven good harvests allowed the government to boast self-sufficiency and an export capacity in wheat from 1977 through 1982, poor harvests the following year threw agriculture into crisis, as the annual average growth rate fell from 3.9 percent to minus 6.14 percent for 1983–84. See Hussain, *Strategic Issues*, 6.

115. As reported in Tom Rogers, "Population Growth and Movement in Pakistan: A Case Study," *Asian Survey* 30, no. 5 (May 1990): 457.

116. Ministry of Food and Agriculture, Government of Pakistan, *Report of the National Commission on Agriculture* (Islamabad: Government of Pakistan, March 1988), xxxv–xxxvi.

117. Government of Pakistan, *The Pakistan National Conservation Strategy*, 113.

118. Ibid., 240.

119. Ibid.

120. Sandhu, *Sustainable Agriculture*, 36.

121. Sajid Akhtar, Senior Research Economist, Applied Economics Research Centre, University of Karachi, Karachi, Pakistan, interview, 19 September 1995.

122. World Bank, Agricultural Operations Division, South Asia Region, *Pakistan: A Strategy for Sustainable Agricultural Growth*, Report 13092-PAK (Washington, D.C.: World Bank, November 1994), 32.

123. See, for instance, National Institute of Population Studies, *Pakistan Demographic and Health Survey: 1990–1991* (Islamabad: National Institute of Population Studies, July 1992), 4, 12.

124. As reported in Hasan and Ali, "Environmental Problems," 16.

125. See M. Nawaz Tariq and Waris Ali, *Managing Municipal Wastes: A Pakistan National Conservation Strategy Sector Paper* (Karachi: IUCN-The World Conservation Union, Pakistan, 1993), 7.

126. Hastings Donnan and Prina Werbner, "Introduction," in *Economy and Culture in Pakistan: Migrants and Cities in Muslim Society*, ed. Hastings Donnan and Prina Werbner (London: Macmillan, 1991), 11.

127. See Sandhu, *Sustainable Agriculture*, 36.

128. Qutub, "Rapid Population Growth," 47.

129. Ibid.

130. Sandhu, *Sustainable Agriculture*, 37.

131. Ibid.

132. United Nations Department of International, Economic and Social Affairs, *Population Growth and Policies in Mega-Cities*, 24.

133. Ibid., 25.

134. Ibid.

135. Kamran Zakaria, "KESC—It's Time to Ponder," *The Globe* (Karachi), July 1994, 37.

136. Ibid., 28.

137. Ibid.

138. Hasan and Ali, "Environmental Problems," 16.

139. Tariq and Ali, *Managing Municipal Wastes*, 1.

140. Hasan and Ali, "Environmental Problems," 15.

141. Ibid.

142. Government of Pakistan, *The Pakistan National Conservation Strategy*, 83.

143. Tariq and Ali, *Managing Municipal Wastes*, 5.

144. Ibid.

145. Thomas Homer-Dixon, "Environmental Scarcities and Violent Conflict."

146. Ibid., 25.

147. Government of Pakistan, *The Pakistan National Conservation Strategy*, 108.

148. Ibid., 110.

149. Ibid.

150. Ibid.

151. Ibid.

152. World Bank, *Trends in Developing Economies*, 384.

153. Sandhu, *Sustainable Agriculture*, 37.

154. See Environment and Urban Affairs Division, Government of Pakistan, *Pakistan National Report*, 31.

155. As reported in Sungi Development Foundation, *Ghazi-Barotha Hydro Power Project*, 2.

156. Zafar Samdani, "Bigger Power Crisis in the Offing," *The Globe* (Karachi), 24 July 1994, 27; K. Qamar and A. Abidi, "Electric Blues," *Newsline*, July 1994, 50.

157. Government of Pakistan, *The Pakistan National Conservation Strategy*, 110.

158. United Nations Department of International, Economic and Social Affairs, *Population Growth and Policies in Mega-Cities*, 19.

159. Ibid.

160. Ibid., 34.

161. Kathy Evans, "Frankenstein's Monsters Terrorize Karachi," *Manchester Guardian Weekly*, 2 April 1995, 7.

162. See Hasan, "What Is Karachi Really Fighting For?" 59.

163. See for instance, Akmal Hussain, "The Karachi Riots of December 1986: Crisis of State and Civil Society in Pakistan," in *Mirrors of Violence: Communities, Riots and Survivors in South Asia*, ed. Veena Das (New York: Oxford University Press, 1990), 205.

164. Azhar Abbas, "Return of the Dacoit?" *The Herald* (Karachi), May 1995, 26–30, 32–33.

165. Ibid., 32. See also "Sindh: Dacoits Active Again," *The News* (Karachi), 29 May 1995, 7.

166. Arif Hasan, "Karachi and the Global Nature of Urban Violence," *The Urban Age* 1, no. 4 (summer 1993): 6.

167. Adams, "Population and Urbanization," 254.

168. "Asia's Answer to Beirut," *The Economist* 336, no. 7921 (1 July 1995): 30.

169. Farhan Bokhari, "Ripple Effect," *The Herald* (Karachi), July 1995, 48.

170. Ibid. See also Farhan Bokhari, "Pakistan—Effects of Karachi," *The Nation*: Islamabad, 31 July 1995, 25.

171. With the notable exception of the dacoits, rural violence has tended to be confined to familial conflicts and isolated disputes over land. See Pervaiz Naeem Tariq and Naeem Durrani, *Socio-Psychological Aspects of Crime in Pakistan*, Psychological Research Monograph 1 (Islamabad: National Institute of Psychology, 1983), 103–106.

172. Lamb, *Waiting for Allah*, 121.

173. Migrants entering cities will not necessarily experience the highest levels of relative deprivation or be those most likely to engage in violent activity. Evidence suggests that newly arriving migrants generally regard urban life as an improvement over their previous rural existence. See, for instance, Yoshifumi Usami, "Rural-Urban Migration and Employment in Karachi and Islamabad," in *Migration in Pakistan: Theories and Facts*, ed. Fritz Selier and Methab Karim (Lahore: Vanguard Books, 1986), 81–82. Nevertheless, heavy migration increases the number of diverse, competing groups within the urban setting and reduces resources available to the urban population as a whole. These processes raise the probability that certain groups—whether migrants or others—will eventually come to perceive themselves as seriously deprived in relation to neighboring groups.

174. For instance, the Karachi Metropolitan Corporation, the body charged with providing essential facilities to the city's residents, has long served as a vehicle for patronage, providing jobs for political activists. Thousands of the corporation's employees have no specific work to do. Almost half of the corporation's budget is spent on salaries, while one-quarter is allocated to development, and reports indicate that over 40 percent of this development budget is lost in pilferage. See Zahid Hussain, "A City Betrayed," *Newsline*, July 1994, 52.

175. Abbas Rashid and Farida Saheed, *Pakistan: Ethno-Politics and Contending Elites*, United Nations Research Institute for Social Development Discussion Paper 45 (New York: United Nations, June 1993), 21–22.

176. Nafia Shah, "Karachi Breakdown," *Newsline*, July 1994, 34.

177. Pakistan Administrative Staff College, *Environmental Issues and Problems*, 48.

178. Quadssi Akhlaque, "It's Tanker Warfare, Capital Flight," *The Nation* (Islamabad), 1, 9. Reports from rural villages in Digri indicate a rise in protest due to closures of water courses and canals. In Mirpurkhas Division, farmers demonstrated against the Irrigation Department for its seeming apathy. See "Farmers Protest Against Water Crisis," *The News* (Karachi), 30 September 1995, 11.

179. Hameed Hasan, "Imperatives of Urban Planning: A Case Study of Mingora," unpublished paper, International Union for the Conservation of Nature–Sarhad Provincial Conservation Strategy Unit, Peshawar, Pakistan, October 1995, 2.

180. Ibid., 2–3.

181. Stephen Fuller, Chief Technical Adviser, IUCN-SPCS Unit, Planning Environment and Development Department, Civil Secretariat, Peshawar, Pakistan, interview, 5 October 1995.

182. For more detailed discussion, see Mohammad Zubair Khan, *The Devastating Impact of Ghazi-Barotha Project on Downstream Water Resources*, Working Paper 21 (Islamabad: Sustainable Development Policy Institute, 1995), and Sungi Development Foundation, *Ghazi-Barotha Hydro Power Project*.

183. Khan, *Devastating Impact of Ghazi-Barotha Project*, 1.

184. Ibid.

185. Ibid., 4–5.

186. Tariq Banuri, Executive Director, Sustainable Development Policy Institute, Islamabad, Pakistan, interview, 9 October 1995.

187. Hasan and Ali, "Environmental Problems," 96–97.

188. Ibid., 98.

189. Ibid., 98–99.

6

The Case of Rwanda

Valerie Percival and Thomas Homer-Dixon

Overview

Some commentators have claimed that environmental and demographic factors were powerful forces behind the recent civil violence in Rwanda.[1] We believe that much of this commentary has been too simplistic.

It is true that Rwanda is predominantly a rural-based society that relies on agriculture to sustain its economy and consequently is vulnerable to the effects of environmental stress.[2] Environmental degradation and population growth are critical issues in Rwanda; before the recent violence, they clearly threatened the welfare of the general population. On first impression, therefore, the recent genocide in Rwanda appears to be a clear case of environmental and population pressures producing social stress, which in turn resulted in violent conflict. But on closer study, this is not an adequate explanation of the genocide. Environmental degradation and high population levels contributed to migrations, declining agricultural productivity, and the weakening of the legitimacy of President Juvenal Habyarimana's regime. *However, many factors were operating in this conflict, and environmental and population pressures had at most a limited, aggravating role.*

We begin with an overview of the recent violence in Rwanda. We analyze the social effects of this scarcity and then discuss the evolution of ethnicity in Rwanda. We present three hypotheses outlining some possible links between scarcity and conflict in the Rwandan context and show how these hypotheses cannot fully explain the events following the 6 April assassination of the president. We conclude by offering a fourth explanation that identifies a more limited role for environmental scarcity and places it in the context of the many other factors that led to the genocide.

Background

Civil War: 1990–1992

The recent violence within Rwanda had its origins in the October 1990 attack by the Rwandan Patriotic Front (RPF) from their bases in Uganda. Predominantly of Tutsi origin, many of the members of the RPF were refugees, or descendants of refugees, who fled Rwanda during the postcolonial establishment of a Hutu-dominated government in the early 1960s. The RPF proved to be a skilled fighting force; its leadership and soldiers had gained valuable military experience fighting with Yoweri Museveni's National Resistance Army in western Uganda. After the expatriates from Rwanda participated in the successful overthrow of Ugandan leader Milton Obote in 1985, they created the RPF. The front's leaders timed an invasion of Rwanda from Uganda to exploit growing domestic opposition against the regime of President Habyarimana.[3] After some initial setbacks, by 1992 the RPF had captured a significant portion of northern Rwanda.[4]

The RPF's invasion and the subsequent two years of civil war placed a great deal of stress on the Rwandan government and its citizens. At the same time, international lenders forced the government to implement a structural adjustment policy, which, coupled with a drought in the early 1990s, fueled domestic opposition to the Habyarimana regime. Simultaneously, therefore, the government faced a threat from the RPF and growing pressure for democratization within Rwanda spurred, in part, by the structural adjustment policy. It systematically arrested anyone suspected of antigovernment sentiments; over 8,000 people were arrested immediately after the invasion. The slow movement toward multiparty democracy ended; local authorities began to actively promote and lead attacks on Tutsi and all those who opposed the government.[5] By 1992, the civil war had displaced one-tenth of the population, and the RPF controlled key tea-, coffee-, and food-producing areas, which greatly reduced government revenues.[6]

As the civil war continued in the north, opposition to the government increased in Kigali. International donors also placed Habyarimana under significant pressure to increase democratization measures and begin a dialogue with the RPF. Habyarimana responded in two ways. First, he introduced a multiparty system and a coalition government in April 1992, but he was able to juggle alliances to retain control of the state apparatus. Second, he conspired with the two political parties that he controlled, the National Republican Movement for Democracy and Development (MRND) and the Hutu-extremist Committee for the Defense of the Republic (CDR), to undermine the democratization and peace processes. Together they formed militias known as the Interahamwe (those who attack together) and the Impuzamugambi (those who have the same goal). The militias received weapons from the army and killed hundreds of civilians suspected of antigovernment activities.[7]

Negotiation and the Arusha Accords, 1992–1994

On 31 July 1992, a precarious cease-fire came into effect in the civil war and negotiations between the RPF and the government began in earnest in Arusha, Tanzania.[8] These negotiations were concluded in August 1993, and the agreement provided for the formation of a broad-based transitional government. The RPF and the Rwandan army together would form a smaller, united national army.[9] Although Habyarimana would remain president during the transition period, specified ministerial positions were allocated to members of the RPF and other political parties. Elections were scheduled to be held twenty-two months after the transitional government took office.[10] Many members of the Habyarimana government, including the CDR, were unhappy with the results of the Arusha negotiations. The accords gave the RPF much power: RPF members would control key ministries and would hold a great deal of influence in the army.

Habyarimana continued his two-track policy: he appeared to cooperate with international efforts to implement the Arusha Accords while simultaneously working to maintain his hold on power through the militias.[11] Habyarimana and the CDR used every possible opportunity to increase social cleavages to create animosity toward the RPF. Two events were exploited to their fullest to incite anti-RPF and anti-Tutsi sentiments. The October 1993 massacres in Burundi were used to create and fuel fears of the RPF—the killings were to a large degree carried out by Burundi's Tutsi-dominated army. And on 21 February 1994, Felicien Gatabazi, the leader of Rwanda's Social Democratic Party, was killed by assassins. In retaliation, a senior CDR official in Gatabazi's hometown was murdered. The CDR quickly organized violence in Kigali; CDR members killed several hundred people, and the majority of those targeted were Tutsi.[12]

Genocide: April to July 1994

On 6 April 1994, Habyarimana's plane exploded in the skies above Kigali. Although those responsible for Habyarimana's death have not yet been identified, Belgian peacekeepers reported seeing two rockets fired toward his plane from the vicinity of a camp belonging to the Rwandan Presidential Guard and army commandos.[13] Within hours of the plane crash, the Presidential Guard, the army, the Interahamwe, and the Impuzamugambi mounted roadblocks. They attempted to exploit the death of Habyarimana and to use it as a spark to ignite an anti-Tutsi backlash. The army and militias began a systematic sweep of the city, killing members of the transitional government and other civilians.[14] The killings had three goals: to eliminate the opposition, to eradicate the country of all Tutsi, and to continue fighting the RPF.[15] The UN forces, present in Rwanda to monitor the implementation of the Arusha Accords, lacked the mandate to act decisively and were refused permission by the UN Security Council to intervene in the massacres. Forced to withdraw from the streets of Kigali, they could only provide shelter and food, but not necessarily protection, for Rwandans hiding from the government troops.[16] Much of the United Nations' attention became focused on establishing a cease-fire between the government forces and the RPF, rather than on stopping the massacre of civilians by the militias and their followers.[17]

From Kigali, the violence spread quickly throughout the country—planned, ordered, and encouraged by the army and Rwandan government officials.[18] The RPF responded with an offensive from the north; by July it had taken control of most of the country and established an interim government,[19] which included many members of the transitional government initially established by the Arusha Accords.[20] Members of the former Habyarimana government, the army, and the militias fled first to the zone established by French troops in the southwest of the country and then to the refugee camps in Zaire (now Republic of Congo) and Tanzania.[21]

The Refugee Camps: August 1994 to June 1995

The former government claims that it is the only body able to represent the predominantly Hutu refugees.[22] At a meeting in early October in Bukavu, Zaire, members of the former government, the former Rwandan army, and the militias decided to take control of the camps. The new Rwandan government and the United Nations have made significant efforts to encourage the two million refugees to go back to Rwanda, yet the refugees are afraid to return. Those refugees who have expressed the desire to go back have been threatened or killed by the militias. The militias also instill refugees with the fear that they will be killed by the RPF upon their return.[23] In the absence of consistent or solid support from the international community, the UN Office of the High Commissioner for Refugees (UNHCR) and other aid groups have been forced to accept the authority of the militias. The militias have taken control of the distribution of humanitarian relief and constantly harass and threaten aid workers.[24] In late September 1994, Care Canada withdrew from the refugee camps in Katale, north of Goma, when its staff received death threats.[25] On 15 November 1994, Médecins Sans Frontières left five camps that had been taken over by approximately 30,000 Hutu troops threatening aid workers and brutalizing refugees.[26]

Reports from Rwanda and refugee camps in Zaire and Tanzania suggest that extensive violence may soon explode again. Médecins Sans Frontières has reported that open military training activities and stocks of arms continue to appear in the camps. They conclude that the former Rwandan forces are preparing for a military offensive in the near future.[27] This conclusion is shared by the UN secretary-general, who stated in a recent report: "It is believed that [the militias and former army members] may be preparing for an armed invasion of Rwanda and that they may be stockpiling and selling food distributed by relief agencies in preparation for such an invasion."[28] Reports also indicate that the RPF's control of its troops in the Rwandan countryside is precarious and cite instances of backlash attacks by some RPF members against Hutu. The RPF and the transitional government established by the RPF are finding it difficult to police or stop these revenge attacks due to a lack of resources and insufficient support from UN troops.[29] The Rwandan government, backed to a certain extent by the UNHCR, is promoting the closure of refugee camps to ensure that the spring planting is completed and to promote stability. The UNHCR has already shut down one camp in southwestern Rwanda;[30] reportedly, all the residents moved to a neighboring refugee camp, rather than return home. It remains to be seen whether Rwanda can peacefully absorb the return of over a million refugees, some of whom are armed and have the intention of destabilizing the new government, if and when the remaining camps are closed.

Environmental Scarcity

Supply-induced Scarcity

Rwanda's ecosystem is extremely diverse, which makes it difficult to generalize about its vulnerability to population pressures and resource degradation. Rwanda is part of the Great East African Plateau; from swamps and lakes along the Tanzanian border, the plateau rises toward the highlands in the northwest and southwest. The country has a moderate climate, with temperature varying according to altitude. Precipitation is sporadic in the east but is more regular in the west.[31] The steep slopes of the western region are vulnerable to erosion, and some of Rwanda's worst environmental degradation is found in the southwest.[32] The central area of the country has been settled and cultivated for centuries, whereas the eastern portion of the country was traditionally the cattle-grazing area and has only recently been brought under cultivation. Due to the low precipitation in this area, agricultural production is unreliable.[33]

Prior to the recent conflict, soil fertility had fallen sharply in some parts of Rwanda. Half of the farming in Rwanda occurred on hillsides with slopes of more than 10 percent; these areas were vulnerable to erosion, particularly under conditions of intense cultivation. On the steepest slopes, heavy rainfall eroded more than eleven tonnes of soil per hectare per year with twelve million tonnes of soil washing into Rwanda's rivers every year.[34] Although erosion was serious in some parts of Rwanda, soil character in other parts of the country kept erosion moderate.[35] In general, rather than erosion, overcultivation appears to have been the principal factor behind falling fertility. Grosse notes that "the major perceived cause of decreasing soil fertility in Rwanda is depletion of soil nutrients by cultivation rather than erosion. Even in Ruhengeri, where erosion is the most severe, farmers mention soil exhaustion as a problem much more often than erosion."[36]

Forest and water scarcity were also serious. Forests cover only 7 percent of the country. Although deforestation rates decreased in recent years, in 1986 the Forestry Department estimated that Rwanda was annually using 2.3 million cubic meters of wood more than it was producing. Ninety-one percent of wood consumption was for domestic use,[37] and the scarcity of fuelwood for cooking was evident as peasants substituted animal manure and crop wastes for fuelwood.[38] Although the Rwandan government began a reforestation campaign, the tree usually planted was eucalyptus, which consumes large amounts of water and nutrients. Water resources were further constrained as watersheds and wetland areas were lost. These problems were compounded, especially in the southern regions of the country, by several droughts in the 1980s and early 1990s.[39] The impact of water scarcity on agriculture was harshest in arid regions, but in other areas water shortages became critical for personal, domestic, and industrial needs.[40]

Demand-induced Scarcity

Until the recent civil violence and mass refugee flows, Rwanda had a high population density and growth rate. In 1992, Rwanda's population was 7.5 million, with a growth rate estimated at 3.3 percent per year from 1985 to 1990.[41] The population density was roughly 290 inhabitants per square kilometer—among the highest in Africa; the per hectare density was 3.2 people in 1993.[42] If lakes, national parks, and forest reserves are excluded from this calculation, the figure increases to 422 people per square kilometer.[43] However, the 1990 census determined that the birth rate was declining sharply. It dropped from 54.1 to 45.9 per thousand, as couples delayed marriage and decided to limit the number of their children. Poor and deteriorating economic circumstances due to worsening land shortages, few opportunities off the farm, and declining agricultural productivity influenced decisions to have fewer children. The decline in birth rates was most dramatic in the southwest and northwest.[44]

Before the recent violence, most Rwandans relied almost exclusively on renewable resources, such as agricultural land, to sustain themselves. Ninety-five percent of the population lived in the countryside and 90 percent of the labor force relied on agriculture as its primary means of livelihood.[45] Rural-urban migration was not significant; only 6 percent of Rwanda's population lived in urban areas in 1990, and the annual urban growth rate decreased from 5.6 percent in the period 1955–60 to 4.9 percent in the years 1985–90.[46]

Social Effects of Environmental Scarcity

With a large and dense population dependent for its livelihood on extraction of natural resources from a deteriorating resource base, Rwanda clearly exhibited both demand- and supply-induced environmental scarcity; structural scarcity was not serious, since land was quite evenly distributed throughout the population.[47] Supply-induced scarcity resulted from falling levels of soil fertility, degradation of watersheds, and depletion of forests. Demand-induced scarcity was caused by too many people relying on Rwanda's low supply of land, fuelwood, and water resources.[48]

These environmental scarcities began to cause the social effects Homer-Dixon identifies: agricultural production started to decrease, migrations out of areas of intense environmental stress were commonplace, and the state began to lose legitimacy.[49]

Declining Agricultural Production

By the late 1980s, environmental scarcity caught up with Rwandan agriculture. Supply- and demand-induced scarcity gravely stressed the ability of food production to keep pace with population growth. The agricultural frontier had closed. There was little land available for agricultural expansion, and the number of people placing demands on existing cropland increased. Farmers were forced to increase the intensity of agriculture, and they began to cultivate their fields two to three times per year.[50]

In terms of per capita food production, Rwanda was transformed from one of sub-Saharan Africa's top three performers in the early 1980s to one of its worst in the late 1980s.[51] Food output had risen 4.7 percent annually from 1966 to 1982, outpacing the average population growth rate of 3.4 percent.[52] But much of this rise resulted from an expansion of cropland area and a reduction in fallow periods, not from an increase in technical inputs, such as fertilizer and improved seeds.[53] These trends continued in the 1980s: Rwanda's cropland area increased by 12.9 percent between 1981 and 1991 and fertilizer use remained negligible.[54] By the late 1980s, however, most available land was under cultivation, as rural migrations had established a relatively even distribution of population across the countryside.[55] As the agricultural frontier closed and population continued to grow, per capita agricultural output began to drop.[56] Although total output increased by 10 percent from the early 1980s to the early 1990s, per capita output fell nearly 20 percent.[57]

As a result of these factors, there was not enough food in the southern and western parts of the country. In 1989, 300,000 people, predominantly southerners, needed food aid due to crop failure. Analysts anticipated another food crisis in 1994:

The US Embassy estimated in early April that 1994 production would fall 9 to 17 percent below the 1990–93 average of 4.38 million metric tons because of drought and that the total 1994 food crop shortfall could run to 150,000 to 320,000 metric tons. Output of bananas was estimated at 8 to 15 percent below average. According to the Embassy, the drought has been hardest on crops normally planted in the September through January growing period and worse in the southern prefectures, including Cyangug, Gikongoro, Butare, southern Kibuye, and western Giatarama. USAID officials calculated in late April that more than 500,000 people were already receiving food aid, primarily beans and corn, from relief organizations.[58]

It is important to incorporate the regional nature of agricultural production into any analysis of environment-conflict links in Rwanda. Farmers in the northwest were able to maintain higher productivity and to grow higher-value produce, such as white potatoes. They also received favorable development investment because of the regional bias of the central government (President Habyarimana's home region was the northwest). Consequently, the situation in the northwest was less critical than that in the southern portion of the country.[59]

Migration

After independence, internal population movements in search of better land and livelihood became common. From 1978 to 1991, 76 percent of all rural communes experienced net out-migration; however, as the agricultural frontier closed, the rural zones of in-migration became few and were mostly of marginal agricultural potential.[60] Environmental scarcity caused people to move to ecologically fragile upland and arid areas. Urban areas had few opportunities for employment, and rural-urban migration was restricted after the onset of the civil war. Migrants had little choice but to move to and settle hillsides, low-potential communes adjacent to western parks and forests, wetlands requiring drainage, and eastern communes near Akagera Park.[61]

Decreasing Government Legitimacy

The Rwandan government based its legitimacy on its ability to provide for the needs of the population. The Habyarimana government was responsible for securing a great deal of international development assistance that allowed it to build a sophisticated infrastructure, undertake anti-erosion and reforestation projects, and maintain support among the population. However, as noted, most of this assistance was channeled into the northwest, the president's home region, causing resentment in the rest of the country. In addition to the decline in per capita agricultural output and the lack of opportunities in both rural and urban settings, the Rwandan economy was seriously affected by decreases in coffee and tea prices in the late 1980s, the structural adjustment policy implemented in 1990, and the civil war.[62] Ninety percent of export earnings came from 7 percent of the land and was mainly derived from coffee;[63] declining coffee prices therefore debilitated the economy. The government's increasing inability to solve the country's problems created a crisis of legitimacy. Opposition parties formed and organized peaceful protests against the regime. Much of this opposition was based in the south and central parts of the country, the areas most affected by environmental scarcity and least aided by government funding.

For these grievances to cause civil violence, opportunities to channel and articulate them had to exist. Rwanda had historical ethnic divisions, which might have provided instruments for mobilizing grievances.

Ethnic Cleavages in Rwanda

The recent violence has been described as a tribal war between Hutu and Tutsi, rooted in centuries-long competition for control of land and power. But a close examination of Rwanda's history shows that the terms Hutu and Tutsi were largely constructed social categories representing differing socioeconomic positions within Rwandan society rather than objective biological or cultural differences.[64] The Hutu-Tutsi distinction derives from a precolonial social structure that distinguished between cultivators and pastoralists.[65] Before the growth of central power and colonial domination, the boundaries between the Hutu and Tutsi were fluid. A variety of criteria determined ethnic affiliation: birth, wealth, culture, place of origin, physical attributes, and social and marriage ties.[66] Perhaps the greatest determinant of ethnicity was the possession of cattle; those who possessed cattle were Tutsi, and those who did not were Hutu.

With the growth of precolonial state power, Tutsi and Hutu became important political categories. With the establishment of colonialism, the boundaries of ethnic categories were thickened; it became increasingly difficult to alter one's social status or ethnic grouping. The disadvantages of being Hutu and the advantages of being Tutsi were sharpened under first German and then Belgian colonial rule.[67] Virtually all the chiefs appointed during this period were Tutsi, and the power of the chiefs grew with the imposition of colonial institutions. These shifts created the popular view that being Tutsi was synonymous with having wealth and power, while being Hutu was synonymous with subordination.[68] Political consciousness and discontent developed among the Hutu. The Hutu leadership articulated and channeled this frustration, producing the Hutu uprisings of 1959 and eventually Rwandan independence in July 1962.[69] Political power remained in the hands of the Hutu majority. Independence was followed by heightened ethnic violence between Hutu and Tutsi, causing flows of Tutsi refugees from Rwanda to Uganda, Tanzania, Zaire, and Burundi.

The perception within Rwanda that independence was an ethnic struggle between Hutu and Tutsi for control of the state apparatus—a "Hutu revolution"—set the tone of politics up to the present. Ethnic categories were fostered and manipulated by the Hutu-dominated government to maintain power and popular support. Identity cards were issued; due to the high rate of intermarriage among Rwandans, it was impossible to establish ethnic identity without them. Employment and education opportunities were limited for Tutsi because of an unofficial quota system introduced in 1973.[70]

The ethnic nature of the recent conflict is undeniable; although significant numbers of Hutu were killed, the Tutsi population was undoubtedly the target of most of the violence. Below we outline four hypotheses that identify possible links between environmental scarcity and the outbreak of this conflict, which seems, prima facie, to be derived from ethnic animosities.

Violent Conflict: Four Hypotheses Linking Environmental Scarcity and Conflict

The preceding account has shown that environmental scarcity was correlated with conflict in Rwanda. But to establish environmental scarcity's causal role, it is not enough to demonstrate that high levels of environmental scarcity were accompanied by conflict. To avoid spurious claims about causation, we must analyze all factors contributing to the Rwandan conflict and the interaction of environmental scarcity with these factors.

We propose four hypotheses specifying possible links between environmental scarcity and violent conflict in Rwanda. The first focuses on high levels of grievance caused by high population growth and decreased food production; this grievance caused increased levels of frustration, aggression, and conflict. The second highlights how state institutions were weakened and how the state became increasingly unable to manage the transition from authoritarian rule. According to this hypothesis, the 1989 famine, continuing food shortages, and population pressures were partly responsible for this weakening of the Rwandan state. The third emphasizes the development and manipulation of ethnic identity by elite groups in order to maintain popular support for the regime within the Hutu community.

The fourth hypothesis synthesizes the first three by identifying elite insecurity as the central variable. The insecurity of Hutu elites increased because of internal and external pressures for democratization and the concessions of the Arusha Accords, both of which occurred in the context of falling coffee prices, structural adjustment, the civil war, and environmental scarcity. The Arusha Accords weakened key segments of the Habyarimana regime; these groups then tried to retain control of the state by harnessing popular support and frustration after the death of Habyarimana. Each hypothesis is discussed in detail below.

Hypothesis 1: High Levels of Grievance

Land scarcity was severe; little new land was available for cultivation in an overwhelmingly agricultural society. The majority of the population was young, and a strong social norm existed that couples needed access to wealth, for example, a plot of land, before they married. The lack of land, combined with few nonagricultural employment opportunities, created resentment and frustration within this large segment of Rwandan society. The population was therefore easily mobilized;[71] there were reports of increased rivalry and conflict among neighbors over land.[72] The structural adjustment program both reduced government aid programs and increased the price of imported goods, such as food,[73] while poor economic conditions reduced alternative employment opportunities for youth in urban areas. Frustration was further intensified by increased corruption in the Rwandan government[74] and the unresponsiveness of both opposition parties and government agencies to the problems of rural society.[75] In the context of ethnic cleavages, these grievances were easily channeled into an ethnic conflict (figure 6.1).

The level of grievance among the population was indeed high, and government propaganda did attempt to create and capitalize on popular fear by stating that the Tutsi, in the form of the RPF, were going to seize land. This was a significant threat. The land belonged to the state, and an RPF-dominated state put in place after the implementation of the Arusha Accords could have forced Hutu farmers off their land.

Although many Rwandans felt aggrieved, grievances do not automatically translate into violence. Three conditions are necessary to establish a relation-

FIGURE 6.1
Increased Mass Grievances and Mobilization Potential

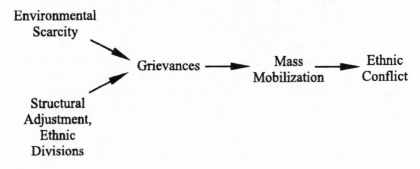

ship between deprivation-induced grievance and violence. It must be shown conclusively, first, that deprivation was increasing; second, that this deprivation was increasing the level of grievance; and, third, that the aggrieved participated in the violence.[76] The first two conditions held in Rwanda, but the third did not. The southwest experienced the greatest scarcities, and the population's ability to sustain itself was clearly decreasing. The political opposition was based in the south. However, the area remained relatively quiet for the first few weeks after the death of Habyarimana. Only when the militias from the north moved in and began their systematic killing of all Tutsi and opposition leaders[77] did violence overtake the south. There is no conclusive evidence that large numbers of Rwandans—especially those experiencing the most severe effects of environmental scarcity—participated in the killings. And for those who did participate in the south, there is substantial anecdotal evidence that peasants were coerced to participate in massacres by militias and local authorities.[78]

Hypothesis 2: the Transition from Authoritarian Rule

The second hypothesis focuses on the transition from authoritarian rule. Regime legitimacy—the government's moral authority—declined because of the 1989 famine, the specter of further food shortages in 1994, and the regime's general inability to meet the needs of rural society. Farmers refused to participate in the central government's one-day-a-week *umuganda* labor system to build roads, dig erosion ditches, and plant trees. Much of this work was seen as useless;[79] the advice of local farmers, often the best experts on soil and farming due to the diversity of Rwanda's geography, was not heeded.[80] The Rwandan government had prided itself on Rwanda's food self-sufficiency, yet the rural food crisis and the failure of its own development strategies combined to undermine popular support for the government.[81] Moreover, these events occurred at the same time as the international trend toward democratization brought pressures from donor countries for similar measures in Rwanda.[82]

The four general stages of the movement toward democratization are the decline of authoritarian rule, the transition from authoritarian rule, the consolidation of democratic institutions, and the maturing of a democratic political order.[83] Successful democratization requires the negotiation of pacts among the elites; hybrid regimes—in which old institutions are combined with new ones—usually oversee the transition periods.[84] Hybrid regimes are often not resilient, which creates a high potential for reversion to authoritarian rule. Adam Przeworski establishes some conditions for a successful transition:

> If reforms are to proceed under democratic conditions, distributional conflicts must be institutionalized; all groups must channel their demands through demo-

cratic institutions and abjure other tactics. Regardless of how pressing their needs may be, the politically relevant groups must be willing to subject their interests to the verdict of democratic institutions. Reforms can succeed under two polar conditions of the organization of political forces: the latter have to be very strong and support the reform program, or they have to be very weak and unable to oppose it effectively.[85]

In early 1994, Rwanda entered a period of transition from authoritarian rule. The Arusha Accords provided for the establishment of a hybrid regime, yet many members of the army and government would have lost their privileged positions within the state under the democratic arrangements outlined in the Accords. At a critical moment in the transition, when the previous regime had lost all legitimacy yet the democratic institutions of the new regime had not fully developed, a coup d'état occurred. Although it is not known precisely who killed President Habyarimana, most experts have concluded that an elite within the Rwandan government—led by the leaders of the two main militias—assassinated him as part of a broader strategy to retain the power and wealth that came with control of the state. These elites tried to garner support within the Rwandan population by exploiting ethnic cleavages; all Tutsi were identified as members of the RPF and targeted for death by the militias and army (figure 6.2).

However, the explanation provided by the second hypothesis is incomplete: it is not clear that there were strong links among environmental scarcity, declining regime legitimacy, the transition from authoritarian rule, and the outbreak of conflict. The regime's agreement to undertake a transition to democracy was mainly a reaction not to its declining legitimacy, but to the RPF invasion and civil war. Internal pressures for democratization, caused only in part by environmental scarcity, were important, but the regime appeared largely able to maintain control of the state apparatus when faced with domes-

FIGURE 6.2
Weakened State Legitimacy and State Breakdown

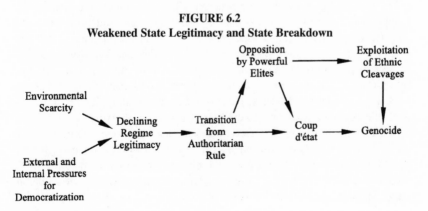

tic appeals for democratization. However, the Arusha Accords threatened members of the Habyarimana regime, in particular the army and militias, as power and wealth would have been shared with the RPF.

Hypothesis 3: Manipulation of Ethnic Identity

In a context in which ethnic affiliation mattered, environmental scarcity created conditions that increased competition between Hutu and Tutsi. Cross-national research shows that cases of severe ethnic conflict share the following characteristics: institutionalized group boundaries and stereotypes, an experience of ethnic domination by one or more groups, the strong perception by one group that the opposing ethnic group has external affiliations, and ethnically based parties with no significant interethnic coalitions.[86] Rwandan ethnic relations exhibited all of these characteristics: colonial rule institutionalized interethnic boundaries, and these boundaries were thickened by Hutu regimes after independence; the Tutsi were the most powerful ethnic group in the pre-independence period, and independence was seen as a Hutu revolution; civilian Tutsi were perceived to have strong affinities with the RPF; and General Habyarimana's ruling party and militias were controlled solely by Hutu.

The scarcity of environmental resources, combined with other factors, created a context within which ethnic affiliations mattered. Ethnic identity was one means that Hutu elites used to establish and maintain control over resources, including environmental resources such as cropland. Economic opportunities for the Hutu elite had been squeezed by the country's general economic crisis due to the structural adjustment plan, the economic strain suffered from the civil war, and the collapse of coffee prices. The importance of access to environmental resources increased as alternative economic options disappeared. Ethnicity was the key to this access, which for the Hutu elite was threatened by the Arusha Accords (figure 6.3).

This explanation also appears inadequate. Anti-Tutsi attitudes were reportedly much stronger among more educated Hutu than among the mass of the Hutu population. Environmental scarcity therefore clearly did not increase the salience of ethnicity among the majority of Rwanda's population, or even among those who were most severely affected by the scarcity. Instead, ethnicity was most important among members of the elite who were least affected by scarcity. A careful review of the evidence shows that ethnic affiliations became salient among the elite, because the predominantly Tutsi RPF threatened the regime's hold on power. Moreover, ethnic divisions were not the only cleavages in Rwandan society: regional cleavages were important, especially under President Habyarimana's rule. Being a Hutu was not enough. One had to be a Hutu from the president's northwestern region or share the sentiments of Hutu extremism,[87] which explains the large number of moderate Hutu targeted by the militias. A hypothesis centered on the multiple forces

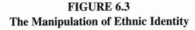

FIGURE 6.3
The Manipulation of Ethnic Identity

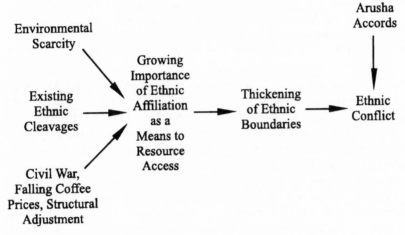

contributing to elite insecurity provides a more powerful explanation of the genocide.

Hypothesis 4: Elite Insecurity in the Context of the Arusha Accords

We believe that the most plausible explanation of the recent conflict, outlined in figure 6.4, is a combination of the three hypotheses above. Elite or regime insecurity plays a central role in this synthesis.

Brian Job, in his recent work on the insecurity dilemma[88] faced by developing states, emphasizes the importance of distinguishing between the state and the regime when analyzing conflict in the developing world. The state has two sets of relations with its environment: external relations with other states and internal relations as its constituent institutions organize, regulate, and enforce interactions among groups within its territory. The norms of international law guarantee that the external relations of the state are rarely threatened, but control of internal relations is often contested by various segments of society.

The regime is the set of individuals that has gained control of the state's internal relations. In developing societies, the regime usually lacks the support of a large share of the population: it represents the interests of a specific ethnic, economic, or military group. The distinction between the internal and external aspects of the state is crucial to our understanding of the Rwandan case: it was the Habyarimana regime, not the Rwandan state, that faced threats to its security. The regime did all it could to maintain its grip on power. According to Job,

[Regimes] are preoccupied with the short term; their security and their physical survival are dependent on the strategies they pursue for the moment. Consequently, it is rational for regimes to adopt policies that utilize scarce resources for military equipment and [humanpower], to perceive as threatening opposition movements demanding greater public debate, and to regard as dangerous communal movements that promote alternative identifications and loyalties.[89]

In Rwanda, regime and elite insecurity was principally generated by the civil war and the Arusha Accords. Even though environmental scarcity's role was limited, it was not insignificant. Environmental scarcities, particularly as they affected food production, undoubtedly increased grievances within the Rwandan rural population and generally weakened the legitimacy of the regime. Scarcities limited the opportunities for wealth creation and for achieving economic and social status within Rwandan society. But there were other significant factors at work: the civil war, structural adjustment, the fall in coffee prices, and Rwanda's position as a landlocked country with little chance for economic diversification also boosted grievances and weakened regime legitimacy. These pressures threatened the preservation of the regime. Rising external and internal demands for democratization compounded elite insecurity by eroding its control of such institutions as the army, the police, and the bureaucracy.

Although the structural adjustment measures, declining food production, and the general economic malaise had hurt the majority of Rwandans, the elite and the armed forces were two groups that did not suffer directly. The army increased from 5,000 to 35,000 soldiers in only 2 years.[90] The Arusha Accords provided for a reduction in the size of the armed forces and for integrating the RPF and the army into a new national force. The Accords also provided for the creation of a transitional government until the elections were held. This government would include not only members of the RPF, but also members of domestic opposition groups. Therefore, the power and privilege of the regime and the army were threatened in a context of general scarcity; those displaced by the Accords would have had few economic or political opportunities in either rural or urban areas.

To maintain its hold on power, the regime began its two-track policy (as indicated in figure 6.4): it negotiated with the RPF, and it undermined the potential transfer of power to the RPF by fomenting anti-Tutsi and anti-RPF animosity in the general population. However, the impending implementation of the Arusha Accords—guaranteed by Habyarimana's final trip to Arusha— was the death knell for the regime's control of the state.

Members of the regime shot down the president's plane in retaliation for his soft stand at Arusha and seized the state.[91] They attempted to gain the support of the population by targeting members of opposition parties and Tutsi as RPF sympathizers who had to be eliminated for national security.[92] But

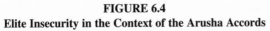

FIGURE 6.4
Elite Insecurity in the Context of the Arusha Accords

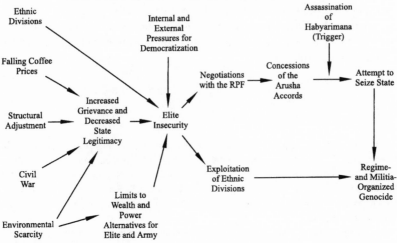

they underestimated the lack of popular support for their strategy and the military strength of the RPF.[93]

Conclusions

The Rwanda case tells us important things about the complexity of causal links between environmental scarcity and conflict. Scarcity did play a role in the recent violence in Rwanda, but, given its severity and impact on the population, the role was surprisingly limited. The role was also not what one would expect from a superficial analysis of the case. Although the levels of environmental scarcity were high and conflict occurred, the connection between these variables was mediated by many other factors. This complexity makes the precise role of environmental scarcity difficult to determine.

The Rwanda example teaches us key lessons for the future study of cases exhibiting a strong correlation between environmental scarcity and violence. If we had focused our analysis solely on environmental scarcity and the social effects it produced, then its contribution to the conflict would have appeared powerful. But by carefully tracing the effects of environmental scarcity and by seriously analyzing competing explanations of the conflict, we determined the best explanation of both the conflict and environmental scarcity's role.

If researchers are to understand complex conflicts like the Rwandan genocide, they must be acutely aware of the issues motivating the conflict's actors. They must not only examine what people do and what physical environment they do it in, but also why they do it. A conflict motivated by different political issues could have occurred in Rwanda in which environmental scarcity played a central role. Although the recent violence occurred in conditions of severe environmental scarcity, because the Arusha Accords and regime insecurity were the key factors motivating the Hutu elite, environmental scarcity played a much more peripheral role.

Notes

This essay was first published as Valerie Percival and Thomas Homer-Dixon, "Environmental Scarcity and Violent Conflict: The Case of Rwanda," *Journal of Environment and Development* 5, no. 3 (September 1996): 270–91. Reprinted with permission. For their valuable help, the authors thank David Campbell, Robert Ford, Scott Grosse, Bruce Jones, Craig Johnston, Phocus Ntombya, Richard Taylor, Peter Uvin, and Vanessa van Schoor.

1. Nancy Gibbs, "Why? The Killing Fields of Rwanda," *Time* 143, no. 20 (16 May 1994): 21–27. "Rwanda serves as a modern laboratory for anyone trying to figure out which factors will matter and which will not in the pursuit of peace and security. It is a crucible full of explosives that nations watching from a comfortable distance have no idea how to handle. War itself is redefined when it is waged within countries rather than between them; when the environment—soil, water, scarce natural resources—become the spoils that cause neighbors to kill neighbors."

2. Although agricultural production accounted for approximately 40 percent of the gross national product, most of Rwanda's foreign-exchange export earnings came from coffee. Geographic Research Paper, *Rwanda: A Geographic Profile* (July 1994), 2.

3. Patrick C. Gaffney, "Rwanda: A Crisis of Humanitarian Security," *Report: The Joan B. Kroc Institute for International Peace Studies*, issue 7 (fall 1994): 2.

4. Catharine Watson, "War and Waiting," *Africa Report* 37, no. 6 (November/ December 1992): 53.

5. Nicola Jefferson, "The War Within," *Africa Report* 37, no. 1 (January/February 1992): 63–64.

6. Watson, "War and Waiting," 55.

7. Lindsey Hilsum, "Settling Scores," *Africa Report* 39, no. 3 (May/June 1994): 14.

8. Watson, "War and Waiting," 52.

9. Hilsum, "Settling Scores," 14.

10. Ibid., 15.

11. Ibid.

12. Paul Watson, "Tribal Feuds Throw Rwanda in Crisis," *The Toronto Star*, 23 February 1994, p. A2.

13. Donatella Lorch, "In the Upheaval in Rwanda, Few Answers Yet," *New York Times*, 3 May 1994, p. A3.

14. Ibid.

15. Catharine Newbury, "A Rwanda Roundtable Discussion" (discussion held at

the Association for African Studies Annual Meeting, Toronto, Ontario, Canada, 5 November 1994).

16. Donatella Lorch, "World Turns Its Attention," *New York Times*, 20 May 1994, p. A10.

17. Hilsum, "Settling Scores," 17.

18. Raymond Bonner, "A Church Became a Killing Field," *New York Times*, 17 November 1994, p. A4.

19. Andre Picard, "Rwandan Rebels Declare Victory," *The Globe and Mail*, 19 July 1994, p. A1.

20. Raymond Bonner, "Rwanda's Leaders Plan Democracy," *New York Times*, 7 September 1994, p. A10.

21. "Tutsi Forces to Occupy Rwandan Zone Where Hutu Fled," *New York Times*, 17 August 1994, p. A12.

22. Médecins Sans Frontières (MSF), "Breaking the Cycle: MSF Calls for Action in the Rwandan Refugee Camps in Tanzania and Zaire," MSF Report, 10 November 1994, 3.

23. Raymond Bonner, "Rwandan Refugees in Zaire Still Fear to Return," *New York Times*, 10 November 1994.

24. Médecins Sans Frontières, "Breaking the Cycle," 5, 7.

25. Ibid., 4, 8.

26. "Wake Up on Rwanda," *Christian Science Monitor*, 24 November 1994.

27. Ibid., 9.

28. "UN Chief Asks Troops for Rwandans," *New York Times*, 22 November 1994, p. A8.

29. Robert Ford, personal communication.

30. Donatella Lorch, "UN Shuts Down Refugee Camp to Prod Rwandans to Go Home," *New York Times*, 1 February 1995, p. A2.

31. Geographic Research Paper, *Rwanda: A Geographic Profile*, 10.

32. Scott Grosse, "More People, More Trouble," draft, Department of Population Planning and International Health, University of Michigan, 16 November 1994, 9.

33. Ibid.

34. David Waller, *Rwanda: Which Way Now?* (Oxford: Oxfam Country Studies, 1993), 23.

35. Grosse, "More People, More Trouble," 31.

36. Ibid., 34.

37. Waller, *Rwanda: Which Way Now?*, 43.

38. Grosse, "More People, More Trouble," 29.

39. John May, "Policies on Population, Land Use, and Environment in Rwanda," *Population and Environment* 16, no. 4 (March 1995): 323.

40. Grosse, "More People, More Trouble," 29.

41. United Nations Environment Program (UNEP), *Environment Data Report 1993–94* (Oxford: Blackwell Publishers, 1993), 217.

42. World Resources Institute (WRI), "Table 17.1: Land Area and Use, 1979–91," *World Resources 1994–95* (New York: Oxford University Press, 1994), 284.

43. Waller, *Rwanda: Which Way Now?*, 18.

44. Jennifer Olson, *Demographic Responses to Resource Constraints in Rwanda*,

Rwanda Society-Environment Project, Working Paper No. 7 (East Lansing: Michigan State University, September 1994), 5–6.

45. Geographic Research Paper, *Rwanda: A Geographic Profile*, 2.

46. UNEP, "Table 4.4: Trends in Urban Population Size and Average Annual Urban Growth Rate, 1950–90," in *Environment Data Report, 1993–94*, 221.

47. The Gini coefficient of land distribution is 0.26 and is indicative of an egalitarian distribution. Grosse, "More People, More Trouble," 41.

48. Grosse, "More People, More Trouble," 29.

49. Economic decline is the fourth factor that is an indicator or social effect of environmental stress. Although the Rwandan economy was suffering, the effect of environmental stress on the Rwandan economy is difficult to isolate from the effect of the falling coffee prices, the structural adjustment policies, and the disruption of the civil war.

50. Geographic Research Paper, *Rwanda: A Geographic Profile*, 2.

51. Grosse, "More People, More Trouble," 19.

52. Geographic Research Paper, *Rwanda: A Geographic Profile*, 4.

53. Olson, *Demographic Responses to Resource Constraints in Rwanda*, 2–3; Scott Grosse, "The Roots of Conflict and State Failure in Rwanda: The Political Exacerbation of Social Cleavages in a Situation of Growing Resource Scarcity," draft, Department of Population Planning and International Health, University of Michigan, 15 November 1994, 11.

54. WRI, "Table 17.1: Land Area and Use 1979–91," 284. Grosse reports that this figure could be inaccurate: "One researcher who has worked at DSA [Data Survey Analysis] reports that the sample frame used for the 1989 and 1990 surveys oversampled relatively degraded areas with low soil fertility in the Southwest and relatively dry areas in the Southeast with larger farm size and also lower productivity. . . . This may account for part of the apparent increase in land area and decrease in soil fertility between 1984 and 1990." Grosse, "More People, More Trouble," 23.

55. David Campbell, *Environmental Stress in Rwanda: A Preliminary Analysis*, Rwanda Society-Environment Project, Working Paper No. 4 (East Lansing: Michigan State University, June 1994), 19–20.

56. Grosse, "More People, More Trouble," 21.

57. WRI, "Table 18.1: Food and Agricultural Production, 1980–82," *World Resources 1994–95*, 292. Grosse states that these data may not accurately represent the existence of significant intercropping.

58. Geographic Research Paper, *Rwanda: A Geographic Profile*, 5.

59. Jennifer Olson, *Factors Behind the Recent Tragedy in Rwanda*, Rwanda Society-Environment Project, Working Paper (East Lansing: Michigan State University, February 1995), 4–5. This piece is based on excerpts from "Behind the Recent Tragedy in Rwanda" published in *Geojournal*, February 1995.

60. Olson, *Factors Behind the Recent Tragedy in Rwanda*, 26.

61. Olson, *Demographic Responses to Resource Constraints in Rwanda*, 15.

62. Numerous Rwandan specialists have remarked on the absence of linkages between rural society and urban society; although the government was affected by agricultural decline in rural Rwanda, it felt the impact of the civil war, structural adjustment policies, and the fall in coffee prices much more.

63. Waller, *Rwanda: Which Way Now?*, 27.

64. Catharine Newbury, *The Cohesion of Oppression* (New York: Columbia University Press, 1988).

65. Gaffney, "Rwanda: A Crisis of Humanitarian Security," 1.

66. Ibid., 51.

67. Ibid., 52.

68. Ibid., 179.

69. Ibid., 181, 196, 198.

70. Grosse, "The Roots of Conflict and State Failure in Rwanda," 8–9.

71. Newbury, "A Rwanda Roundtable Discussion."

72. Grosse, "The Roots of Conflict and State Failure in Rwanda," 12.

73. Ibid., 19.

74. Waller, *Rwanda: Which Way Now?*, 33.

75. Newbury, "A Rwanda Roundtable Discussion."

76. James Rule, *Theories of Civil Violence* (Berkeley: University of California Press, 1988), 206.

77. Romeo Dallaire, public lecture at the University of Toronto, 15 March 1995.

78. Reports indicate that the militias attempted to recruit locals to participate in the killing. The easiest people to recruit were peasants and uneducated, unemployed young men. However, figures on how many and who participated are difficult to confirm. This said, Rwanda could be considered an excellent example of how it takes relatively few aggrieved people to incite mass terror. Raymond Bonner, "Rwandans in Death Squad Say Choice was Kill or Die," *New York Times*, August 14, 1994, p. A1.

79. Grosse, "The Roots of Conflict and State Failure in Rwanda," 15.

80. Waller, *Rwanda: Which Way Now?*, 26.

81. Grosse, "The Roots of Conflict and State Failure in Rwanda," 20.

82. Ibid.

83. Doh Chull Shin, "On the Third Wave of Democratization," *World Politics* 47, no. 1 (October 1994): 143.

84. Ibid., 144, 161.

85. Adam Przeworski, *Democracy and the Market* (Cambridge: Cambridge University Press, 1991), 180.

86. Donald Horowitz, "Making Moderation Pay: The Comparative Politics of Ethnic Conflict Management," in *Conflict and Peacemaking in Multiethnic Societies*, ed. Joseph Monteville (Lexington, Ky.: Lexington Press, 1990), 455–56.

87. The prime minister designate at the time of the conflict, Faustin Twagiramugu, was a Hutu from the south. The government perceived him as an enemy. Hilsum, "Settling Scores," 15.

88. The insecurity dilemma results from competition among various forces in developing societies. This competition means less effective security for all or segments of the population. Therefore the capacity of centralized state institutions to provide services and order is lower, and the state and its citizens are more vulnerable to outside influence, intervention, and control. Brian Job, "National, Regime, and State Securities in the Third World," in *The Insecurity Dilemma*, ed. Brian Job (Boulder, Colo.: Lynne Rienner, 1992), 18.

89. Job, "National, Regime, and State Securities in the Third World," 27.

90. Waller, *Rwanda: Which Way Now?*, 12.

91. Evidence is needed to determine three things. Who shot down Habyarimana's plane? Did the army act independently, with members of the government responding to their initiative after the fact and colluding with them? Or was the seizure of the institutions of the state a cooperative effort by both the government and the army?

92. Execution lists were reportedly created months in advance, which raises interesting questions about how long these events had been planned. Kim Gordon-Bates, "The Hard Lessons of Rwanda," *Crosslines* 2, no. 4–5 (October 1994): 3.

93. Gordon-Bates, "The Hard Lessons of Rwanda," 3.

7

Key Findings

Thomas Homer-Dixon and Jessica Blitt

In chapter 1, we outlined a general theory of the causal links between environmental scarcity and violent conflict. In the five subsequent chapters, we examined the cases of Chiapas, Gaza, South Africa, Pakistan, and Rwanda. By means of these case studies, we sought to determine how the physical, economic, and social factors identified in chapter 1 actually operate in the real world. In this final chapter, we conclude the book by highlighting eight key findings of this research, and we illustrate these findings, where appropriate, with examples drawn from the case studies. The findings are as follows:

1. *Under certain circumstances, scarcities of renewable resources such as cropland, fresh water, and forests produce civil violence and instability. However, the role of this "environmental scarcity" is often obscure. Environmental scarcity acts mainly by generating intermediate social effects, such as poverty and migrations, that analysts often interpret as conflict's immediate causes.*

Environmental scarcity—in interaction with other political, economic, and social factors—can help generate conflict and instability, but the causal linkages are often indirect. Scarcities of cropland, fresh water, and forests constrain agricultural and economic productivity; generate large and destabilizing population movements; aggravate tensions along ethnic, racial, and religious lines; increase wealth and power differentials among groups; and debilitate political and social institutions. Migrations, ethnic tensions, economic disparities, and weak institutions in turn often appear to be the main causes of violence.

The relationship between environmental scarcity and violence is invariably complex. Scarcity interacts with such contextual factors as the character of the economic system, levels of education, ethnic cleavages, class divisions, technological and infrastructural capacity, and the legitimacy of the political regime. These contextual factors determine if environmental scarcity will produce harmful intermediate social effects, such as poverty and migrations. Contextual factors also influence the ultimate potential for instability or violence in a society.

As the Rwandan case showed, the mere existence of a correlation between environmental scarcity and violence does not prove that the scarcity was an important cause of the violence. To determine whether or not causation actually occurred, researchers must carefully examine the individual causal steps from scarcity to its social effects, and they must then determine if these social effects significantly contributed to violence. In the process, researchers must pay special attention to the social, political, and economic factors unique to each case that can interact with scarcity to mitigate or worsen its impacts. In the Rwandan case, such analysis showed that the severe environmental scarcity experienced by the country played at most only an aggravating role in the genocide.

2. *Environmental scarcity is caused by the degradation and depletion of renewable resources, the increased demand for these resources, and/or their unequal distribution. These three sources of scarcity often interact and reinforce one another.*

A simple "pie" metaphor illustrates the three sources of environmental scarcity. A reduction in the quantity or quality of an environmental resource shrinks the pie; population growth and increased per capita demand for the resource boost demand for the pie; and unequal distribution can cause some groups to get portions of the pie that are too small to sustain their well-being. For example, environmental scarcity in Gaza was caused by three phenomena: the degradation and depletion of the aquifer waters, which reduced the available water supply; population growth, which increased the demand for water; and inequitable distribution between Palestinians and the Israeli settler community, which reduced the amount of water available for Palestinian consumption.

3. *Environmental scarcity often encourages powerful groups to capture valuable environmental resources and prompts marginal groups to migrate to ecologically sensitive areas. These two processes—called "resource capture" and "ecological marginalization"—in turn reinforce environmental scarcity and raise the potential for social instability.*

Resource Capture

The degradation and depletion of renewable resources can interact with population growth to encourage powerful groups within a society to shift resource distribution in their favor. Powerful groups secure or tighten their grip on a dwindling resource and often use this control to generate profits. At the same time, resource capture intensifies scarcity for poorer and weaker groups. In Pakistan, for instance, as timber became increasingly scarce and as demand for wood climbed, a timber mafia appropriated many community and government forests. These groups—often run by traditional tribal leaders in collusion with forest officials, forestland owners, and logging contractors—used state development funds and manipulated legislation to open up forests for exploitation and immense profits. In turn, this process impoverished and displaced villagers who traditionally depended on forest resources for their livelihood.

Ecological Marginalization

Unequal resource access can combine with population growth to cause large-scale and long-term migrations of the poorest groups within society. They move to ecologically fragile regions such as steep upland slopes, areas at risk of desertification, tropical rain forests, and low-quality public lands within urban areas. High population densities in these regions, combined with a lack of knowledge and capital to protect the local ecosystem, cause severe environmental scarcity and chronic poverty. In the Mexican state of Chiapas, for example, cropland was scarce in highland regions due to inequitable distribution, population growth, and soil degradation. Peasants were often compelled to migrate to marginal regions, such as the Lacandón rain forest in the eastern lowlands of the state. As population densities increased in the Lacandón, and as the newly arrived peasants progressively burned and degraded the land along the fringe of the rain forest, acute shortages of cropland developed.

4. *If social and economic adaptation is unsuccessful, environmental scarcity constrains economic development and contributes to migrations.*

Societies that adapt to environmental scarcities can avoid undue suffering and social stress. Strategies for adaptation fall into two categories: societies can use their indigenous environmental resources more efficiently or they can reduce their dependence on these resources. But some poor countries are ill-equipped to adapt. They are underendowed with key social institutions, including research centers, efficient markets, competent government bureaucracies, and uncorrupt legal mechanisms. Such social institutions are essential prerequisites for an ample supply of the social and technical ingenuity that produces solutions to scarcity. None of the societies investigated in this book successfully adapted to environmental scarcity.

Developing economies tend to depend on their environmental resource base for a large part of their economic production and employment. If the supply of social and technical ingenuity is inadequate, therefore, scarcity constrains local economic development, affects the overall health of the economy, and causes economic hardship for marginal groups. To escape this hardship and improve their lives, large numbers of people migrate. For example, in the 1980s, Rwanda's high population densities and soil erosion made good cropland very scarce in some parts of the country. Falling agricultural yields depressed incomes. In search of better land, therefore, many people migrated to upland and arid areas. Similar large-scale migrations—especially to urban areas—occurred in South Africa and Pakistan.

5. *In the absence of adaptation, environmental scarcity sharpens existing distinctions among social groups.*

Environmental scarcity can strengthen group identities based on ethnic, class, or religious differences. Individuals identify with one another when they perceive they share similar hardships. This shared perception reinforces group identities and, in turn, intensifies competition among groups, a process called "social segmentation." Within South Africa's townships and squatter settlements, economic hardship forced residents to rely extensively on urban environmental resources for their daily needs. Competition within and among groups grew as resources such as land and water became scarce. Influxes of migrants further increased the demand for these resources and exacerbated group cleavages. Powerful warlords, linked to Inkatha or the African National Congress (ANC), took advantage of weakened community institutions and resource competition to manipulate group divisions within communities. As the apartheid state crumbled, warlords mobilized large numbers of alienated and unemployed young men for the battle for political control between Inkatha and the ANC. Warlords often tried to maintain power by pointing to resources in neighboring townships and informal settlements and mobilizing their communities to seize them.

6. *In the absence of adaptation, environmental scarcity weakens governmental institutions and states.*

In some poor countries, the multiple effects of environmental scarcity increase the demands on governmental institutions and the state, stimulate predatory elite behavior, reduce social trust and useful intergroup interaction, and depress tax revenues. These processes in turn weaken the administrative capacity and legitimacy of governmental institutions and the state. Unable to prosper in the degraded former homelands, large numbers of migrants flooded the townships and squatter settlements of South Africa. This influx worsened urban environmental scarcity and social segmentation. Greater demands were placed on local institutions, yet rivalry among social groups weakened institutional ability to respond to the population's needs. Warlords then easily stepped in to seize control over resources, further undermining institutional capacity. In Karachi, Pakistan, environmental scarcity caused similar strains. As people migrated into Karachi from rural areas often severely affected by environmental scarcity, demand skyrocketed for urban services such as housing, potable water, and electricity. The state was unable to meet these demands, and an informal system of illegal occupation and subdivision of state land emerged, managed by corrupt elites and government officials.

7. *The above intermediate social effects of environmental scarcity— including constrained economic productivity, population movements, social segmentation, and weakening of institutions and states—can in turn cause ethnic conflicts, insurgencies, and coups d'état.*

Migrating groups can trigger ethnic conflicts when they move to new areas. Declining or stagnant economic welfare can generate deprivation conflicts, such as rural insurgencies and urban riots. The weakening of the state shifts the social balance of power in favor of challenger groups (whose identities have often been strengthened by social segmentation) and increases opportunities for violent collective action by these groups against the state. Whether violence actually occurs, however, depends on a variety of additional conditions, including the conceptions of justice held by challenger groups, the opportunities for alliances among diverse social groups, and the capabilities of the leaders of the state, challenger groups, and elites.

Chiapas, for example, saw a peasant rebellion against the Mexican state because of the convergence of a number of these factors. Extreme land scarcity and the predatory behavior of land-owning elites boosted the grievances of peasants, neoliberal reform weakened the local PRI regime, and the activities of nongovernmental organizations and liberation theologians helped peasants focus and act on their discontent. In South Africa, scarcities in the homelands caused huge migrations of blacks into townships and squatter settlements, which aggravated intergroup cleavages, weakened institutions, and produced violent competition over urban environmental resources. In Gaza, economic stagnation, which was in part a consequence of water scarcity, increased grievances against both Israel and the Palestinian Authority. These grievances in turn encouraged terrorist attacks against Israelis, as well as intra-Palestinian violence; border closures designed to contain the situation only serve to further constrain economic productivity, giving a further push to the cycle of violence. In the Pakistani cities of Karachi and Islamabad, riots occurred regularly among ethnic groups competing for power and resources in an urban environment supercharged by rapid population growth and migrations from the countryside.

8. *Conflicts generated in part by environmental scarcity can have significant indirect effects on the international community.*

Environmental scarcity can contribute to diffuse, persistent, subnational violence, such as ethnic clashes and insurgencies. This subnational violence is not as conspicuous or dramatic as interstate resource wars, but it may have serious repercussions for the security interests of both the developed and developing worlds. It can cause refugee flows and produce humanitarian disasters that call upon the military and financial resources of developed countries and international organizations. Subnational violence can also have significant economic consequences beyond a country's borders. For instance, the Zapatista rebellion in Chiapas helped trigger a crisis for the Mexican peso that had consequences for international money markets and cost Mexico and its NAFTA partners—the United States and Canada—billions of dollars in their efforts to stop the dramatic decline of the peso's value. In coming decades, the incidence of violence caused in part by environmental scarcities will probably increase as these scarcities worsen in many parts of the developing world.

Note

The material in this chapter is modified from Thomas Homer-Dixon and Valerie Percival, "Key Findings," in *Environmental Scarcity and Violent Conflict: Briefing Book* (Washington, D.C.: American Association for the Advancement of Science and the University of Toronto, 1996), 5–10.

Index

Adams, John, 186
adaptation failures, 7–9, 225–26
Afghan refugees, 181, 190
African National Congress (ANC), 110, 112–13, 133–36, 226
Agrarian Law of 1992 (Mexico), 45–46, 51
agricultural lands, 3–4; Chiapas, 28, 30–32, 35–39, 41–47; decline of, 44, 85–87, 124–25, 176–77, 207–8; Gaza, 80, 85–88, 102(n53); Pakistan, 149, 160–66, 171–72, 176–77, 197(n114); Rwanda, 207–8; South Africa, 116–17, 120, 124
al-Hout, Shafiq, 94
al-Masri, Mustafa, 68
American Association for the Advancement of Science, 12
American Foundation for Peace in the Middle East, 79
ANC. *see* African National Congress
Applied Research Institute in Jerusalem (ARIJ), 82
Arab-Israeli War of 1948, 68–69
Arafat, Yasir, 67, 70, 71–73, 92–94, 97
ARIJ. *see* Applied Research Institute in Jerusalem
Arusha Accords, 203–4, 210, 213–18

Baluchistan (Pakistan), 149, 153, 159, 169
Bellisari, Anna, 83–85
Bengalis, 153
Bhutto, Benazir, 151
Bhutto, Zulfikar Ali, 154
Botha, P. W., 112, 113, 133

British Empire, 150, 156
Buthelezi, Mangosuthu, 133

caciques, 53
campesinos, 22–24
Cañadas (Chiapas), 22, 47
Canal Command Area (Pakistan), 167
capital availability, 8–9
Care Canada, 204
Catholic Church, 52–53
cattle industry: Chiapas, 35–38, 41; Gaza, 89; South Africa, 117
Central Highlands (Chiapas), 21, 32–35, 41, 47
certificados de inafectabilidad, 45
CFCs. *see* Chloroflourocarbons
Chamula (Chiapas), 32–33
Chiapas, 13–14, 225; agricultural lands, 28, 30–32, 35–39, 41–47; background, 20–26; cattle industry, 35–38, 41; class relations, 22–24, 40, 51; coffee industry, 22, 38–39; deforestation, 27–30, 62–63(n51); demand-induced scarcity, 26–27; demography, 22; ecological marginalization, 35–36, 39–48; economic marginality, 57; elites, 24, 35, 39, 40, 44–46, 54, 227; environmental scarcity, 26–39; geography, 20–22; history, 39–47; indigeous peoples, 19, 22–26, 56, 57, 62(n48); intellectuals and church leaders, 24, 51, 52–54; land base, 26–27, 35–39, 49, 54; landholding, forms of, 25, 40–41; land reform, 40–46, 64(nn 60, 61); liberalization and, 43–44; Mexican Constitution and, 40–41, 45,

About the Contributors

Jessica Blitt is a Research Assistant of the Peace and Conflict Studies Program at the University of Toronto. She received her B.A. in Peace and Conflict Studies and Philosophy from the University of Toronto. From September to December 1996, she interned with the National Peace Council of Sri Lanka. Currently, she is an M.A. candidate in International Affairs at the Norman Paterson School of International Affairs in Ottawa.

Peter Gizewski is a Research Associate at the York Center for International and Security Studies (YCISS), York University, Toronto. He was educated at the University of Toronto and Columbia University, where he was a MacArthur Fellow in Conflict, Peace and Security. Gizewski has published on a variety of topics in international security.

Thomas Homer-Dixon is Director of the Peace and Conflict Studies Program and Associate Professor of Political Science at the University of Toronto. Between 1994 and 1996, he led the Project on Environment, Population, and Security in collaboration with the American Association for the Advancement of Science. He received his B.A. in Political Science from Carleton University in Ottawa in 1980 and his Ph.D. from the Massachusetts Institute of Technology in 1989. He is author of *Environment, Scarcity, and Violence* (Princeton, New Jersey: Princeton University Press, 1999).

Philip Howard received his B.A. in Political Science from the University of Toronto, and an MSc in International Relations from the Development Studies Institute of the London School of Economics. He has worked as a consultant to the World Resources Institute and the Canadian International Development Agency. Currently, he is a Ph.D. candidate and University Fellow in the Department of Sociology at Northwestern University.

Kimberley Kelly received her B.A. in History from Queen's University and her M.A. in International Affairs at the Norman Paterson School of International Affairs in Ottawa. Currently, she is working for ScotiaMcleod as a Broker's Assistant.

Valerie Percival received her B.A. in Peace and Conflict Studies from the University of Toronto and her M.A. in International Affairs at the Norman Paterson School of International Affairs in Ottawa. She has worked at the International Peace Research Institute, Oslo (PRIO), as the lead researcher for the *Preliminary Project on Environment, Poverty and Conflict.* Currently, she is working for the UNHCR in Guinea.